Mapping Literary Modernism

Ricardo J. Quinones

Mapping Literary Modernism

Time and Development

PRINCETON UNIVERSITY PRESS

Copyright © 1985 by Princeton University Press
Published by Princeton University Press, 41 William Street,
Princeton, New Jersey 08540
In the United Kingdom:
Princeton University Press, Guildford, Surrey

All Rights Reserved
Library of Congress Cataloging in Publication Data will be
found on the last printed page of this book

ISBN 0-695-06636-1

This book has been composed in Linotron Galliard

Clothbound editions of Princeton University Press books are
printed on acid-free paper, and binding materials are chosen for
strength and durability

Printed in the United States of America
by Princeton University Press
Princeton, New Jersey

Contents

	ACKNOWLEDGMENTS	vii
	INTRODUCTION	3
I	The Collapse of Historical Values	21
II	The Family, the Machine and the Paradox of Time	40
III	Transformations	87
IV	The Modernist Sensibility	120
V	"The Songs That I Sing"	164
VI	Three Major Works	192
VII	The Bite of Time	222
	CONCLUSION: Purviews and Purposes	246
	NOTES	259
	INDEX	297

Acknowledgments

In completing this book, I was assisted notably by numerous summer financial grants from my home institution, Claremont McKenna College. I am grateful to several deans of faculty and the president, Mr. Jack Stark, for these subsidies. I would also like to thank Mr. Alvin White, who headed the Claremont Colleges' New Interdisciplinary Holistic Approach to Learning (Fund for the Improvement of Post-Secondary Education), for a generous grant in the summer of 1979.

I am also aware how useful it has been to me to have been able to teach the material of this book off and on over ten years at Claremont McKenna College and Claremont Graduate School. The earliest version of this work was read as a paper at the Second International Conference for the Study of Time, Hotel Mt. Fuji, Japan, 1973. My thanks to that organization's indefatigable founding secretary, Mr. J. T. Fraser.

I was helped quite specifically by my colleagues at the Claremont Colleges, particularly Professor Monique Chefdor of Scripps College, with whom in 1982 I helped organize the Claremont Colleges' Comparative Literature Conference on Modernism. My own views on Modernism were enlarged and complicated considerably by the proceedings of this highly successful conference.

Of the many friends and colleagues who have offered counsel, I can single out those stalwart souls Willis Barnstone, Matei Calinescu and Harvey Gross, who read my typescript, alas, on numerous occasions. The unnamed reader for the Princeton University Press gave the typescript a reading that was extraordinary in its scrupulousness and helpfulness.

It is with particular pride that I dedicate this book to my teacher and friend, that *magister ludi*, Harry Levin.

ACKNOWLEDGMENTS

EXCERPTS FROM "The Love Song of J. Alfred Prufrock," "Preludes," "The Waste Land," and "Marina" in *Collected Poems 1909-1962* by T. S. Eliot are reprinted by permission of Harcourt Brace Jovanovich, Inc.; copyright 1936 by Harcourt Brace Jovanovich, Inc.; copyright 1963, 1964 by T. S. Eliot.

Excerpts from *Four Quartets* by T. S. Eliot are reprinted by permission of Harcourt Brace Jovanovich, Inc.; copyright 1943 by T. S. Eliot, renewed 1971 by Esme Valerie Eliot.

Excerpts from *Mrs. Dalloway* and *To the Lighthouse*, both by Virginia Woolf, are reprinted by permission of Harcourt Brace Jovanovich, Inc.; copyright 1925, 1927 by Harcourt Brace Jovanovich, Inc.; renewed 1953, 1955 by Leonard Woolf.

Excerpts from *Finnegans Wake* by James Joyce are reprinted by permission of Viking Penguin, Inc.; copyright 1939 by James Joyce, renewed 1967 by George Joyce and Lucia Joyce.

Excerpts from *The Rainbow* by D. H. Lawrence are reprinted by permission of Viking Penguin, Inc.; copyright 1915 by David Herbert Lawrence; renewed 1943 by Frieda Lawrence.

Excerpts from *Apocalypse* by D. H. Lawrence, copyright 1931 by the Estate of D. H. Lawrence; Excerpts from *Women in Love* by D. H. Lawrence; Excerpts from *Kangaroo* by D. H. Lawrence, copyright 1923 by Thomas Seltzer, Inc.; renewed 1950 by Frieda Lawrence; Excerpts from *Sons and Lovers* by D. H. Lawrence, copyright 1913 by Thomas Seltzer, Inc.; Excerpts from *Aaron's Rod* by D. H. Lawrence, copyright 1922 by Thomas Seltzer, Inc.; renewed 1950 by Frieda Lawrence are all reprinted by permission of Viking Penguin, Inc.

Excerpts from *The Collected Poems of Wallace Stevens* are reprinted by permission of Alfred A. Knopf, Inc.; copyright 1923, 1931, 1935, 1937, 1954 by Wallace Stevens.

Excerpts from *The Necessary Angel* by Wallace Stevens are reprinted by permission of Alfred A. Knopf, Inc.; copyright 1942, 1944, 1947, 1949, 1951 by Wallace Stevens.

Excerpts from *Death in Venice and Seven Other Stories* by

ACKNOWLEDGMENTS

Thomas Mann, translated by H. T. Lowe-Porter, are reprinted by permission of Alfred A. Knopf, Inc.; copyright 1930, 1931, 1936 by Alfred A. Knopf, Inc.; renewed 1958, 1959, 1963 by Alfred A. Knopf, Inc.

Excerpts from *Buddenbrooks* by Thomas Mann, translated by H. T. Lowe-Porter, are reprinted by permission of Alfred A. Knopf, Inc.; copyright 1924 by Alfred A. Knopf, Inc.; renewed 1952 by Alfred A. Knopf, Inc.

Excerpts from *The Magic Mountain* by Thomas Mann, translated by H. T. Lowe-Porter, are reprinted by permission of Alfred A. Knopf, Inc.; copyright 1927 by Alfred A. Knopf, Inc.; renewed 1955 by Alfred A. Knopf, Inc.

Excerpts from *Joseph and His Brothers* by Thomas Mann, translated by H. T. Lowe-Porter, are reprinted by permission of Alfred A. Knopf, Inc.; copyright 1944 by Alfred A. Knopf, Inc.

Excerpts from *Remembrance of Things Past* by Marcel Proust, translated by C. K. Scott Moncrieff, are reprinted by permission of Random House, Inc.; copyright 1924, 1925 by Thomas Seltzer, Inc., copyright 1934 by The Modern Library, Inc.

Excerpts from *The Past Recaptured* by Marcel Proust, translated by Andreas Mayor, are reprinted by permission of Random House, Inc., copyright 1970 by Chatto & Windus, Ltd.

Mapping Literary Modernism

Introduction

As a literary movement and broad cultural force, Modernism has made its mark and has had its impact. It has entered into history and needs now to be discussed with the same comprehensive scope and yet with the same historical imagination that we might muster in discussing the Renaissance or Romanticism. Certainly, the time is long past when a distinguished literary historian (who here shall be nameless) could refer to the use of the term "modernism" as pretentious.[1] Modernism has become, in that celebrated Modernist phrase, "a climate of opinion," and now permeates the everyday life and common patois of the time, it being with us when we know it not. All the more reason, then, to disentangle ourselves from a presence that is so pervasive and try to make some sense—if only from the limited perspectives that I employ here, those of time and development—of a movement that has been so epoch-making.

To be sure, we cannot write about Modernism with the same fervor of discovery as did men of letters such as Ernst Robert Curtius, Valéry Larbaud or Edmund Wilson in the 1920s—their works have in part entered into the very canon of Modernism; they themselves were participants. Nor can we write about Modernism with the same wise appreciation and reliable judgment shown by such later witnesses as Stephen Spender and Harry Levin. And yet our historical distance offers opportunities as well. Stragglers in the lower foothills, we might be better able to get a sense of the shape of the mountain.

There is no question but that as a literary movement Modernism has steadily been coming into our view. We are better able now to look at the movement as a whole, so to speak, to map the Modernists' comings and goings, mark their points of connection, the convergences that make for grand clusters

INTRODUCTION

and interchanges. This is possible in part because enough fully detailed monographs on individual Modernists have appeared that we are in a position to bring together the separate studies and speculate about the patterns that they form.[2] Now it becomes easier to place the various Modernists under one roof, to provide a frame for them, a Modernist *épistémè*.

Ever since Harry Levin's essay, "What was Modernism?" (1960), where the verb indicates that its subject's time has clearly passed, discussions of Modernism have increased remarkably.[3] Not only have they increased numerically but the rate of increase has accelerated. At the 1976 meeting of the Modern Language Association of America, no less than six sessions were directly devoted to questions of Modernism; but at the 1979 meeting nine sessions had *post*-Modernism as their subject. These meetings revealed a need: one had the impression that the speakers were talking through one another (although this is perhaps the nature of such meetings), and that the issues had not been profitably joined. It was almost as if, in this time of rapid change, Modernism had been passed by before it had been fully understood. What is needed is a coherent picture of the major forces at work in Modernism, its own principles of change and development, and some sense of its philosophic unity. It is toward these goals of understanding that the present study aspires.

Mapping Literary Modernism, as its subtitled emphasis on time and development suggests, is a highly individual approach to important but not all-inclusive segments of the subject. In its use of time, it positions itself as something of a sequel to my earlier study, *The Renaissance Discovery of Time*.[4] As it was in the Renaissance, so with Modernism: time is at the forward point of the changing consciousness; it performs the function of an indicator-theme. Joachim's rebuke of Hans's heightened susceptibility to the rampant temporal speculations of *The Magic Mountain* ("From the very beginning you began bothering about time,") could very well stand as the motto of this study.

One justification of a theme is the number of superior works

INTRODUCTION

it forces us to consider. Another is the critical violations or abortions that would be perpetrated were this theme to be avoided in discussions of these works. *The Magic Mountain* (the opening chapter of most new sections is devoted to a sustained discourse on the subject of time), *Four Quartets*, the last volume of Proust's *Recherche*, the intervening "Time Passes" chapter of *To the Lighthouse*, *Ulysses*, Gudrun's "internal monologue" at the end of *Women in Love*—these are works of the first rank that the theme of time compels us to consider. In fact, not to consider time when discussing these works would be an extravagance only the most serendipitous among us could afford.

Time is further useful as a centering principle: by its very amorphousness it lends itself to a gathering of kindred ideas and concepts, ideas about fame and children, history and causality. Since I have been making this argument for years, it might be more useful to quote from Malcolm Bradbury's introduction to his co-edited volume of essays, *Modernism*:

> ... one feature that links the movements at this center of sensibility we are discerning is that they tend to see history of human life not as a sequence, or history not as an evolving logic; art and the urgent now strike obliquely across. Modernist works frequently tend to be ordered, then, not on the sequence of historical time or the evolving sequence of character, from history or story, as in realism and naturalism; they tend to work spatially or through layers of consciousness, working towards a logic or metaphor of form.[5]

While this suggests a particular perspective, it does show time to be an underlying principle, allowing us to "center" a broad group of writers.

The connection with the Renaissance is, of course, more substantial. Time is more than a centering principle, a means of gathering in related concepts. Its main use is as a principle of historical placement. Modernism can be located historically in regard to those countries or individuals that enjoyed an advanced notion of time, that is, those countries or individuals whose national past included the formative stage of a Renaissance (or a Reformation), and were thus well along in the processes and effects of industrialization. This remarkably simple idea will further help distinguish between what I would call High Modernism and some of the other avant-garde movements, particularly in the Hispanic and Latin worlds, part of whose idea of Modernism was precisely to adapt for their countries just that sense of time the more advanced Western countries had evolved since the Renaissance and which the more gifted talents were now abandoning.[6] *Mapping Literary Modernism* is thus based upon the understanding that the particular time-world establishing a connection among the nineteenth-century industrialized countries (England, Germany, America and, to a certain degree, France) had its origins in the Renaissance. Consequently, the confrontation with the Renaissance is an essential one for Modernism.

Of the studies establishing the important connection between time and Modernist authors (think only of Poulet, Meyerhoff and Mendilow),[7] several more recent works stand out, and they do so mainly because they also place the conceptions of time and Modernism in clear cultural and historical perspective. I refer to Octavio Paz's *Children of the Mire: Modern Poetry from Romanticism to the Avant-garde* (Harvard University Press, 1974) and Matei Calinescu's *Faces of Modernity: Avant-garde, Decadence, Kitsch* (Indiana University Press, 1977). (A kindred work is Suzi Gablik's *Progress in Art* [New York: Rizzoli, 1977], which, from the viewpoint of space and perspective, establishes important confrontations between the plastic arts of the Renaissance and those of the Modern period.) While differing in style, essential method and focus, each of these two works shows a broad recognition of a distinctive sensibility and style that resulted in the Modernist masterpieces of twentieth-century literature, and each shows how a new conception of time—one that insists on up-to-date involvement in the changing present—is crucial to the development of aesthetic Modernism (as well as to its counterpart and arch-enemy, social modernity). And whether explicitly

INTRODUCTION

(Calinescu, pp. 19-22) or implicitly (Paz, p. 8) each locates the origins of this dynamic conception of time and art in the Renaissance (Paz even utilizes a broader backdrop—one that is not without its difficulties—when he suggests that this conception of time could only have occurred in Western Christendom, with its sense of linear, irreversible time).

At the moment, under the press of post-Modernist revisionism, one of the most interesting and vexing questions attending the problem of Modernism is its relationship with Romanticism. The Renaissance, Romanticism and Modernism—these are the three pivotal cultural movements and mutations of the modern world. The question is to what extent the Romantics anticipated the Moderns in their hostility to the time world that emerged from the Renaissance, and to what extent the Modern is "continuous with" the Romantic and its literary styles only "transformations" of the Romantic. In my early chapters I write of the two aspects of time, the predictive and the innovative, that seemed to enjoy a happier coherence in the time of the Renaissance. I attribute a key concept, the paradox of time, to the almost total suppression of one (the innovative) by the other (the predictive) in the course of the nineteenth century. It is argued that the process of division that occurred between these two forces (also known in their later dress as the mechanistic and the intuitive) was initiated, or, more likely, aggravated, in the period of Romanticism, when the "two modernities" (Calinescu), social modernity with its commitment to prediction and control of events, and aesthetic Modernism with its commitment to innovation and artistic "up-to-dateness" split apart, and have ever since maintained an adversarial and ambiguous relationship.[8] Our problem will be to explain why the Modernist opposition to this overwhelming triumph of the mechanistic, or the predictive, was based upon a new and different style, sensibility and philosophy.

AS FOR the second controlling concept of this study—development—I have been convinced for some time of the advan-

INTRODUCTION

tages to be gained by discussing Modernism in terms of its phases of growth. Throughout the body of this text and summarily in its concluding section, I indicate ways in which awareness of Modernism's development helps us to resolve cruces, or simply helps us to comprehend the fuller picture of its contributions. There is something in the very logic of Modernism's inception and purpose that seems to require development. For instance, as Nietzsche, who was something of a prototype and very much of a prophet of Modernism, foresaw, the very negativity that marks so strongly the preliminary phase of Modernism looks to future growth. Only by first advancing a negative critique, by disturbing "the current optimism that had treated the universe as knowable, in the presumption of eternal truths, and space, time and causality as absolute and universally valid laws," only after that work was accomplished could the kind of art be revived that possessed the realism, the pessimism and, finally, the evocative mythic dimensions of Greek tragedy.[9] The first phase, while necessary, is by itself incomplete, and hence must not be judged until the fuller logic of the Modernist position is realized. How useful this formulation is when analyzing such headstrong young Modernist characters as Paul Morel or Stephen Dedalus. "The struggle of the modern," in Stephen Spender's useful phrase, implies a development, a movement toward an ultimate but hard-won end, whose basic directions, even when unrealized, have become clear.[10] T. E. Hulme, in his essay, "Modern Art and Its Philosophy," refines this idea, making the development of Modernism a three-step process, one of break-up, transformation and culmination (that is, beginning with a necessary negative critique), and these three rubrics might very well describe the first three of the four phases I consider.[11]

Nor, it should be added, are these "phases" merely pedagogic conveniences: they are very palpable occurrences and consistencies in time. For almost all of the writers whom we consider (and many of those whom we do not), the crucial years of break-through and the beginnings of transformations

INTRODUCTION

were those immediately preceding World War I. This generalization encompasses the individual careers of Proust and Mann, Kafka (and Rilke), Joyce, D. H. Lawrence, Eliot, Pound and Stevens (and Robert Frost). This period of stylistic innovation and discovery continued through the war years and resulted in the great harvests of the early twenties. (Curiously enough, the war did not bring a new creative consciousness but rather intensified one already present.) This period of historical consistency was followed by another that extended into and through the thirties. It, however, is decidedly different, with its own common interests and solidarities. We have only to compare *The Waste Land* with *Four Quartets*, *The Magic Mountain* with *Joseph and His Brothers*, *Ulysses* with *Finnegans Wake*, *Jacob's Room* and *Mrs. Dalloway* with *The Waves*, *Harmonium* with *Ideas of Order*, to see the clearly distinctive orders of interest that rule in these successive phases.

The first phase, that which charts Modernism's point of departure, is discussed in the first two chapters, "The Collapse of Historical Values" and "The Family, the Machine and the Paradox of Time."[12] In Modernism, at least, break-through required a break-up, and this is experienced in the first stage of Modernist negativity—itself a necessary prelude to future development. As Nietzsche and others saw, it was necessary to show that this time-complex, inherited from the Renaissance, and its attendant assumptions about art were not absolute but, as it were, historically derived and, as such, subject to historical revision. In obvious ways, these chapters form the book's prologue. Relying on discrepancies between some key phrases in Thomas Mann's *Buddenbrooks* and their renderings in the standard English translation, my aim is to establish what is meant by historical values and the time-complex here involved and to show why and how the break with such values is the necessary Modernist point of departure. From this early resistance much of the character of Modernism derives. Here the central conception, that of the paradox of time, is developed in regard to such generational works as *Buddenbrooks*, *The Rainbow* and *Women in Love*. These works of cre-

INTRODUCTION

ative imagination are complemented by well-known achievements of twentieth-century philosophy and social thought.

If the first phase considers Modernism in its response to the social and historical conditions of the late nineteenth and early twentieth centuries, the second, in the subsequent chapters called "Transformations" and "The Modernist Sensibility," shows the stylistic and thematic consistencies of Modernism. In these chapters I trace the more positive expressions of the formal and aesthetic consciousness of Modernism, particularly as they move beyond (and derive from) the largely negative critiques of the earlier works. In the words of one critic, describing Eliot's movement from *Prufrock* to *The Waste Land*, this development was marked by a "resolute advance upon experience."[13] This phase shows the Modernist need to record the "given" of their time and their experience. But this "constatation of fact," of fact that is stubbornly irreducible, is part of a larger range of experience, of a greater readiness to include within the frame of aesthetic consciousness the infrahuman, the social and the ethical, and the religious as distinguishable but necessary parts of experience. Behind this most decisive phase of Modernist development there stands a philosophy, the hierarchic one of T. E. Hulme, that seeks to provide a unifying frame to these many strands of complex consciousness. In this phase, Modernists began to evolve a new typology, one that went beyond the "negative heroes" of their earlier works. In this regard, Tiresias, Bloom, Hans Castorp and Marcel, as others have recognized, are all brothers under the skin.

The even fuller and more positive purpose of Modernism is met in its third phase, in the chapters entitled "The Songs That I Sing" and "Three Major Works." If, following Hulme's formulation, the second phase involved "transformations," it is tempting to think of this third as the "culmination" (but that will remain one of the essential critical and aesthetic questions confronting the student of Modernism; whether, indeed, as works of art, *Four Quartets* is superior to *The Waste Land*, *Finnegans Wake* to *Ulysses*, or *Joseph and His Brothers* to

INTRODUCTION

The Magic Mountain). This phase of Modernist development shows the goal of Modernism, for the sake of which the linear time-complex had first to be disrupted, to be mythopoetic art (which is, of course, the end Nietzsche had in mind for the art of the new era), and the recovery of some sense of the self in relation to the past and to the individual's own inner being. One can see why this phase has been labeled "neo-Romantic" (particularly in relation to Wallace Stevens), and, indeed, the question of Romanticism's relation to Modernism is particularly complicated at this period.

The last phase (in the chapter I call "The Bite of Time"), represents something of a pullback, with most Modernists here expressing a revived sense of the reality of history, of the event and of time itself. This is the point of return, which while not as marked a historical moment as the two preceding ones, still owes a lot to the chastened attitudes of the thirties as well as to the new political and economic consciousness of a rising generation. As a moral pattern it completes the paradigm of Modernist development and prepares the way for many of the political and social values of the 1950s. This point of return has a fitting purpose in the Modernist order of development, since without exception it only occurs after the greatest liberties have been taken with time, history and event; only then do the Modernists feel compelled to right the balance and reinvoke the reign of consequence after the play of consciousness.

WHILE THESE are some of the interesting issues that emerge when we discuss Modernism in the light of its own internal dynamic of development, there is also a contemporary critical need for devising a paradigm of Modernist development. In reaction to the overwhelming triumph of the historical method in the nineteenth century, literary criticism of the twentieth century—in its newer waves—has tended to be antihistorical, or at best ahistorical. As a consequence, we hear more about contiguity studies than about continuity studies, more about synchrony than about diachrony, more about structure than

INTRODUCTION

about dialectic or development, and more about myth than about history. Yet it would appear that the more admirable literary critics are those who have explored both ways of human knowing. Erich Auerbach, for instance, has written about *figura*, but also about mimesis, and more importantly has shown their intersection in the works of Dante.[14] Indeed, the richness of such complexity is not in keeping the two approaches separate, but in showing their interconnection. There cannot be a coherent structuralism (as the late Jean Piaget has shown) apart from constructivism; but neither should literary history be blind to the helpful formulations to be had from studies of patterns and structures.[15]

Piaget, a clinical psychologist but in truth a philosopher (and how interesting to learn that he began his career as a zoologist), was admirably situated to help us contain within the frame of our speculations some of these dichotomies of contemporary critical thinking. In such theoretical works as *Genetic Epistemology* (trans. Eleanor Duckworth [New York: Norton, 1971]) and *Structuralism* (trans. Chaninah Maschler [New York: Harper and Row, 1970]), he has rendered an immense service to literary history in his suggestions of a fusion of the paradigmatic and the developmental. A structuralist himself, he nevertheless asks that if we are not to believe that the anthropological structures of Claude Lévi-Strauss or the *épistémès* of the late Michel Foucault are innate or permanent, how are these structures then obtained? What are their initiating conditions and how do they develop? Piaget has provided a theoretical and practical justification for returning literary study to its true bases in time and history, to preoccupations with causality and change, origins and principles of transformation, genesis and development.

On the other hand, the importance of structures for literary history is that they help us to see. They are perceptual. They raise to the level of discussion elements of a work that might have remained buried. We must rise above the dogmas of empiricism and share in the benefits of speculative and systematic criticism. Oddly enough, E. H. Gombrich, who is himself a

INTRODUCTION

perceptualist, has urged the cultural historian to concern himself with the "individual and the particular rather than with the study of structures and patterns."[16] Yet, if literary criticism is a method, it is also a process involving movement from the particular to the general (the best schema are those that emerge internally from the deepest immersion in the particularities of a work) and from the general to the particular (the test of any pattern or structure must lie in the individual readings that it yields). We begin with the text, the passage and the line, and by our own "commodius vicus of recirculation" we must return to them.

Points of departure, initiating conditions; points of return, arresting conditions, the end of a movement—these are means of delimiting a phenomenon as complex as a literary movement. Between these termini, the great literary movements undergo an evolution, with phases of development. As we, following Piaget, must ask how the initiating conditions of a movement are obtained, so we must account in a genetic way for its successive phases. We must see not only that one phase follows another, but the ways in which one phase actually derives from the preceding. In my earlier study of the Renaissance, I made use of the schema Ernst Cassirer proposed in his *Individual and Cosmos in the Philosophy of the Renaissance*. The beauty of his schema (graduated mediation, chorismos and methexis) was that it was internally developed, that it was susceptible of extension to writers like Montaigne and Shakespeare, whom Cassirer did not have in mind, and that it explained how one stage of development grew out of and in relation to the preceding.[17] I am attempting a similar sort of thing in *Mapping Literary Modernism*: an internal, generational schema of Modernist development, with a point of departure, with distinct, recognizably valid phases that cover in their extent the fullest growth of the major Modernists, with some basis for understanding how subsequent phases emerged from the preceding, and how and why the Modernist movement came to an end.

INTRODUCTION

ANOTHER advantage to be gained from establishing a paradigm of development for Modernist writers is that such a paradigm suggests the range of their complex vision. It is as a consequence of this complex range that Modernists individually and as part of a movement exceed the normal tendency to be misunderstood, a situation that comes about when one quality or one phase of their evolution is singled out and made to speak for the others. One student has regarded the Modernist movement primarily as Dionysian, while another has emphasized its formal, reflexive qualities (to the declared exclusion of D. H. Lawrence).[18] Modernism has been denounced by Marxist critics and others of the left as reactionary, and attacked by reactionaries for being part of the liberal froth of modern times. It has been said to be overly intellectualized and yet to lack ideas; formalistic and devoted to the Word, while erotic, primitivistic and given over to the unconscious; heroic élitist and yet common, attached to the self and yet in search of myth. The surprisingly contradictory extent of the testimony points to the multiform range of Modernist concern.

Premonitions of this Modernist complexity may be seen in Baudelaire and Nietzsche—they are among the "solitary precursors." The French poet, one of the crucial voices in the development of the Modern, explicitly regards it as an artistic vindication of the aesthetic validity of present-day life (see "On the heroism of modern life," in *The Salon of 1846*). Art must be up-to-date; the only advantage we might have is in the newness of our experience. Yet, in "The Modern Artist" (part of *The Salon of 1859*), Baudelaire chastises the Modern artist as being the spoiled child of his century: he knows nothing of the past; he is uneducated. In his *Painter of Modern Life* (1863), while describing one half of modernity as being concerned with the "transitory, the fugitive and the contingent," the other half records the "eternal and the immutable. . . ." On a public street in full day a spirit accosts a passer-by.[19]

Nietzsche's most interesting works reveal a similar modu-

INTRODUCTION

lation and complexity (qualities Anglo-American readers, accustomed only to the fulminations of *Thus Spake Zarathustra*, do not normally associate with his thoughts). On the one hand, Nietzsche deplores the defeat of the present by the past. The triumph of history in his time has only brought about an enfeebled sense of decline: "we are latecomers and epigoni, . . . we are, in a word, born with gray hair." This conception of history is only disguised theology, inherited from the Middle Ages.[20] In Nietzsche we can see how potent was the myth of the Renaissance, resistant to any idea of decline, and urging the men of the present to make solid their own places in time. Yet, Nietzsche can only ridicule the presumption of the idea of progress: that the latecomer is elevated to the godhead, that the men of his time seem to be the culmination of the entire process of history. Indeed, this latter twist makes Nietzsche all the more congenial to the curious double nature of the Renaissance, its young heroes set in opposition to the historical sense of decline, as if there were nothing more to be done, while at the same time looking to the greater heroes of the past for sparks of illumination, as well as direct models to imitate. The myth of the Renaissance as heroic revival was part of Nietzsche's spirit, tragically so, since as we shall see, it brought with it aspects of the will and ego that were not congenial to the real needs of the twentieth-century Modern.

These examples of Baudelaire and Nietzsche show how difficult it is to pin down the nature of the Modern. As we work to suggest more positively the nature of Modernism, we find a sensibility that is neither neo-Romantic nor neoclassical, yet one that combines elements of each into a third entity and that is capable of bringing together figures as nominally diverse as T. S. Eliot and D. H. Lawrence (a conjunction, it is interesting to note, that the later F. R. Leavis had no difficulty in accepting).[21] In a similar way, in their reactions to the effects of bourgeois industrialized society, Nietzsche and Marx, Bergson and Lukács may be joined. T. E. Hulme, whose own gropings toward hard-line truths are strangely bound up with the sense of a buried, more fundamental self (that can nevertheless be described in very precise terms), reflects this Mod-

INTRODUCTION

ernist ambivalence. He was very much in sympathy with the anti-Romanticism expressed in two books by Pierre Lasserre, and yet was troubled when this member of the *Action Française* attacked Bergson: "I was in agreement with both sides, and so I wondered whether there was any real inconsistency in my own position.[22]

Perhaps the fullest statement made by a Modernist showing his sense of the new attitude—that almost paradoxical combination of qualities that seems to defy categorization—was made by Thomas Mann in his essay on Schopenhauer, in whom he finds a sensibility, a style and a philosophy that prefigure the Modern. Antitheses like classic and Romantic do not apply to Schopenhauer: "He stands nearer to us than do the minds who in their day were occupied with such distinctions and ranged themselves accordingly." And "Schopenhauer's mental life (*Geistesform*), the dualistic, over-strained irritability and fever of his genius, is less Romantic than Modern." This mixture in Schopenhauer's nature combined the rationalism of Voltaire with the mysticism of Jacob Boehme, and "resulted in the paradox of a classic pellucid prose employed to illumine the darkest and lowest purlieus of being"—a sentence that could in fact be used to describe Freud.[23] Similar attempts to raise up models that bring together other such combinations of qualities is a marked feature of the Modernist essayists. Mann's essay on Kafka comes to mind, as do Eliot's most influential pieces on the metaphysicals, Andrew Marvell, and George Herbert.

Schopenhauer's role, in which Mann as a Modernist involves himself, was to test humanism against hard facts, to extend the Enlightenment into areas of darkness and irrationality, and, in a larger sense, as Nietzsche himself advocated, to qualify at its depths the bourgeois, liberal and scientific worldpicture of the nineteenth century. This is evidence, of course, that the source of Modernism is not only to be sought in stylistic experimentalism. "In short," Mann concludes, "what I called his pessimistic humanity seems to me to herald the temper of a future time."

INTRODUCTION

If our concern is to extend the pavilion of what constitutes critical fact, certainly there is meaning in the controversies surrounding Modernism, a meaning that points to an essential truth, namely that Modernism is both and neither, both neo-classical and neo-Romantic and neither at the same time, that it transcends each in the formation of a new type of sensibility, style and philosophy. It is for this reason, then, that approaches to Modernism must be as comprehensive as its own complex and evolving nature. Since the extraordinary range of the Modernists' register is in some way the basis of their development, to follow this development will help suggest their true complexity.

FINALLY, I would like to establish some ground rules and general principles governing this study. Its historical center of gravity extends from about 1900 to about 1940; in other words, from the decade prior to World War I into the early years of World War II (if we date Romanticism from about 1790 to roughly 1830, we see that like it Modernism spans some forty years). But once the critical mass of a movement has been established there is not too much point in arguing over exact beginning or ending dates. For instance, I have no objection to pushing the beginning of Modernism as a movement back to 1890, which has in its defense clear evidence that in the earlier decade the content of the term "modern" shifted. Prior to that time the modern was identifiable with what we mean by modernization, technological progress, new attitudes on social issues, the spreading franchise, hygiene, liberal democracy—"to cut and sew, be neat in everything / In the best modern way." It is in this sense of the word that Ibsen, Shaw, Bennett and Wells were and remain modern. In the 1890s, however, the impact of Nietzsche's long-neglected work began to be felt.[24] After Nietzsche had lapsed into incompetency, the Danish critic Georg Brandes endeavored to make his thought known to Germany and Europe. The impact of this collaborative effort gave to Modernism a new ingredient of pessimism, irony and even hostility to democratic programs

17

INTRODUCTION

and scientific progress. The children stare in wonder at "a sixty-year-old smiling public man," but Yeats is dreaming of a "Ledaean body." Modernism itself begins with the dilemma of these two modernities and never escapes their polar pulls, pulls that are reflected in two divergent critical alignments over the purpose of Modernism (see "Purviews and Purposes").

At the other end, however, there is more of a problem. If the purpose of the years we suggest as outer limits is to allow the full articulation of Modernist development, then there is a serious loss if we stop that development short at around 1930 (as Bradbury and McFarlane do in their much-used collection of essays, *Modernism*). We lose that superb decade of Modernist development, where many of the fuller implications of their earlier positions were brought out and expanded. In the 1930s Joyce was working on *Finnegans Wake*, Mann on *Joseph and His Brothers*, Eliot on *Four Quartets*, Virginia Woolf had moved on to *The Waves* and that "late-blooming genius" Wallace Stevens was about to break a more than ten-year-long period of silence and to write again in a rich and new manner. If we arrest Modernist development at about 1930, we do indeed cover the "mythic method" of the 1920s, but we miss that period of further growth, the natural consequence of the interests of the 1920s, when these writers went beyond "method" into the very heart of myth itself.

An epoch is not a movement, as E. H. Gombrich reminds us in his valuable essay, *In Search of Cultural History*.[25] Not all the writers within this time-period were Modernists (here we can make use of the distinction made by Stephen Spender—and by Valéry before him—between Moderns and contemporaries, separating the Moderns from those of their coevals, who nevertheless held to older conceptions of style, of sensibility and of self).[26] As is apparent, the focus of this study will rest on the "high" or "classical" Modernists, whom tradition tends to group in by now familiar litanies: Proust, Mann, Pound, Eliot, Stevens, Joyce, Virginia Woolf, D. H. Lawrence, Kafka. . . .[27]

This study does not pretend to be a history, and the figures

INTRODUCTION

it chooses to present are more illustrative than exclusionary. It will not attempt to sort out the complex relations between Modernism and all the avant-garde movements of the early part of this century. Obviously there are real and intricate connections. For this reason and other personal reasons I find it very hard to disagree with Renato Poggioli's inspired conviction, expressed in his *Theory of the Avant-garde*, that the Modernist genius is essentially avant-gardistic.[28] In its origins this is doubtlessly true, but in the final achieved masterpieces of the twenties and thirties, the major Modernists went beyond their earlier associations with the avant-garde and brought to their works a sense of personal appropriation that resulted in fuller aesthetic experiences. This is perhaps what is meant when Eliot remarked that Imagism had served a critical function (thereby denying it a creative function), or when Lawrence complained that Futurism lacked a sense of naïveté (Apollinaire, too, after having been an earlier supporter, later separated himself from Futurism), or when Stevens, in his *Adagia* writes, "The essential fault of surrealism is that it invents without discovering."[29]

Of the older writers, I regretfully neglect Yeats. I can very well understand why David Perkins in his recent study places Yeats among the grand masters of Modernism.[30] Yet, since Yeats already had had a fuller career and mature style prior to his contact with the young Modernists, his involvement does not seem to have the same freshness and personal identification as that of others his juniors, whose own careers were coincidental with the rise of the Modern. And of the young writers, born in this century, treatment will even be sketchier (think of Malraux and Beckett, Sartre, and Camus, Hemingway, Fitzgerald and Faulkner, the Joycean Broch). If I am indeed approaching the philosophic unity of Modernism, then I may not be avoiding these writers at all, but rather using other figures to suggest the intellectual climate in which they participated and out of which they grew.[31]

As this study progressed and as I became more aware of its own unfolding character, it became clear that what I was de-

INTRODUCTION

veloping, one of its personal centers, was the intellectual background of the generation of the 1950s, the last generation to take to the works of the Modernists with anything like avidity. If this "historical" work does have a contemporary resonance, it has it by reminding us of the intellectual continuities between Modernism and this later post-World War II generation. In this sense, the watershed separating us from a genuine contemporary participation in Modernism was not only formed by the attitudes of post-Modernism but also by the new needs of the activist sixties, the values of community and commitment, the new moral feeling and fire, and the convictions that smashed through the prevailing sense of ambivalence, studied complexity, divided loyalties and unacceptable alternatives—by all the events that drove a younger generation to seek liberation from the moral schizophrenia that had bedeviled the later heirs of Modernist attitudes, the aesthetic correlations and structurings, the complex consciousness and the aesthetic and moral distancings of Modernism.

CHAPTER I

The Collapse of Historical Values

Two questions bring into preliminary focus some of the more basic issues motivating this study. If we date the commencement of Modernist activity from about 1900, or even if we push back the initiating conditions to 1890 and include that decade of ferment, we must reflect that either date locates a crucial contradiction. At those times European civilization and culture exercised a practically world-wide hegemony. "European civilization overshadowed the earth."[1] "Europe dominated the world politically as well as economically."[2] Yet, at that very time, two remarkable works of literature appeared, the forerunners of many more, that clearly showed strong dissatisfaction within European society itself, and among some of its most gifted talents, with the very principles upholding that world-wide supremacy. To be sure, there had been other barometers of defection, but few of those works summarize as potently this particular contradiction as do Joseph Conrad's *Heart of Darkness* and Thomas Mann's *Buddenbrooks*, or are as profound in their analyses of the causes of the European malaise. These works are not centered on out-of-the-way protests of peripheral characters, but show the afflictions of the most representative adherents to the codes of nineteenth-century values. Their defeats come by their allegiances to the very values of their culture. "All Europe contributed to the making of Kurtz." *Buddenbrooks* actually shows that it is the values underlying the powerful Western dynamic that lead to stagnation and yield little satisfaction. The question to be asked is

COLLAPSE OF HISTORICAL VALUES

why in these decades of the nineties and before World War I so many writers and thinkers found their most active creative mode, that which led to a recognition of their style and material, in devastating critiques of the foundations of a society that was apparently so flourishing and so abundant in the rewards and satisfactions it offered.

This contradiction can be stated another way. One of the most consistent and yet astonishing phenomena of America undergraduate education is the way—by now—generations of students respond to *The Waste Land*. Why should these students, whose untutored and probably unvoiced preferences are still romantic, democratic, and filled with secular optimism, be so fascinated by a poem whose author not long after its publication would make known his classical, royalist and Anglo-Catholic allegiances? This contrast of Eliot's professions with principles of liberal democracy is not an isolated instance. Witness what can only be called the "Dostoevsky phenomenon." If given a choice, whom would the literate undergraduate of ten years ago or more have preferred, Dostoevsky or Dickens? A new kind of voice entered literature in the later nineteenth century, a voice represented by the names of Baudelaire, Dostoevsky, Nietzsche and Rimbaud, and this voice had a resonating appeal in twentieth-century literature. With what bitter passion does Paul Morel recite Baudelaire to Miriam in *Sons and Lovers*! Thomas Mann summarizes this voice in the French expression spoken by Mme. Chauchat to Hans Castorp (Russian sentiment by way of French expression summarizes the literary tradition in Mann's historically accurate, synoptic novel). We must be *aventuriers dans le mal*, she tells him in the voice of a new Modernism that sweeps away the precautions of the older Modernism of the liberal humanist, Settembrini. These are the experiences that must remain with us as we try to understand the motivations of Modernism.

One might ask, in addition, why what is primarily a literary study would bring into foremost position such cultural questions. There is a reason for devoting, as this first chapter will do, substantial space to the philosophical or ideological bases of Modernism. Perhaps the most intriguing and substantial criticism of Modernism derives from a not unsympathetic critic, Graham Hough, whose charge is a crucial one. He argues that, unlike Romanticism, Modernism represented no spiritual shift in values.[3] That is, Modernism primarily represented a change in the style but not in the substance of our culture; it may have altered the diction of Romanticism but not its prevailing spirit. Modernism had no prevalent character. Against this view we argue that literary Modernism was part of a significant shift in values, one whose impact is still with us, and whose ideology and style are practically inseparable, each having their roots in the higher stages of industrialization. This historical placement, as the Introduction indicated and as the next chapters argue, is a determining factor in the nature of Modernism.

1. *Time and History: The Renaissance Connection*

We sometimes need to be reminded that almost without exception the high classical Modernists were also the greatest essayists of their day. Nor were they only random essayists; rather, they were actively engaged in giving a valid historical structure to their thought and work. They made bold and speculative incursions into history in order to carve out niches for their own positions. Modernism, in its initiating conditions, was set directly against the values of historical continuity that this chapter will delineate, but Modernists were quite capable of using history to alter the perspective of historicism. As innovators they knew the dimensions of the circle that they were breaking, and they were able to rearrange the pieces of the design that they had voided.

For the Modernists no period was in greater need of revised thinking than the Renaissance—that most formative period of our cultural past. T. E. Hulme was able to write with some categoricalness: "A proper understanding of the Renaissance seems to me to be the most pressing necessity of thought at the present moment."[4] And most certainly he was not alone. Such influential writers as Wilhelm Worringer and Ortega y Gasset saw that the requirements of their culture undermined the hegemony of the naturalistic humanism that had prevailed in the arts since the Renaissance. In his monumental novel, *The Magic Mountain*, Thomas Mann sensed that the crisis his age was experiencing was a crisis of culture—one that Mr. Bradbury regards as being typical of Modernism—and that the culture which was ending was one that had originated in the Renaissance. In his lengthy essay, "Goethe and Tolstoy," Mann asks the question that he was in the process of dramatizing in *The Magic Mountain*:

> Is there not also in western Europe a feeling alive that not only for Russia, but for it, for us, for all the world there is at hand the ending of an epoch: the bourgeois, humanistic, liberal epoch, which was born at the Renaissance and came to power with the French Revolution, and whose last convulsive twitchings and manifestations of life we are now beholding?[5]

In an essay more than a decade later, where Mann's changed ideological emphases produce a different Goethe, "the representative of the bourgeois age," the same problem remains:

> For us who are witnessing the end of an epoch, the bourgeois, whose fate it is to search, in the midst of the great stress of the transition, for the path into the new worlds, new orientations within and without, for us this third angle of vision is the most immediate and natural: to see him, that is, as representative of the five hundred years which we call the bourgeois epoch, from the fifteenth to the turn of the nineteenth.[6]

And although in this later essay (1932) Mann has revised his estimation of the bourgeois, middle-class morality, still vigilance over time is one of its characteristics. Goethe was a prime representative of the bourgeois "time-cult" and "time-economy"—"Time was his field (Sein Acker die Zeit)," Mann concludes.[7]

To alter the conditions of the thought and of the society under whose burdens they suffered, leading Modernists felt they had to place those conditions in historical perspective (to remove them from the categories of the absolute, or the permanent) to take them back to their source, which was the Renaissance, and by showing the historical moment of their origins, that from which they emerged, to suggest alternative possibilities. There were, of course, ambivalences in the Modern attitudes toward the Renaissance. On the one hand, that period contains the classics of the modern world, and where ideological objection is the strongest—precisely in a writer like T. E. Hulme—admiration is still the due of their artistic accomplishments. On the social, religious and philosophical planes, however—and this particularly in the most highly industrialized countries in Europe, like Germany and England—reservations are apparent as to the tendencies of Renaissance thought and society and their later developments.

It should be obvious that by invoking the Renaissance we are doing more than perfunctorily providing "valuable cultural background." The contention with the Renaissance enters vitally into the very nature of Modernism and in very particular ways. If a key conquest of the Renaissance was the modern notion of time, one so crucial to the mentality of our industrialized societies, then it is not surprising that in a time of disenchantment with that industrial base, the formative concept of time should itself undergo revision. This explains why time is more than a convenient guy-wire, or even centering principle: it is a major article in the debate with the Renaissance.

No one knew this better than Nietzsche, who was the first thinker to set the pattern for the Modernist attitude toward the Renaissance and toward time. As a young philologist, the possibilities Nietzsche perceived in the German victory over France in the war of 1870 are responsible for the contemporary resonance of his brilliant early work, *The Birth of Trag-*

edy.[8] That "external" triumph was to have provided both the occasion for the German people to shed the relics of Romance culture and the inspiration for a more "inward" regeneration worthy of the heirs of Luther. (Nietzsche's attitude toward his people was soon to change when it became evident that the splendid opportunities presented by the military victory were not being fully exploited by the German people.) By this strange mixture of a Romantic quest for a national mythology with a remarkable classical culture, Nietzsche heralded a new German Renaissance, perhaps even a Northern Renaissance, to compensate for the one his nation never had and to replace the Latin Renaissance that had gone wrong. The Italian Renaissance had developed into the rational civilization of the French Enlightenment. The figure at the head of that culture was Socrates, who epitomized the forces of rationalism that had undermined Greek tragedy. This Socratism was revived in the fifteenth century and placed itself at the center of Western intellectual life. Now, four hundred years later, the fact that Socratic culture has crumbled stands clearly revealed. The war has brought home this higher truth. But the German nation must take advantage of the greater possibilities afforded by its military victory: it must thoroughly refashion Western intellectual life out of Germany's two most significant contributions, philosophy and music. Adherence to the spirit of these achievements will, by a strange reversal, bring back the tragic pessimism (the essay's subtitle is "Greek Pessimism") that had prevailed in Greek tragedy before it was eroded by the Socratic rationalism of Euripides.

Nietzsche is a Modernist in responding to this urgent contemporary need. A critical moment has presented itself, one representing a new juncture in Western society. Another critical period from the past—the end of Greek tragedy—may, by a kind of "reverse parallel," give directions to present actions. Nietzsche is consciously aware that he is using history to defeat history: "History must solve the problem of history, science must turn its sting against itself." (*The Use and Abuse of History*, see below.) In short, the inherited way of regarding

COLLAPSE OF HISTORICAL VALUES

things, the rationalism that had prevailed since the Renaissance, is shown to be not permanent but rather the product of an historical development, a development that may itself be reversed. The eternal conflict between Socratism, or theoretical optimism, and tragic pessimism works itself out on the wheel of history. For a term one will prevail, to be succeeded under different historical conditions by the other. Now, Nietzsche's time is ripe for the reassertion of the second opposing pole of that eternally recurrent duality. Just as Socratic culture replaced Greek tragedy based upon myth, so, by "inverse dialectic," going in "reverse order," or what we have called "reverse parallel," the Socratic culture originating in the Renaissance will be replaced by Germanic culture with its own tragic myth.[9]

The consequence of this reliance on Socratic culture has become clear for all to see, showing itself in the development of Faustian man (a type, Nietzsche avers, that would be incredible to the Greeks, so imbued with a sense of limits—what Ortega would later call "finitism"). The end of Faustian man is imminent and is detectable by the same symptoms that presaged the dissolution of Greek culture (again working in reverse order): "Today we experience the same extravagant thirst for knowledge, the same insatiable curiosity, the same drastic secularization, the nomadic wanderings, the greedy rush to alien tables, the frivolous apotheosis of the present or the stupefied negation of it." Curiously enough, Nietzsche regards the unrest of the proletariet, themselves now infected with this restless drive toward the future, as the most disquieting sign of dissolution.[10] Looking ahead for a moment and in a context where we are stressing Nietzsche's great relevancy for Modernism, we must also suggest that in this impatience with fragmentation, his evident quest for unity and identity, Nietzsche shows his Romantic roots—he does not show the Modernist capacity to exploit and develop the virtues of cosmopolitanism, diversity and fragmentation.

Nietzsche's early work performs many services for the development of the Modernist temper. First, of course, he makes use of startling historical parallels to undermine the assumed permanence of the inherited Renaissance world-view. Secondly, he suggests that the symptoms of the end of a culture are to be found everywhere and in all aspects of life. He shows the human consequences over a wide field of activities, and in this he will be followed by many novelists and poets. And thirdly, he shows how he has philosophical support in his efforts, the suport of German philosophy, the most interesting philosophy of the nineteenth century. In particular, Nietzsche's emphasis on the philosophical attack on the inherited conception of time shows why a new concept of time would be so important for Modernism. Just as the larger culture was presumed to be permanent, so this concept was presumed to be absolute. In attacking its notions of time, German philosophy was attacking not only the foundations of modern science but also the bases of Socratic and historical culture:

> The extraordinary courage and wisdom of Kant and Schopenhauer have won the most difficult victory, that over the optimistic foundations of logic, which form the underpinnings of our culture. Whereas the current optimism had treated the universe as knowable, in the presumption of eternal truths, and space, time and causality as absolute and universally valid laws, Kant showed how these supposed laws served only to raise appearance—the work of Maya—to the status of true reality, thereby rendering impossible a genuine understanding of that reality....[11]

The discontent that Nietzsche detected extended across a wide range of associated values, of which the central, most potent one was the inherited conception of time. In the Renaissance the new sense of time emerged with a new order of historical values. This is the connection I am trying to make, one that shows up so clearly in Nietzsche's early thought. The older conception of time and causality—which had previously seemed to be so formidable a part of reality and which, following Newton, seemed so absolute—is the basis for the new triumph of history in the nineteenth century. History—not only in the

COLLAPSE OF HISTORICAL VALUES

sense of historiography but as a way of knowing and of being—seemed to take over the more individual qualities of life, and this usurpation was a further extension of the victory of Socratic man.

Consequently, Nietzsche's *Use and Abuse of History* (*Vom Nutzen und Nachteil der Historie für das Leben*, written in 1873, published in 1874) is the natural ally of *The Birth of Tragedy*. In the earlier work he already shows some of the larger needs of Modernism when he argues against the process of secularization that had begun in the Renaissance and was associated with the name of Socrates, all things coming to be viewed *sub specie saeculi*. He foresaw the mythic needs of Modernism, the need to have, as in Greek tragedy, "the immediate present appear *sub specie aeternitatis*, and in a certain sense timeless," and to give to everyday experience "the stamp of the eternal." Nietzsche anticipates the positive creative impetus of the Moderns, present in Mann and in Kafka, in Joyce and Eliot and in Lawrence, the active goal behind their need to break up the continuities of history, to disrupt the linear, to shed routine, and that goal was to look at experience with the vision of the timeless, or mythic. In the very passage of *The Birth of Tragedy* where Nietzsche distinguishes between life led *sub specie aeternitatis*, where the individual partakes of the typical as a constant source of universal reference, and life considered *sub specie saeculi*, he writes that the opposite of the universalizing and timeless vision occurs "when a nation begins to conceive itself historically *(sich historich zu begreifen)* and to demolish the mythical bulwarks that surround it."[12] This process, Nietzsche tells us, began in the Renaissance.

There will be other opportunities for detailing the many other values—also triumphant in the nineteenth century—that were so dependent upon the development of concepts of time and of history. For the moment, I want to fix on their necessary association and origin in the Renaissance. If Claude Lévi-Strauss is right in declaring that in the modern world, history has replaced myth, providing connections with past and future and a charter for action in the present (which, inciden-

COLLAPSE OF HISTORICAL VALUES

tally, is a superb way to describe the role of history in Shakespeare's history plays), we can be historically more explicit and say that it was in the Renaissance that this replacement began to occur.[13] History, as Lévi-Strauss's phrase would indicate, is not only knowledge of the past, it implies connections, continuities, and a "charter" or justification for action in the present. Shakespeare's history plays—that very significant generic contribution of the Renaissance—confirm the emergence of these values of time and historical continuity. Prince Hal must learn the new valuation of time if he is to escape the fates of Richard II and Falstaff. He must extricate himself from their great illusions if he is to avoid the vanity that ends in nothingness. To redeem the time for him means to come into possession of his historical identity. In becoming his father's son and true successor, Hal, with a rare show of exhilaration, finds redemption in historical continuity:

> The tide of blood in me
> Hath proudly flowed in vanity till now.
> Now doth it turn and ebb back to the sea,
> Where it shall mingle with the state of floods
> And flow henceforth in formal majesty.
> (2 *Henry IV*, V. ii. 129-133)

The Renaissance discovery of time carried with it a complex of values that could be called historical. More faith came to be placed in those earthly things that promised continuity: the polis, marriage, family, children and fame. These were redemptive counters, significant achievements in man's need to rescue himself from nothingness. In this sense, Shakespeare's history plays are not only historical in subject, they are historical in value. And these achievements and values were dependent upon a new and aroused militancy toward time. Temporal linearity and historical lineality, or succession, merge. "Fair sequence and succession."[14]

When we come to the first stirrings of Modernism, it is clear that something has happened to this code. History, once redemptive in its processes for Hal, has for Stephen Dedalus become nightmarish. Eliot will voice an old man's fatigue with the saeculum: "I am tired with my own life and the life of those after me." His sense of "redeeming time" is not the secular one of Prince Hal, rather it is the Pauline: "Redeem / The unread vision in the higher dream."[15] It is no accident that the need for a larger vision should coincide with a feeling of ennui with history. The nineteenth century witnessed the triumph of the values of history and continuity that had emerged from the Renaissance. One of its great faiths held that man could save himself or was in the process of saving himself by being part of a collectivity, a system, a stream of continuity. Maurice Mandelbaum, in his *History, Man and Reason*, argues that the paramount belief in the nineteenth century was "that an adequate understanding of the nature of any phenomenon and an adequate assessment of its values are to be gained through considering it in terms of the place which it occupied and the role which it played within a process of development."[16] Yet in the midst of this triumph, Nietzsche proclaimed the crisis of historical values, their failure to satisfy, and portentously declared that there can be "no salvation in process."[17] The imposing first sentence of T. E. Hulme's "Humanism and the Religious Attitude," confirms this view of the nineteenth century: "One of the main achievements of the nineteenth century was the elaboration and universal application of the principle of continuity." He follows this with a typical call to arms, "The destruction of this conception is, on the contrary, an urgent necessity of the present."[18]

Discussions of time and history unavoidably bring in close association other concepts of a wide range and interest. This is because time is so amorphous that it is almost impossible to consider it as a pure, isolated idea. It has been called a "socialized" concept by a Japanese physicist; it almost naturally must be considered together with other features of human life.[19] By itself it is hard to visualize: like the wind we only see it when the trees bend. Consequently, when Nietzsche denounces the scientific rationalism epitomized by Socrates, which rationalism, revived in the Renaissance and come to fruition in the nineteenth century is based upon definite conceptions of space, time and causality, he means, as we have suggested, an entire complex of qualities originating in the most formative period of our culture. And so, too, the Modernists, while directing the vanguard of their attack against such concepts as time and linear causality still had to extend their efforts to many other closely related concepts.

The suicidal Rhoda in Virginia Woolf's most experimental novel, *The Waves*, gives us some idea of what enters into this complex of ideas—the kind of associations that are germane to the inherited notion of time. That she is an eventual suicide should not deter us from accepting her thoughts (frequently in Virginia Woolf—think of Septimus Warren Smith in *Mrs. Dalloway*—the suicidal speak essential truths, truths that they carry to an extreme solution). As Septimus Warren Smith is the surrogate for Mrs. Dalloway so Rhoda can be ours. Rhoda perceives her group of friends in the distance, "how [they] stand embedded in a substance made of repeated moments run together. . . ." Their involvement with time shows an inner coherence, it hangs together, bestowing a solid quality to their beings. And she goes beyond that to draw other meaning from the order and coherence of time: "[they] are committed, have an attitude, with children, authority, fame, love, society; where I have nothing. I have no face."[20]

Virginia Woolf is instinctively insightful here. The terms that are contrasted are almost precisely those that are set against each other in Shakespeare's *Richard II*, but in reverse order. In Shakespeare's play it is Richard II, representing an older dispensation, who is incapable of mustering a more vigorous, realistic conception of time. And it is Richard who has no children, who loses authority, identity, and is finally confronted with namelessness and nothingness. In contrast to Richard is his conqueror, Bolingbroke, who seems so settled in the solid world of connections and consequences. Prince Hal, on the verge of being dispossessed, of suffering discontinuity, profits from fatherly counsel (this lineal connection is pivotal in each part of *Henry IV*) and is moved to accept his

COLLAPSE OF HISTORICAL VALUES

historical identity, with all of its implications. As Rhoda declares of her friends for whom time seems to cohere: "[they] are committed, have an attitude."

This historical world of sensed connections and continuities involves choice, decision and character, "attitudes and commitments." By a reasonable extension of the word, it has been called the "ethical."[21] If we accept this terminology, contrasting the transformations of Hal with the trends of Modernism (using Rhoda's words as an illustrative example), we can say that in the Renaissance time had distinctly ethical importance. Richard relies on metaphysical being, while Henry and Hal enter into time and history (hence the larger cultural significance of Shakespeare's "history" plays). The Renaissance shift moves from the metaphysical to the ethical. In Modernism the reverse is true, and for considerable reason. The shift is not toward the "ethical" but away from it. One feels cast out of the world of time and its connections. One such connection is brought home in Malraux's *La Condition humaine*, when old Gisors mourns over the body of his son, "son espoir mort," thinks that now he is thrown outside of time ("rejeté hors du temps"): "the child was the submission to time, to the flow of things (à la couleé des choses)."[22] Others, too, will sense not the ethical solidity and coherence of time, but rather its emptiness, its vacuity, not the direction of time, but rather its pointlessness. In this same way, for other Modernists time is intimately involved with other forces of human experience: history, the ethical, marriage and children, fame and commitment to the state. Across this wide range of human allegiances—perhaps most aptly summarized as "historical values"—the Modernists experience a sense of disruption. Their values no longer satisfy: something has happened to the historical momentum and sense of coherence. And this is the Modernists' point of departure. Hovering above the line of human experience and yawning beneath it is empty space.

A few years ago after I had sent off the typescript of my book dealing with Renaissance time, I reread *The Magic Mountain* and was intrigued by the realization that what Mann had in his novel (and more particularly in the character of Settembrini) described the end of, I had, in my study, described the beginning of. Settembrini was not only the fading voice of nineteenth-century liberal humanism, he was also the figure embodying its origins in the Italian cities of the Renaissance, with their growing awareness of time, of the need for energetic action, and their code of civic identity, a figure summarizing, in Mann's essayistic and intellectual *Zeitroman*, the very continuities and confrontation of Renaissance and nineteenth-century thought it is the purpose of this section to present.

Settembrini is of course the spokesman for the acutely time-conscious dynamic of the West. And as an Italian humanist he is sensitive to the regressive nature of the sanatorium, in fact, to its resemblance to the medieval world before the Renaissance. Time there is in effect nonexistent. Joachim shocks Hans by referring to an event that occurred eight weeks in the past as having taken place "just the other day (neulich),"—transformations at which Hans himself will later prove to be adept. (53/57)[23] Meeting Settembrini he declares that his planned length of stay is to be about three weeks; his teacher in time-values laughs and ironically explains that "up here" "Our smallest unit (*Zeiteinheit*) is the month. We reckon in the grand style—that is a privilege we shadows have." (58/63)

The issues are entered into contemporary history, and brought up to date when the encroaching remedievalization of the West comes out of the East, and in Mann's mind, out of Russia. "Up here there is too much Asia," the warning, but weakened voice of Settembrini declares, "that is why the place is so full of Muscovite Mongolians." Hans Castorp has already taken to "flinging months about." This lavishness with time, Settembrini calls barbaric and Asiatic. "Have you ever noticed that when a Russian says four hours, he means what we do when we say one." They have great space and as a consequence they think they have great time. Whereas in the West, in Europe, "we have as little time as our great and finely articulated continent has space, we must be as economical of the one as of the other, we must husband them. . . ." And Settembrini, the latter-day voice of the Renaissance, goes on to declare, with great historical accuracy, that the Western sense of time was a conquest of those who had the least amount of space, the city-dwellers. Time was an urban victory: " *'Carpe diem!'* That was the song of a dweller in a great city. Time is a gift of God, given to man that he might use it, Engineer, to serve the advancement of humanity." (242-243/257-258) When teaching the lessons of time it is hard to avoid this imploring tone, and even the interlocutors are the same as those in the Renaissance argument of time: an experienced and alarmed older person and a generally unheeding younger person. The use of the Latin utterance, suggesting the close association between the return of Roman aspiration and the Renaissance conceptions of time, the idea that time is merely loaned (*verliehen*, not as the translation suggests, "given"), and that man is thus obliged to make full use of his bequest ("auf Nutzung, Nutzung"), and the implied utilitarian doctrine and sense of exploitation—these are the very contents of the argument of time that the literature of the Renaissance amply confirms. Like Virginia Woolf, Mann was on historically sound footing when he detailed the time-world that the Modernists were bound to transform.

But he also shows that world being challenged. Hans differs from the young man of the Renaissance pattern—he is not pre-Settembrini; he is post-Settembrini. To be sure, Hans is influenced by the malaise of the sanatorium, but in fact he is being moved by an inner directive, one that is reacting against the tired sound of Settembrini's words. The true problem is not the influence but rather the susceptibility—and the causes for that susceptibility are the primary matter of the early chapters of this study.

Very late in the novel, immediately before the prevalent abrogation of time is revoked and external events begin to accumulate and history acquires a physiognomy, that is, something happens, Hans sits smoking his cigar and is a perfect representative of the graduate of the new education. His cigar, that pleasant narcosis to which he had from the beginning yielded himself, now serves in its splendidly veined ash as a time marker, "for he no longer carried a time-piece. His watch had fallen from its night-table; it did not go, and he had neglected to have it regulated, perhaps on the same grounds as had made him long since give up using a calendar, whether to keep track of the day, or to look out an approaching feast: the grounds, namely, of his freedom."[24] We can think of that highly symbolic gesture, whereby Rousseau, before arriving at Paris, discards his own watch, thus rejecting his native Geneva and the order it represented. Hans's freedom, though, is more of a metaphysical conquest: "Thus he did honor to his abiding-everlasting, his walk by the ocean of time, the hermetic enchantment to which he has proved so extraordinarily susceptible. . . ." (708/749)

What Mann has detected and successfully adumbrated, as have the other Modernists, is the readiness of the younger representatives of the West to yield to the new doctrine that is so hostile to the foundations of their society. While not quite willing to throw themselves in with Naphta (who is strictly reactionary and who evolves no new livable philosophy) still they find that the message of Settembrini has worn thin. And, throughout, the points of crucial difference are made by temporal speculation and its coordinates. Joachim relies upon accurate measurement, he then knows what a minute or seven of them (the time it takes to establish a temperature) "actually" amounts to. To which Hans, not accustomed to philosophize, replies, "You say, 'actually,' . . . but after all, time isn't 'actual.'" (66/70-71) Prior to the arrival of Naphta, Hans shows himself ready for the pre-Renaissance values: he thrills at the zodiacal speculations of the Egyptians and the Chaldeans, "those Arabic-Semitic old necromancers, who were so well versed in astrology and soothsaying." (369/391) And into one of the heated debates between Settembrini and Naphta—they are really arguing over the direction of Hans's soul—he interjects that the true basis of their opposition is the differences between time and eternity: "only in time was there progress; in eternity there was none, nor any politics or eloquence either. There, so to speak, one laid one's head back in God, and closed one's eyes. And that was the difference between religion and morality. . . ." (463/487) All of his own interjections tend to reassert the metaphysical properties of time and human life rather than the ethical. That is where his capacity for freedom shows itself.

Mann asserts that the sense of time is psychic, that it is intimately bound up with the consciousness of life. (104/110) The weakening of the Western time sense must be connected then with the attenuation of the Western life sense. Of course, the commanding question is why this should have happened, why the Renaissance ethic of productivity and exploitation should have been so vulnerable to collapse from within? To answer this question is to set the stage, to provide the historical occasion for the Modernist point of departure. Speaking only in the most general terms, without specific argument or example, the explanation I offer I call the paradox of time; it has to do with the complex nature of time in the Renaissance and its more simplified dimension in the nineteenth century. As part of its dual nature, time in the Renaissance lent itself to important ethical and historical conclusions. But since it was a discovery it imparted fervor as well as practicality, passion as well as precision.[25] The fates of those (Richard II, Falstaff) who ignored the new meaning of time were too apparent, the sense of the pending nothingness from which characters like Hal were escaping too pressing, not to place in a metaphysical perspective this new means of organizing human life. This new discovery brought validation to action (as Lévi-Strauss concluded, history bestowed a "charter" on the present), it was a principle of legitimation, providing the metaphysic to Shakespeare's political ethic. As a great discovery, with metaphysical and cosmic reverberations, time led to practical decisions and mundane consequences, such as scheduling one's activities (the newly devised *emploi du temps*). Time was a fervent discovery that lent itself to quantitative precision and an increased control over human life.

These two aspects of time can be called the innovative and the predictive. At a world symposium on time (1973), a Japanese scholar regarded the latter as instrumental in the birth of time: "The sheer need for a more precise control of predictions thus might have helped give birth to the notion of time as such."[26] In a very helpful journal article on entropy, R. Schlegel looked to the other dimension: "In a human culture in which there is an active development of new knowledge and new ways of living there is concomitantly an emphasis on history and the role of time."[27] Oddly enough, Professor Schlegel's understanding of the innovative roles of time and history comes closer to helping us understand the emergence of great drama in fifth-century Athens and the revival of high literature in the Renaissance, when poets were naturally "historians," than do Nietzsche's strictures against history.

Briefly, the paradox of time means that when the predictive, controlling aspect of time triumphed in the late nineteenth century, and triumphed so thoroughly and one-sidedly, it paradoxically produced its opposite effect, the triumph of space. Predictive time, without innovation or simple freshness of human appeal, leads to a kind of repetitive sameness, and this is what we mean by the paradox of time. Nietzsche noted this phenomenon in another way. "To those who have ever on their lips the modern cry of battle and sacrifice—'Division of labor! fall into line!' we may say roundly: 'If you try to further the progress of science as quickly as possible, you will end by destroying it as quickly as possible; just as the hen is worn out when you force it to lay too many eggs.' The progress of science has been amazingly rapid in the last decade; but consider the scientists, those exhausted hens."[28]

That the aggressive, predictive controlling Western dynamic fell from within may be explained by the paradoxical nature of time. That dynamic bred its own nemesis, and that nemesis was the attenuation of its own resources, as Nietzsche predicted, by reason of its very triumph. The triumph of time produced the triumph of space, that is, a new, haunting metaphysical perspective that called into question the very bases for action. Animal faith and vigor are left daunted. This is the primary record of T. S. Eliot's *The Waste Land*, particularly its fundamental encounter with the Emersonian jauntiness of his American past:

> (Come in under the shadow of this red rock),
> And I will show you something different from either
> Your shadow at morning striding behind you
> Or your shadow at evening rise to meet you;
> I will show you fear in a handful of dust.

The first reactions of the early Modernist works will register these experiences.

CHAPTER II

The Family, the Machine and the Paradox of Time

1. Early Miniatures

The dominant experience at the Modernist point of departure is one of a powerful drive and energy, a persistent will and a prevalent code all coming to an end. There are large and dramatic types who exemplify this dissolution—large and dramatic because of the fullness of their relationships (think of Thomas Buddenbrook and Gerald Crich)—and they will be discussed at length later in this chapter. But there are also miniature portraits (certainly not minor), Kurtz in *The Heart of Darkness*, Aschenbach in *Death in Venice*, Gabriel Conroy in *The Dead*, Prufrock and Mauberley in Eliot's and Pound's poems of those names, and the characters from Kafka's *The Judgment*, *The Metamorphosis*, and *In the Penal Colony* (all originally intended to be published together under the collective title, *Strafen*, or Punishments), and Joseph K. from *The Trial*. In each of these works, the experience is distinct of a suddenly revealed cosmic emptiness behind human experience, of the unresponsiveness of alien surroundings that seriously questions humanistic ideals or simple endeavor, and even of the dissolution of the known, ordinary, solid world. These early classics show the evolution of a negative typology as well as principles of future Modernist development.

Typifying this negativity, these earlier types are divided between those who went too far in their needs to escape and those who did not go far enough (we recall that Nietzsche prophesied that the antidote to the triumph of history was

FAMILY, MACHINE AND PARADOX OF TIME

itself toxic). "Ceaseless labour," T. S. Eliot wrote in *Choruses from "The Rock,"* is the lot of man, or "ceaseless idleness," and the latter is harder.[1] In *The Crown*, D. H. Lawrence makes a similar division: "shall we know the barren triumph of the will?—or the equally barren triumph of inertia, helplessness, barren irresponsibility?"[2] For the Modernists, among the most tragic intellects of the nineteenth century were those who did not quite complete the break-through that they themselves required. For Eliot, Tennyson was, like Dante's Virgil, "the most instinctive rebel against the society in which he was the most perfect conformist."[3] Joyce, in his second lecture on Irish matters at the Università Popolare in Trieste in 1907, saw in James Clarence Mangan the keen example of those who failed to escape. "The history of his country encloses him so straitly that even in hours of extreme individual passion he can barely reduce its walls to ruin" (a highly relevant commentary on the last paragraphs of *The Dead*).[4]

Against this background Prufrock should be read as a negative example, a type trapped in his own mundane order. His days of small habit result in the same triumph of space as does the enormous will of a major character like Gerald Crich:

> For I have known them all already, known them all:—
> Have known the evenings, mornings, afternoons,
> I have measured out my life with coffee spoons. . . .

Behind all his aborted statements and gestures of defiance Prufrock hears the snickers of eternity and senses the vast spaces that reduce to insignificance (and ultimate futility) all human endeavor.

The same problem—even at times in the same rhythms as those of *Prufrock*—is described by Virginia Woolf. It is as if everything had come down to their generation second- and third-hand, and even time—which Ovid and his Renaissance followers thought to be stirring and fresh, or, when destructive, at least powerful—seems worn out (muffled and swaddled), before reaching their generation. In *Jacob's Room*, the problem seems to be metaphysical as well. Each action, insulated and distant, has little horizontal relation to that which goes before or that which follows, but is rather encased vertically in vast and empty space:

> Spaces of complete mobility separated each of these movements. The land seemed to lie dead. . . . The worn voices of clocks repeated the fact of the hour all night long.[5]

For the time-vacuous and for the time-harried, as we shall see, the result is the same: the standardization or the routinization of experience, the triumph of the predictive and ordered face of time, has resulted in the triumph of space. It is because they derive from the same historical conditions that opposites in this case meet.

As examples of those who go too far, Kurtz and Aschenbach may be compared, particularly in this context emphasizing Renaissance connections. "Aschenbach's whole soul, from the very beginning was bent on fame. . . ." The remarkable historical prologue to *The Heart of Darkness* provides an Elizabethan perspective. Lending some nobility to Kurtz's original energies, his spiritual ancestry is suggested from the adventurers of other times, "the great knights-errant of the sea," "adventurers and settlers," "hunters for gold or pursuers of fame. . . ."[6] But in each of these earlier works the experience that emerges is one of a blankness in existence, an unresponsiveness to which the protagonists' own energies have led them.

The wilderness had found Kurtz out. "I think it whispered to him things about himself that he did not know, things of which he had no conception till he took counsel with this great solitude . . . It echoed loudly within him because he was hollow at the core. . . ." His "magnificent eloquence" could not hide this lack; in fact, it may have been prompted by it. The blankness outside uncovers the hollowness within. The alien setting shows the kind of high idealism preached by Kurtz to be fantastical, and he turns against it with a civilized brand of extreme vengeance.

Gustav von Aschenbach's methods may have been different, but his ends were similar. By sheer force of will, by persistence and struggle (indeed, showing some of the traits that later Mann will describe as his own), he wrote works that became typical of his age: they provided the image of forbearance, of greatness achieved in spite of burdens that an historical culture required. His hero and the subject of his major work was Frederick the Great, whose motto was "*Durchhalten.*" The bourgeois artist has standing behind him the Prussian conqueror; he held to his work "with an endurance and a tenacity of purpose like that which had conquered his native Silesia. . . ."[7] He began every morning with a cold shower. (The mood, the tone, of something having happened to his native Germany, of some old-fashioned ease having been squeezed from its life by the rigors of a new system—this was also the purpose of Mann's *Buddenbrooks*, which, at its beginning, still basks in the pleasant Enlightenment geniality of the old grandfather, and, at its end, struggles under the Prussianized grip of the new educators.) Although concerned with a writer, this story of repression, a modern *Bacchae*, is also a summary of the bourgeois ethic: Aschenbach is kin to Buddenbrook.[8]

Oblivion is not only something that befalls him, it is the object of his deepest pursuit. The stable world dissolves, much to Aschenbach's gratification, when he travels by boat to Venice:

> Beneath the sombre dome of the sky stretched the vast plain of empty sea. But immeasurable unarticulated space weakens our power to measure time as well; the time-sense falters and grows dim. Strange, shadowy figures passed and repassed—the elderly coxcomb, the goat-bearded man from the bowels of the ship—with vague mutterings through the traveler's mind as he lay.[9]

To be sure there is erotic infatuation, and this is one of the pleasures that the suspension of the orthodox Western time sense seems to promise. But the story's title is, after all, *Death in Venice*. The true object of Gustav's quest is obliteration, hence the mixture of his erotic fancies with images of rank corruption and menace. The crouching tiger that he imagines fills his heart with terror, but also with "inexplicable longing." This dream from the beginning of the novella is linked with another near the end. Here Aschenbach makes himself part of the mad bacchanalian rout; he throws himself into the orgy, "and in his soul he tasted the bestial degradation of his fall."[10] So perverse indeed has become the singular attachment to the discipline of the will that it transforms objects of pleasure into ulterior means of destruction. The will in self-revulsion is willing its own end. Oddly enough, Aschenbach and Prufrock are nearly one.

Unlike some heroes of nineteenth-century fiction, whose possession of a competency, or independent means, allows them (and their authors) to avoid the rigors of work, a code of labor is definitely in the backgrounds of many twentieth-century characters, particularly Mann's (Buddenbrook, Aschenbach, and even Hans Castorp, except that his illness prevents him from assuming his position as an engineer), D. H. Lawrence's (most notably Gerald Crich), and even Kafka's. It is not necessarily the case that we see them work. All we need to know is the background code and ethic of work from which they are suddenly jarred loose by the intervention of another labor and another consciousness. Kafka's heroes seem to have allowed themselves no reprieve from the day-in day-out drudgery of work. They are called to a new awakening, but a terrible one, fraught with all the revenges that their neglected physiques and psyches have accumulated. They suddenly look at their lives from the blankness toward which their own efforts have led them. A kind of metaphysical or cosmic space surrounds their past efforts, in regard to which their doctrines of labor offer little satisfaction. Here we can see a pattern that links the works of Mann with those of Kafka and D. H. Lawrence, most clearly, but with those of other Modernists as well, marking the point of departure.

2. *Buddenbrooks*

Remarkably enough, these exceptional works are in most cases preparatory, staging grounds for greater efforts of fuller

FAMILY, MACHINE AND PARADOX OF TIME

dramatic scope and power, where more detailed implications of the collapse of historical values are presented. In such works as *Buddenbrooks* (written some ten years before *Death in Venice*, which, therefore, ought more properly to be allied with the genesis of *Magic Mountain*), *The Rainbow* and *Women in Love*, we see depicted a much fuller format of the values that had emerged from the Renaissance, a real complex of values involving time and history, linearity and lineality, children, marriage and the family—all in the process of disintegration.[11] Summarily put, the essential confrontation is between the values implicit in such works as *Henry IV*, or Shakespeare's second tetralogy, and the same values in the state of disintegration in *Buddenbrooks*, and works like it, between what I have called "the argument of time" and the phenomenon, widespread in Modernism, that represented the former's undoing, "the paradox of time."

Quotations will be specific showing how the problems of time and history in the nineteenth century were given living embodiment in these great works of fiction and brought home into the family—it having become the great shelter for the burdens of continuity and remembrance. Quite brilliantly Phillipe Ariès has shown in his *Western Attitudes Toward Death* that the family became almost a surrogate religion in the nineteenth century, that it became the emotional center, the shrine of values and attachments, and that it was incumbent upon the family to keep alive the memory of those who had died.[12] The tendency in the nineteenth century to "endow the family as such with new and deeper meaning," suggested by John Demos, will be discussed in chapter 4.[13] For now we stress the development and devolution of the family as a source of continuity and value in some remarkable works of Modernist fiction.

The first part of *Buddenbrooks*, the chronological starting-place of this work, delineates the differences between two earlier generations of Buddenbrooks, the older Johann, the son of the Enlightenment, and his son, the Herr Consul. In all of these contrasts, it seems that the older man, the grandfather of the novel, enjoys the better qualities (expressing a constant

45

phenomenon in Modernism—the prestige attributed to the eighteenth-century personality, although not to the programs of the Enlightenment). Where the father was witty and irreverent, the son was pietistic. Where the father was liberal and urbane, the son was something of a practical-minded grind. Where the father was both nonchalant and decisive, the son fretted and was troubled. A delightful contentment with the superficies of life is contrasted with a Romantic yearning and need for probing of depths. This same oppositeness is reflected in their attitudes toward history. While the father is humming in his bedroom, the son is deriving sustenance from the family ledger—as constant a piece of stage property in *Buddenbrooks* as is the Book of Account in *Everyman*. "What a pity," the son thinks, "he had so little taste for these old records!" And then, perhaps continuing his thoughts, or more likely an intervention of the narrator: "He [the father] stood with both feet firmly planted in the present, and concerned himself seldom with the past of his family." (40/41)[14] This insight by Mann precedes some of the conclusions of Foucault and others, today, who find in the nineteenth century the development of an historical sense that was absent in the eighteenth, when those of the earlier century were more concerned with general laws and paradigms of how things ought to have happened.[15]

This same sense of history combined with family compels Tony Buddenbrook to foresake a summer romance and marry Grünlich, the family's choice, an objectionable man who had in fact deceived the family. In the proximity of the sea, the normal time-world of the city and its pressures disappear and man recovers a kind of natural simplicity. The sea for Mann, at least in *Buddenbrooks*, represents this release from pressurized existence. The Consul Buddenbrook's letter brings Tony back to reality; it could be used as a forbidding example of the sclerosis that had made its way into a code formerly so full of individual choice and lively response. And while it would probably be unfair to contrast it with Gargantua's famous letter to Pantagruel, where the father's insistence on the respon-

FAMILY, MACHINE AND PARADOX OF TIME

sibilities of family continuity is in its Renaissance context inspiring, still the general point would be clear. The Herr Consul writes:

> My child, we are not born for that which, with our short-sighted vision, we reckon to be our own small personal happiness. We are not free, separate, and independent entities, but like links in a chain, and we could not by any means be what we are without those who went before us and showed us the way, by following the straight and narrow path, not looking to right or left. Your path, it seems to me, has lain all these weeks sharply marked out for you, and you would not be my daughter, nor the granddaughter of your grandfather who rests in God, nor a worthy member of our own family, if you really have it in your heart, alone, willfully, and light-headedly to choose your own unregulated path. (114/111)

At first, Tony finds no consolation in brother Thomas's suggestion that she will forget young Morten Schwartzkopf ("Forgetting—is that any consolation"). (121/118) But after she has returned to her native city, and her environment re-establishes its hold, she happens to page through the historical family ledger, "accidentally" left out of its drawer by her father. Her sense of historical identity is confirmed by this reading:

> What she read were mostly simple facts well known to her; but each successive writer had followed his predecessor in a stately but simple chronicle style which was no bad mirror of the family attitude, its modest but honourable self-respect, and its reverence for tradition and history. The book was not new to Tony; she had sometimes been allowed to read in it. But its contents had never made the impression upon her that they made this morning. She was thrilled by the reverent particularity with which the simplest facts pertinent to the family were here treated. She propped

herself on her elbow with growing absorption, seriousness and pride. (122/119)

She reflects that the events of her life there recorded would be read by future generations "with a piety equal to her own." She thinks back to the phrase from her father's letter "like a link in a chain," and comes to accept with "reverence for herself" this historical identity:

Yes, yes. She was important precisely as a link in a chain. Such was her significance and her responsibility, such her task: to share by deed and word in the history of her family. (123/120)

With a sense of drama she then marks her own acquiescence to the family's wishes by inscribing in that same ledger the fact of her betrothal to Herr Grünlich.

Both young Buddenbrooks enter adulthood by sacrificing their personal lives (two scenes later, in chapter 15, Thomas makes a similar renunciation of a woman who would have brought him some comfort and solace), and in each case acceptance of their roles in the family and its historical values is responsible for the misstep. Not only is it the cause of the initial error, but it is also the cause of any later inability to change, to break out of the extremely constrictive atmosphere. Pathetic to be sure, nevertheless, a large, dramatic type emerges from these straitened circumstances, the type of the "suffering hero" who perishes because of his stature and the responsibilities he shoulders. The antagonists who fill out this type are locked into their choices and we are obliged to follow them to their terrible final ends. Somewhat like Gerald Crich in Lawrence's *Women in Love*, Mann's "suffering hero" is a representative of the Western dynamic in its state of exhaustion and weariness, and a man whose breakdown, because of his values, would reveal a more general disease.

Very early, Thomas senses imaginative possibilities in assuming the direction of an honorable firm like that of the Buddenbrooks. This is what distinguishes him and his father

FAMILY, MACHINE AND PARADOX OF TIME

from the step-uncle, Gotthold, he thinks, as he stands at Gotthold's deathbed:

> To cherish the vision of an abstract good; to carry in your heart, like a hidden love only far sweeeter, the dream of preserving an ancient name, an old family, an old business, of carrying it on, and adding to it more and more honour and lustre—ah, that takes imagination. (215/208)

Thomas is something of a test case to answer the question, whether the consolations of history and the continuities of firm and family are sufficient to support a philosophy, are sufficient against death. His being was historical; when people saw him they saw not an individual but a totem; when he was elected to the Senate, "people honored in him not only his own personality, but the personalities of his father, his grandfather and his great grandfather as well . . . he was the representative of a hundred years of honourable tradition." (321/310) But like other men in all vocations, Thomas, who thought he had imagination, found he only had energy. And as he encounters the limits of his attainments, with no new worlds to conquer, Thomas is hard put to find any strength in his values, something upon which to rely. Summarily expressed, the values of history had failed to satisfy, they failed to answer the questions raised by Nietzsche or, later, Eliot and Lawrence, the one felt but left unformulated by Hans Castorp in *The Magic Mountain*, the question of *"Wozu?"* To what end all of this endeavor? Thomas did not have the healthy eighteenth-century irreverence and flexibility of his grandfather, nor the Restoration religious piety of his father. He was the perfect representative of the man of the seventies of the last century (that is, Nietzsche's contemporary), born to live through and to question, without any personal or metaphysical and religious supports, the crisis of historical values. "He ended by finding in evolution the answer to all his questions about eternity and immortality." A mistranslation in this standard English version calls our attention to the true values under discussion. Mann did not write that Thomas tries to find his values in evolution, but rather in *history*: "Hatte er sich die Fragen der Ewigkeit und Unsterblichkeit *historisch* [my italics] beantwortet." What he means by "historisch" (what we would call "historical values") is explained in the next clause, "dass er in seinen Vorfahren gelebt habe und in seinen Nachfahren leben werde (that he had lived in his forbears and would live on in his descendants)." (509/495)

There is even more convincing proof that this apotheosis of history is for Mann as it was for Nietzsche synonymous with the underlying nineteenth-century notions about time. The guiding purpose of Thomas' life had been his "sense of family, his patrician self-consciousness, his ancestor-worship," but in the shadow of death these values proved illusory; not bearing a philosophy they provided him "with not a single hour of calm or readiness (Bereitschaft) for the end." It is at this time that he makes his stirring, but tragically belated discovery of Schopenhauer. He is thrilled by the passionate freedom of the discourse on the indestructibility of the soul, and for once feels liberated from the responsibilities that had so weighed him down. "Have I hoped to live on in my son? In a personality yet more feeble, flickering, and timorous than my own? Blind, childish folly. What can my son do for me—what need have I of a son? Where shall I be when I am dead? ... I shall be in all those who have ever, do ever, or ever shall say 'I'—especially ... in all those who say it most fully, potently and gladly!" (513/499) For the first time in his adult life, he has broken with the bonds of continuing historical existence. They now seem to be products of accident, far from his real being. Mann's narration then proceeds to link this rejection of historical values with Schopenhauer's (and through him, Kant's) own thoughts about space, time and history, and for our purposes brings the novel *Buddenbrooks* and its issues squarely within the mainstream of modern temporal speculations, which indeed it helps define:

> The deceptive perceptions of space, time and history, the preoccupation with a glorious historical continuity of life

in the person of his own descendants, the dread of some future dissolution and decomposition—all this his spirit now put aside. He was no longer prevented from grasping eternity. Nothing began, nothing left off. There was only an endless present. . . . (514/500)

This passage clearly is indebted to that of Nietzsche quoted earlier in chapter 1, section 2, where he credits Kant and Schopenhauer, those men of genius, with being the first to break through the illusion that the Western conceptions of space, time and causality were absolute, "unobjectionable *aeternae veritates*" (in fact, in his later essay, "Schopenhauer," Mann essentially repeats this passage, this time giving credit to Kant). Two false steps in the translation of the passage above could mislead the reader as to Mann's intellectual origins and preoccupations. He does not use the phrase, adequate as it is, "deceptive perceptions"; he instead writes, "Die trügerischen Erkenntnisformen des Raumes, der Zeit und also der Geschichte. . . ." To write "Erkenntnisformen" is to place the passage clearly in a Kantian philosophical tradition. But even more important, the German original reveals what has been the contention of these sections, that is, the tight nexus of relationships existing between conceptions of space and time and the development of the values of history: "und also der Geschichte." History is a consequence (". . . and therefore of history") of these conceptions of space and time. And the next clause reveals what is involved with history: "the preoccupations with a glorious historical continuity of life in the person of his own descendants."

Familial continuity for Mann, as it did for the bourgeois society of the nineteenth century, clearly provided the flesh-and-blood meaning of historical value. And the same was true for Shakespeare's royal history plays. Indeed in Shakespeare, capping several centuries of development and speculation of continental and English society and thought, temporal linearity and generational lineality merge. If Richard II confiscates Gaunt's property and deprives Bolingbroke of his inheritance, he is striking at time, whose prerogatives include "fair sequence and succession." In Mann (and Modernism) fatigue with linear sequence dashes hope in generational succession. These two efforts, Shakespeare's account of the rise of Prince Hal to full acceptance of the historical code of time and continuity, and Mann's account of the dissolution of that code, deserve to confront one another across the centuries. If Shakespeare's histories were historical in value as well as in subject, Mann's first novel, indeed one that sets the stage for his later works as well as those of other Modernists, might well be historical in subject but certainly not in value. *Buddenbrooks* shows not merely the decline of generations, but the decline of the generational ideal. Shakespeare's historical plays center upon the time-conscious father who saves and who is saved by his son. The great dualities of historical antagonism are transcended by the emergence of Hal as Henry V, England's grandest monarch. Mann's novel has been called a "reckoning" with the world of the fathers, where redemption can lie only outside its processes.[16] Hanno does not help Thomas, whose fearful preoccupations only serve to crush his son. Dualities are not transcended but left bitter and bare. And finally, there is no great wedding to celebrate symbolically the continuity of the race, but rather, as in tragedy, only the counting of the dead. In his *Sincerity and Authenticity*, Lionel Trilling associates the decline of the family and narrative style. "Traditionally, the family has been a narrative institution: it was the past and it had a tale to tell of how things began, including the child himself. . . ."[17] If this is the case, *Buddenbrooks* is the last great narrative novel that traces the decline of those very values that made narration possible.

3. *The Rainbow*

Time as a theme inevitably involves one in the issues of society and of history (we have referred to it as a "socialized" concept). The study of time entails not a single idea, but rather idea-complexes. (Such clusters of related concepts and attitudes we saw reembodied in Mann's Settembrini and suggested by Rhoda's thoughts in *The Waves*.) Furthermore, time as a concept is usually placed at the forward post of experience. In D. H. Lawrence, as well as in Mann, a new consciousness is formed by virtue of the rejection of older values of continuity, just as in the Renaissance (think of Rabelais or Shakespeare), a new consciousness was formed by their adoption. When one encounters a change in time one encounters change in a host of related issues. Thus, as an example to be pursued in this chapter, along with the concept of temporal linearity, the values of family and continuity through children—lineality—must also suffer.

It is not an accident that Mann and Lawrence should emerge as major spokesmen in this first chapter. Each of their respective countries was highly industrialized (leaders in Europe in the production of coal and steel), each was Protestant, each had been foremost in the Romantic movement and each was increasingly dominated by the ethic and values of the middle class. A valuable paragraph in Whitehead's *Science and the Modern World* (necessary reading for any understanding of Modernism) links the two countries not only in the development of technology but in the development of the disciplined method of acquiring knowledge. "The greatest invention of the nineteenth century was the invention of the method of invention. . . . The possibilities of modern technology were first in practice realized in England, by the energy of a prosperous middle class. . . . But the Germans explicitly realized the methods by which the deeper veins in the mine of science could be reached. . . ." We have seen carried in Germany to its farthest extent "the triumph of the professional man." This is the fulfillment of Francis Bacon's prophecy.

At the same time, this triumph is disquieting. Whitehead finds the last twenty years of the nineteenth century to be "one of the dullest stages of thought since the time of the First Crusade. . . . The period was efficient, dull and half-hearted."[18] Nietzsche, writing in the early seventies, did say the same thing, and found his assertions confirmed by coming events. White-

53

head, from his perspective of scientific thought, helps us to understand the situation that Thomas Mann was depicting in the malaise, that initiating condition of Modernism, that besets his characters. Obviously the stage was set for a literary revolution as well as a scientific one.

In a Freudian age the family is seen more as a source of struggle than of continuity.[19] Gerald Crich's mother in *Women in Love* can—with good reason, given her own destructive rejection of her son—madly exclaim: "Pray for yourselves to God for there's no help for you from your parents."[20] The great danger does not come from the fathers in literary modernism; they are mainly passive. This already indicates an alteration of historical values, since the Renaissance prince entered history by accepting the adult world of the father. Paideia was secular and fatherly. But by the end of the nineteenth century, whatever the ideal, the fact of the father's role had been diminished considerably. Stephen Dedalus desires a spiritual father more commensurate with the freedom of his speculative, heroic self (in *Ulysses* he finds that sensual, tragic man, Bloom); his real father is too much a part of the dismal history of dissolution and decay—national as well as familial. "Fatherhood is a mystical state, an apostolic succession. . . ." In *The Waste Land*, part of whose biographical background was the recent death of Eliot's father, the grief of the son and the hope of the resurrection find no modern corollary. The lines of Ariel's song from *The Tempest*—"Full fathom five thy father lies"—are broken, and left incomplete, as if an emotional circuit had been interrupted. In *Sons and Lovers*, the father, Walter Morel, after a futile attempt at rebellion, remains a defeated outsider in his own family—and this, as Lawrence later knew, was a deadly Pyrrhic victory for mother and sons. Kafka's fathers are not the Titans overwhelming their sons that they are thought to be: rather they are pensioners on the shelf whose pathetic lot creates a self-destroying guilt in their sons, who could otherwise readily surpass them. In Proust the father also abdicates—especially in relation to his will-less son. In fact, the breakdown in continuity could very well constitute

FAMILY, MACHINE AND PARADOX OF TIME

a sub-theme of his enormous work, for the fact is that in the *Recherche* every parent who trusts herself or himself to the kindly later ministrations of their children is sadly disappointed, or betrayed.

But as is evident in Proust and Lawrence, it was the maternal relationship that inspired the most poisonous behavior. In fact, rather than needing to liberate themselves from their fathers—an all-too-easy task, in most cases—the real problem for many of the Modernists was to achieve freedom from the mother. Few Modernists would be as pronounced as Lawrence, when in that revealing tract, *Education of the People*, he bursts out, "À bas les mères."[21] He looks to legend to support his need—the founders of virile Roman society had no mother; or in *The Plumed Serpent* to his own adopted mythology—Quetzalcoatl, who replaces the Santissima, "He has no mother, he."[22] In chapter 4 we shall explain more fully why it was the mother—particularly in death—who weighed so heavily upon Modernists, and why Modernism as an aesthetic is consequently more in search of the virile hard-line.[23] For the moment we are dealing with the break-up in the forces of continuity. Lawrence, as usual, has a strong statement. In "The Lemon Gardens," faith in continuity through children is placed in the middle of the large social problems of the northern and industrialized West. Unlike the Italians, who, Lawrence seems to believe, have the capacity to enjoy the flesh as it is, "we [of the Northern races] set ourselves to serve our children, calling them 'the future.'" This abnegation of the self and of the living present is part of the larger sacrifice to the on-going collectivity, where devotion to progeny is part of the great mechanized society we have created on our way to perfection. And this great mechanized society, being selfless, is pitiless."[24] This is the new monster—pitiless in its demands—that slouches to be born.

Joyce's need to liberate himself from the mother is equally as strong as that of Lawrence. In the purposeful Telemachus section of *Ulysses* Stephen cries out to the dream of his mother: "No mother, let me be and let me live."[25] As a consequence he stresses the fatherly role in religion: Jesus is the son of God the father not of the Virgin. In the Nausicaa episode the devotions to Mary intersperse Gerty's coy Romantic imaginings. Ireland is included in the resistance to mothers: she is the old sow that eats her farrow. (595) From the father, Dedalus, Icarus-Stephen must learn to fly, since the mother is earthbound in her loyalties. In fact, submission to her will, symbolized by making his Easter duty, would for Stephen be a yielding to all the forces of religion and nationalism that would enmesh him. In "The Dead" the mother of Gabriel Conroy disapproves of his marriage to the girl from the west of Ireland, from whence in the story comes all mutinous and finally liberating passion. The mother has become for Modernism the voice of submission to that which is conventionally social, to the larger general processes of life, foremost among which, for her, is the procreative. Stephen has to remind his mother "religion was not a lying-in hospital," and he consistently rejects the procreative as the basis of aesthetics as well as of religion.[26]

As one of our purposes here is to manipulate cultural parallels between the Renaissance and Modernism, we find that almost in all respects the elements of their patterns are opposites. In the Renaissance, to enter into the stirring processes of history was to enter into the ethical. That is, it meant precisely—as the quotation from Hal would indicate—the subjection of the more individualized self to the larger demands of the race and the nation. At the heart of this decision, if Shakespeare's history plays are prototypal, is the crucial father-son link. In his history plays those figures whose fathers are absent or dead (Richard II, Henry VI, Hotspur, or almost all of Marlowe's figures, Edward II, Faustus) meet with disaster, as if they are individually separate and hence alienated from the great code of historical continuity. In Modernism, the necessary first step—the break with historical values—begins with the absence of the father. Hans Castorp's spiritual journey begins with his departure from his "Elternhaus" and his "Vaterstadt"—where the rudimentary German composite words sug-

FAMILY, MACHINE AND PARADOX OF TIME

gest more than their English renderings. In Modernism the mother's voice urges continuity and the ethical, and for her sons this seems more the counsel of resignation and submission to a dead hand—rather than the daring setting-out for new experience, for transcendence of the *saeculum* that was required. What we witness further in Modernism—again unlike the Renaissance—is the separation of the procreative from the spiritual. Their merger in the nineteenth century—and anticipated in the Renaissance—had become intolerable. We shall look at this problem further in the next chapter; here it should be remarked that the horizontal disruption in continuity carries with it vertical divisions and separations as well. As Stephen separates from his own family into a position of "fosterage," so the spiritual meaning of his quest must be separated from the procreative, and the religious or more intensely spirited must be separated from the historical.

Thomas Mann quite consciously fleshed out the implications of the nineteenth-century triumph of time; he showed its consequences to be historical values based, in the realm of his greatest expertise, upon familial continuity. D. H. Lawrence was in a better position to make another addition to this line of thought. To the nexus of linear time, historical values and bourgeois continuity he adds the machine. For him this does not merely mean implements of production, but mechanical thinking as well and organizations set up with a static will, one that seems perverse and suicidal in its determination to control experience. In Lawrence's novels and essays we have one of the most acute presentations of the consequences of linear time for the human will and ego. His work shows how prophetic were Nietzsche's fears that the triumph of historical values would reduce man to being no more than a cog in a machine.

Ursula Brangwen in Lawrence's *The Rainbow* is a heroine more in the mold of Paul Morel and Stephen Dedalus. Some spiritual hunger and personal restlessness, some need for adventure inclines her, like them, to experience dissatisfaction with the *saeculum*. In fact, as with them, and key to this first section of time and Modernism, a Nietzschean hostility to secularization—in its true sense—brings her up against the nineteenth-century triumph of historical values. "She was an enemy of those who insisted on the humanity of Christ. . . . It was the vulgar mind which would allow nothing extra-human, nothing beyond itself to exist. . . ." (273)[27] Requiring the ultimate, "she was always in revolt against babies and muddled domesticity." (273) The very word "fecundity" became abhorrent. "She knew as a child what it was to live admidst storms of babies, in the heat and swelter of fecundity. And as a child, she was against her mother, she craved for some spirituality and stateliness." (262-263)

Given the time, it was natural that this quest for spirituality should strike at historical values. Like Tony Buddenbrook Ursula very early thought to find peace and consolation in being part of some great process. She loved to hear her grandmother tell of her two grandfathers, the Pole, Lensky, whom she never knew, and the Englishman, Tom Brangwen, whom she did.

> Here from her grandmother's peaceful room, the door opened on the greater space, the past, that all it contained seemed tiny, loves and births and deaths, tiny units within a vast horizon. That was a great relief, to know the tiny importance of the individual, within the great past. (258)

But the "Flood" chapter in *The Rainbow* marks a great divide, and for Lawrence a new covenant needs to be created, independent of the hold of historical values. The above sentiment comes to sound wearying, when the soldier and diminished lover, Skrebensky, talks of duty:

> What did a man matter personally? He was just a brick in the whole great social fabric, the nation, the modern humanity. His personal movements were small and entirely subsidiary. The whole form must be ensured, not ruptured. . . . One had to fill one's place in the whole, the great scheme of man's elaborate civilisation, that was all. The Whole mat-

FAMILY, MACHINE AND PARADOX OF TIME

tered—but the unit, the person, had no importance, except as he represented the Whole. (326)

The mistress of the High School gives the same advice. (357)

One can see the appeal of the "chronicle" for Mann and Lawrence as being the perfect receptacle for the historical values it was their purpose to break. In *Buddenbrooks* Mann uses the form of the family chronicle to destroy the very validity of the generational ideal; in *The Rainbow*, another story of three generations, Lawrence destroys even that form. The most striking feature of his "chronicle" is its *achronicity*. In Mann's novel there is no event that is not given a date: "what happened next occurred in 1855" is a typical indication. But in Lawrence's novel it is remarkable and yet true that there is only one historical date given in the entire novel, that of 1840, when, ominously enough, a canal was constructed to connect the newly-opened collieries. Reference without date is later made to the Polish revolution, presumably of 1848, and then to the need to deal with the Mahdi at Khartoum and, finally, declaration of war on the Boers (these last two put to interesting aesthetic effect). This achronicity emphasizes that, while not severed from external history, still *The Rainbow* is more concerned with emotional realities and personal drama. History—while present—has a more subtle, even unconscious influence on character. In his second foreword to *Women in Love* Lawrence explains that the background of World War I must be assumed in the novel although it is never specifically the concern: "I should wish the time to remain unfixed, so that the bitterness of war may be taken for granted in the characters." (vii)

The generations are like the waves of the sea, having their moment of freedom and central position in the drama where it is incumbent upon them to reach consummate being, to realize themselves. This is strictly a relationship between man and woman, where they must achieve the only kind of absolute—that of fulfilled being—or part forever maimed. "Immortality is not a question of time, of everlasting life. It is a question of consummate being." This quotation comes from *The Crown*, a work called by Lawrence's biographer the "essay of an inspired amateur philosopher."[28] It offers the best gloss on *The Rainbow*, showing that his work was not accidental, but rather the product of sustained thought, and providing the key to understanding human failure in love—particularly among the men, Will Brangwen, the younger Tom Brangwen and Anton Skrebensky (early forms for Gerald Crich). In *The Rainbow* Lawrence discovered his great and true theme: the terrible pathos of men defeated by the superior will of independent and restless women. Only in Ursula do we see the beginnings of the positive formation of the Modernist consciousness, and this by way of rejection of the values of historical continuity represented by her mother.

Lawrence seems even to imply that Ursula's new quest has old religious backgrounds. As a child she lived through the rhythm of the Christian calendar, with its drama of birth and death and resurrection, "the epic of the soul of mankind . . . the rhythm of eternity in a ragged, inconsequential life." Its incitements and expectations persisted even when the Christian ritual had become itself "mechanical action." (279) Her own spiritual passion contrasts with Skrebensky, whose response to the sermon ("The very hairs of your head are all numbered") was flat and unimaginative: "He did not believe it. He believed his own things were quite at his own disposal. You could do as you liked with your own things, so long as you left other people's alone." (324)

In *The Rainbow* it is the women who pass beyond this egotism, who seem to have the miraculous capacity for innocent joy and wonder, and who experience in their own fulfillment a thorough loss of the preoccupations that harry the self-involved; when their men (Will and Anton) are unable to muster the same freedom or cannot tolerate the differences, the result is injury, spleen, a kind of onset of consciousness that desires futilely and pathetically to control the other person. In chapter 6 of *The Rainbow* we see this happen specifically to Will and Anna. Will's insistence intrudes upon Anna's free-

FAMILY, MACHINE AND PARADOX OF TIME

dom and places him in a position of dependence. He required fusion: "He was afraid. He was afraid to know he was alone. For she seemed fulfilled and separate and sufficient in her half of the world. He could not bear to know that he was cut off. Why could he not be always one with her." (175) His sullen, injured and dark yearning becomes offensive to her own peace. He feels lost in space, drowning: "He would let go. . . . Yet he wanted her still, he always, always wanted her. In his soul, he was desolate as a child, he was so helpless. Like a child on its mother, he depended on her for his living." (186) This pattern of male dependency, repeated on a larger scale but with the same details in Gerald Crich, finds its compensation in timelessness.[29] That this "timelessness" is a product of personal defeat shows the importance of Ursula's quest to find a new sense of eternity *within* the flux of time.

This double need is at the heart of the Modernist quest. Very early Nietzsche was caught on its two horns: a disbelief in conventional religion and morality and yet a fine enmity against the corrosive effects of positivism, the *petits faits* of fearful reckoning. For Proust the tragedy of Swann was his reliance on these *petits faits* and his entrapment within the cynical nihilism of the Guermantes way; and yet equally necessary to Marcel's education was the expansion of his consciousness beyond the known certainties of the Méséglise way. The dilemma is epitomized in the Scylla and Charybdis episode of *Ulysses*, where Stephen must move between the etherealized wisdom, the "spiritual essences" of a faded Romanticism and the cunning total disbelief of Mulligan, between the Yankee yawp and the Saxon smile, and finally between his own belief and unbelief. And Eliot in the same line of Modernist thought affirms that only through time is time conquered.

Oddly enough, sheer "timelessness"—never admired in Modernism—seems to be the goal not only of those who are religiose, but who, like the younger Tom Brangwen or Anton Skrebensky (and later Gerald Crich) are devoted to the public world of management, business and controlled experience.

Given their personal dynamics they arrive at the same ends. The old ego-consciousness with its need to control, the unfree static will that always wants the same thing to happen (what Lawrence condemns when he writes "only perpetuation is a sin")—these qualities seem to require conditions free from change, some larger totality in relation to which they can let go of themselves.[30]

The industrial world of the colliery produces such an effect, it too depending upon a kind of resigned submission to the "great machine" that even extends its values to marriage and child-bearing. As represented by the younger generation of Winifred Inger and Tom Brangwen, what had been the richly procreative values of Ursula's mother, Anna, have become corrupted by their mixture with the machine and the static will:

> Brangwen had reached the age when he wanted children. He wanted children. Neither marriage nor the domestic establishment meant anything to him. He wanted to propagate himself. He knew what he was doing. He had the instinct of a growing inertia, of a thing that chooses its place of rest in which to lapse into apathy, complete profound indifference.

The insistence of his will is almost drab—hence the repetition of the simple sentences beginning, "He wanted . . ." The unholy alliance between machine-like apathy thoroughly leveling all distinctions and the dull instinct of perpetuation is completed in this summary passage:

> He would let the machinery carry him; husband, father, pit-manager, warm clay lifted through the recurrent action of day after day by the great machine from which it derived its motion. (351)

Clearly in the nineteenth century—and this is the basis of Ursula's rejection of her mother's values—the biological and the historical had merged with the spiritual. Against this process of secularization was aroused the more questing Modernist

FAMILY, MACHINE AND PARADOX OF TIME

spirit. In Tom Brangwen's choices we see very specifically the further alliance between what we mean by the historical and the machine—all resulting in a primeval and uncreated physical and moral apathy, the repetitive sameness of experience. Strangely enough, this apathy finds its support in Tom's abstracted sense of linear time: "He believed neither in good nor evil. Each moment was like a separate little island, isolated from time, and blank, unconditioned by time." (344) We gain here an inkling of a crucial paradox to which we shall shortly return, the paradox that by some curious and far-reaching reversal, the triumph of time at its most advanced produces a reversion to life at its most primeval. Nietzsche referred to the product of this new conjunction as a "civilized barbarism."

In the Renaissance when studying the new consciousness of time, it seemed almost inevitable that discussion should be extended to its application in education. In Modernism, where time is again at the forward point of experience, education follows closely. In his previously noted book, *From Hegel to Nietzsche*, Karl Löwith introduces sections on work and education (in a larger part aptly called, "Studies in the History of the Bourgeois-Christian World") with this sentence that is stunning in its simple power: "In the nineteenth century, work and education became the substance of the life of bourgeois society."[31] One needed to work at education in order to work better later on. If work has become the end of existence, education must lose whatever attendant spirit of graciousness or liberality it once possessed. If one's being is limited to one's function, then education suffers an irreparable constriction. "Education shrinks daily because hurry increases daily."[32] This explains why in both *Buddenbrooks* and *The Rainbow* seemingly incongruous chapters are devoted to education. In the concluding section of Mann's first novel the Prussianization of the schools crushes the last of the Buddenbrooks. Significantly, the chapter opens with this harsh awakening! "The alarm-clock went off with cruel alacrity. It was a hoarse rattling and clattering that it made, rather than a ringing. . . ." (548)

FAMILY, MACHINE AND PARADOX OF TIME

In the much later *Rainbow*, Lawrence goes beyond this coarse vigor represented by the new education to the system's final regression toward nothingness (as Mann will also do in *The Magic Mountain*). That the weather is gray and wet does not seem to matter to the staff of the Brindsley Street school, Ursula's new place of employment. In there "it seemed that neither morning nor weather really existed. This place was timeless." The first person she encounters, "spoke in an occupied voice, like an echo." (369) The school itself is the perfectly realized product of the mechanized will of the headmaster, and his assistants fall in line: "She could always hear Mr. Brunt. Like a machine, always in the same hard, high inhuman voice, he went on with his teaching, oblivious of everything." (376)

This "man's world" Ursula is able to escape easily, but the penetration of its values to the worlds of marriage and continuity she finds somewhat harder to manage. Such an escape requires a break-through from one level of consciousness to another. Skrebensky has been revealed to be the weaker vessel; he withers before the greater passion, the naked self-abandon, and the innocent unself-consciousness of Ursula. Her simple capacity to become absorbed in delightful experience destroys his egotism. And yet all around her are pressures urging her to marry him. It is not only her mother's example, the whole argument of time demands to know who she thinks she is to go against the great machinery of the race. In a moment of weakness she relents:

> What did the self, the form of life matter? . . . Who was she to be wanting some fantastic fulfillment in her life? Was it not enough that she had her man, her children, her place of shelter under the sun. Was it not enough for her, as it had been enough for her mother? She would marry and fill her place simply. That was the ideal. (483-484)

We can see how the mother's choices, rich in their context, have become impoverished when applied as models for Ursula. These thoughts are followed by a letter that can, *mutatis mutandis*, be compared with the one received by Tony Buddenbrook from her father. In its simple expression of *mauvaise foi* it suggests that Ursula's marriage with Skrebensky would be tantamount to that of Tony with Grünlich—again recognizing the differences. Unlike Tony, though, Ursula has a Modernist hunger—one that was left unsatisfied in Thomas Buddenbrook. She passes through a time of hallucinogenic experiences and a fortnight of bed-ridden delusion and pain. The movement from the Old to the New World (493) required just such a period of traumatic experience that was indeed beyond her consciousness. Physically the trauma aborted Skrebensky's child that she was carrying. But this was only a signal of the past that she needed to slough off psychically and abort, because, as expressive of her new consciousness, she felt she could have kept the baby without feeling the need to bind herself to Skrebensky. In fact, looking at the conclusions of all three of Lawrence's major novels, we see that they end with a striking rejection and defeat of the codes of marriage and continuity: Morel's merciful killing of his mother, Ursula's abortion and Gerald Crich's final letting-go and suicidal reversion to the womblike emptiness of the Tyrolean Alps.

4. *The Paradox of Time*

The problem is an enormous one. In the full glory of its achievements, and with the full promise of abundance, scientific industrial culture had created its own dissidence, and in those who had most fully accepted its premises, its prime representatives. Within the terms of this study, the theory that accounts for this strange reversal whereby the temporally most sophisticated come to resemble the most primitive—as we have seen in the case of the younger Tom Brangwen and shall see more fully in Gerald Crich of *Women in Love*—I call the paradox of time. It helps us to understand why what had been a highly effective and inspiring code had reached a state of exhaustion by the end of the nineteenth century. It also helps to dispel that misguided notion that Modernism was a response in kind to the new energetic dynamic of modern life, to the new bustle, movement and change, the accelerating pace of life. Perhaps in regard to some of the stylistic devices, this might be true, but when it comes to the substance of the life, Modernists did not find the new energy to be terribly exciting. In fact, they found it rather repetitive, representing only quantitative but not qualitative changes in the order of experience. Unlike Futurists (with whom they shared many common origins), Modernists did not feel a need to identify with the forward movements of industrial society. They felt the end-products to result in stagnation, showing no real change based upon heterogeneity and variety, but rather repetitive sameness. The paradox of time helps us to understand this phenomenon. I have deliberately postponed the fuller treatment of this explanatory theory (alluding to it only briefly in previous chapters) in order to accumulate illustrative examples from the younger Modernists themselves as to the liabilities of their culture. What is clear (and will become clearer) is that the illustrations are consistent and, more importantly, reasoned—they themselves promote the formulations we offer.

We have repeated enough the notion that in the Renaissance time was predictive as well as innovative. But it is worthy of note that there was some effort on the part of Modernists to reassert that former relationship—it is at least implicit in their depictions of the victims of the triumph of the predictive. D. H. Lawrence explicitly expressed a similar need for human control over experience as well as the need to participate in newness. Lawrence's speculations on labor and the machine in his *Study of Thomas Hardy* should be placed in the line of those German thinkers that Karl Löwith discusses so effectively in *From Hegel to Nietzsche*. Yet, Lawrence's considerations are so typically Modernist. He regards the machine as the fullest development of man's need for and delight in work. Lawrence's Modernist, as distinct from Romantic, tendencies may be seen in his refusal to go back on the means of his time: "Now there is a railing against the machine, as if it were an evil thing. And the thinkers talk about the return to the medieval system of handicrafts. Which is absurd." (426)[33] (Like Freud's thought in *Civilization and Its Discontents*, Lawrence's disinclination to return to the past is accompanied by a lack of hope in future reformations on a mass scale—the workingman is just the opposite side of the same coin as the rich man. He only wants riches. "Why try to alter the present industrial system on behalf of the workingman, when his imagination is satisfied only by such a system?") (427).

Several things are striking in this argument. One is the evident struggle behind the inspired intuitiveness of Lawrence's writing. This struggle is a product of the dualistic nature of his thought. He does not wish to assert only a single truth, but rather to assert the simultaneous importance of several truths, as well as their interrelations. He wishes to affirm the intellectual significance of the machine and at the same time assert that all of man's actions are not to be confined to this predictable expertise. But the main point is the relation established by a major Modernist thinker between the predictive and the innovative (as I have stated, other paired terms could be used) aspects of time. If the Modernists had more forcibly to assert the innovative—the venture into the unknown as a postulate of human freedom—that was only because around them predictive control held such preponderant sway, and they, expressing an instinct that will become more evident later, felt the need to right the balance.

When the predictive aspect of time establishes such hegemony that it thoroughly eclipses the innovative, when experience has become so standardized and homogeneous, then, according to the paradox of time, we obtain a condition exactly the opposite of that which had prevailed in the Renaissance, we obtain the triumph of space. In Modernist literature, especially in the great exponents of the Western dynamic, Thomas Buddenbrook and Gerald Crich (we could of course offer Aschenbach, Prufrock and others as examples), this encounter with the barrenness of repetition as the product of the strongest efforts to control time is the point at which the Western dynamic breaks down. This phenomenon, whereby time by virtue of uniformity becomes transformed into space, is the subject of another brilliant expository analysis in two chapters of *The Magic Mountain*.

In "By the Ocean of Time" Mann expresses his own concern for the time-lostness of Hans Castorp, for whom the routines of the sanatorium hold such interest. The emptiness of the bleak mountainous snowscape appeals to Hans by reminding him of the ocean he knew and loved as a child, but whereas the ocean in *Buddenbrooks* provided a release from pressurized temporal existence, here it is threatening by its very lack of measurability:

> there is the same as here, once upon a time the same as now, or then; time is drowning in the measureless monotony of space, motion from point to point is no motion more, where uniformity rules; and where motion is no more motion, time is longer time. (547/576)

The ocean, as well as the mountain, becomes correlative to Han's own temporal indifference. All things become the same.

In the earlier section called "Excursus on the Sense of Time," Mann confronted this problem more directly. Time passes quickly, we think, when many things happen; it passes slowly when we are bored, and nothing seems to happen. In the long run just the reverse occurs. Routine, tending towards sameness, causes the temporal markers to meld and lose their distinctness: "the perception of time tends, through periods of unbroken uniformity to fall away. . . . Vacuity (Leere), monotony have indeed the property of lingering out the moment and the hour and of making them tiresome. But they are capable of contracting and dissipating the larger, the very timeunits (Zeitmassen) to the point of reducing them to nothing at all (verkürzen und verflüchtigen sie sogar bis zur Nichtigkeit)." This is why, of course, the sense of time and the sense of life must necessarily go together, influencing one the other, and why boredom is not merely a physical, but rather a psychic experience of time: "etwas seelisches—es ist das Erlebnis der Zeit." (104/110-111)

It can be argued of course that what Mann is here describing is actually the "Asiatic" time-menace implicit in the remedievalized atmosphere of the sanatorium, and that he does not mean to include the Western time-dynamic, which would be in strong opposition to this devastating routine (as we can infer from its spokesman, Settembrini). But the fact remains that this demoralizing experience of repetition and routine was the breaking-point for Thomas Buddenbrook as well as for the tight-fisted, time-diligent Gustav von Aschenbach—that is, for the two prime representatives of the Western need to control experience. Furthermore, as we saw earlier, it is Hans's own experience of the moribund bourgeois ethic that predisposes him to find attractiveness in the timeless.

Whether caused by Western dynamic or counter to it, the deadening effects of uniformity that Mann describes and so brilliantly analyzes is confirmed by other Modernists—and in no debatable context. Ortega y Gasset, in his *Revolt of the Masses*, defends the twentieth century against the view that it was merely a decayed and fallen-away descendant of a fuller culture. Furthermore, he contends in pages that could very well serve as a gloss on the fate of Thomas Buddenbrook, the nineteenth century was not the period of plenitude previously imagined. Its outer satisfaction, its sense of having "arrived" might only shield an inner death. "When a period satisfies its desires, its ideals, this means that it desires nothing more; that the wells of desire have been dried up. That is to say, our famous plenitude is in reality a coming to an end."[34] When Modernists looked at the nineteenth century they saw more than its productive energies and bountiful life.

In *Orlando* Virginia Woolf gives a dramatic version of this phenomenon. In Orlando's imagination all of the Victorian traffic along Park Lane has suddenly coagulated into golden blocks. While awed by this transformation she is also disturbed by one thought, a thought familiar to all who beheld great elephants, or whales of an incredible magnitude, and that is, how do these leviathans to whom obviously stress, change and activity are repugnant propagate their kind? Perhaps, Orlando thought, looking at the stately, still faces, their time of propagation is over; this is the fruit, this is the consummation. What she now beheld was the triumph of an age.[35]

And, as Lawrence pronounced in *The Crown*, it perishes by virtue of its triumph.[36] We are reminded that Thomas Buddenbrook's collapse comes after he has achieved the utmost of his possibilities. For him, also, the time of propagation is over. His destroyed son Hanno draws a line through the family ledger, "I thought, I thought," he stammered, "there was nothing else coming." (411/397) This obvious dissatisfaction with the triumph of an age explains why, as C. A. Patrides has written, "the nineteenth century terminated in claustrophobia."[37]

The very linearity of time itself, become mere monotonous extension, adds to the sense of fatigue and nothingness. In contrast D. H. Lawrence looks in *Apocalypse* to a more pagan and cyclical sense of time:

> Our idea of time as a continuity in an eternal straight line has crippled our consciousness cruelly. The pagan conception of time as moving in cycles is much freer, it allows movement upwards and downwards, and allows for a complete change of the state of mind at any moment. One cycle finished, we can drop or rise to another level, and be in a new world at once. By our time-continuum method, we have to trail wearily on over another ridge.[38]

Indeed, even progress is seen by Ortega to be a gloomy faith, implying no creative reassessments on a large scale, but rather the addition of small lines to the chart of local adjustments. Progress meant that "tomorrow was to be in all essentials similar to today; [it] consisted merely in advancing, for all time to be, along a road identical to the one already under our feet."[39] Both Lawrence and Ortega relate fatigue and weariness of spirit to similitude, the essential sameness of experience involved in conceptions of linear time, which ends in the triumph of space. The triumph of space as we have described it in the paradox of time places the weight of eternal sameness upon the human spirit whose energy is dependent upon variety. Time itself requires distinctions, for where there are none, there is uniformity. Hence the combination of lethargy and the absence of any aroused sense of time in Renaissance portraits of their medieval predecessors (seen in the different stages of Gargantua's education), and the fact that in the Renaissance new conceptions of time were closely bound up with the love of variety and an energized reawakening. By a strange and yet perfectly understandable turn of events, the Modernists, in attacking what the Renaissance time-consciousness had become, were about that very business we associate with the word "renaissance."

The paradox of time here set forth is not the insight of writers of fiction and of poetry only; it is shared by modern philosophers such as Bergson, Whitehead and, as we have seen, Ortega. They, like other Modernists, undertook a critique of fundamental assumptions and found that the way that time had been regarded in the West after the scientific revolution was not in fact an accurate representation, but rather a transference whereby the laws that suited laboratory physics had been converted into absolute principles governing life. A methodology had become a philosophy. Following Bergson in his analysis, Whitehead went on to call this the fallacy of misplaced concreteness. By virtue of this fallacy the lapse of time is "accidental" to any investigation. "The material is fully itself in any sub-period however short. Thus the transition of time has nothing to do with the character of the material. The character is equally itself at an instant of time." The world is made up, then, of a "succession of instantaneous configurations of matter" without any connections.[40] As a consequence, nature at any given period does not refer to or include nature at any other period. Although Whitehead does not draw the psychological implications, other writers do—one thinks immediately of Virginia Woolf—and are pained by the isolation of things, as if they bore only their own weight, measured against an otherwise empty existence. Thinking back to D. H. Lawrence, we see that precisely this sense of time was the basis of Tom Brangwen's apathy.

As Whitehead acknowledges, the master of this analysis is Bergson, who in his early *Essai sur les données immédiates de la conscience* (1889; trans. *Time and Free Will*, 1910), declared directly that time in the West had become spatialized. Let us notice, Bergson alerts us, that when we speak of time we generally refer to a "homogeneous medium in which our conscious states are ranged alongside one another as is space, so as to form a discrete multiplicity"—where the multiplicity is strictly quantitative, meaning identical yet separate counters.[41] And a few pages later, "It is true that when we make time a homogeneous medium in which our conscious states unfold themselves, we take it to be given all at once, which amounts to saying that we abstract it from duration. This simple consideration ought to warn us that we are thus unwittingly falling back upon space, and really giving up time." (98)

Treated as moments in space our states of consciousness become discrete multiplicities (that are yet homogeneous, and in the same line of succession), impermeable, like matter, one to the other. For Bergson, however, real states of consciousness do permeate one another, to such an extent that "in the simplest of them the whole soul can be reflected." (98) Duration for Bergson might well be "nothing but a succession of qualitative changes, which melt into and permeate one another without precise outlines, without any tendency to externalize themselves in relation to one another. . . ." This "duration" would be pure heterogeneity where "heterogeneity" implies, unlike "discrete multiplicity," a mixture of qualitatively different experiences. (104) Hence in Modernism the need for a break-up of linearity, of the succession of spatially discrete but in fact uniform experiences. Bergson himself calls for some bold novelist to tear aside the curtain—he calls it

FAMILY, MACHINE AND PARADOX OF TIME

"cleverly-woven"—of our conventional ego and show us "under this appearance of logic a fundamental absurdity, under this juxtaposition of simple states an infinite permeation of a thousand different impressions." (133) A multitude of twentieth-century novelists and poets answered his call. Against the worn-down homogeneity of experience they would look for and present the freedom of difference, discrepancies based on qualitative intensities rather than on linear sameness. They would look for the permeable presence of the past, undying and strangely reappearing in the unthinking moments of the present, and finally, rather than the smoothly running machine they would look for something that had, in Bergson's words, "the bite of time" in it. (152)

Perhaps closer to our literary purposes is the most accessible of Bergson's studies, his classical *Laughter: An Essay on the Meaning of the Comic*.[42] What is laughable, Bergson indicates, is "something mechanical encrusted on the living." (37) Life and thought being animated never repeat themselves; consequently, that which is repetitive—like a machine working automatically—is risible. "Wherever there is repetition or complete similarity, we always suspect some mechanism at work behind the living." (34) At one instance this mechanism is referred to as a "clockwork arrangement," (36) and at another, "this idea of regulating life as a matter of business routine...." (48) Requisite suppleness of response in face of the ever-changing elements of life is thus lost to fixation, which society tries to exorcise by laughter. While Bergson uses as models in this essay many traditional practices of comedy, still it is clear that his particular formulations and theoretical understanding could only have come forward in modern times.

In the next chapter we indicate some of the stylistic consequences of the paradox of time and of the search for heterogeneity. At the moment it is sufficient to point out that one of the leading theoreticians of Imagism, T. E Hulme, makes use of Bergson's ideas to vindicate the role of art in twentieth-century society. What Bergson perceived as a dominant need for action gives, unfortunately, a forward acceleration to our thoughts and our responses to the external world; as a consequence the objects of the world have become streamlined and standardized. They have become conventional counters that have lost any communication of freshness, or possibilities of an "actual contact with reality." The mechanical, utilitarian means of society finds its corollary in an equally mechanical and conventionalized imagery. Ordinary language or prose takes us along as if we were travellers on a train, with scant attention to the world whizzing by. Hence, the "function of the artist is to pierce through, here and there, accidentally as it were, the veil placed between us and reality by the limitations of our perception engendered by action."[43] As we shall see, such concerns will have great influence in the Modernist movement, well beyond the major writers upon whom I center this study. What will come to matter in good writing is not the universal quality, nor any classical generality or inherent dignity of subject matter, but rather the skill of the poet in making certain physical details stand out. Things must be redeemed from the nothingness to which our standardized experience relegates them: "it doesn't matter if it were a lady's shoe or the starry heavens."[44] To render precisely an object or an experience—the aim of Hemingway—thus becomes one way of giving some definite meaning to experience.

The disciplinary differences of the points of view—philosophy, history of science, sociology and literature—and yet the common language as well as similar conclusions indicate that when dealing with the paradox of time we are dealing with a fundamental stratum of twentieth-century experience. This evidence is reinforced when the most prestigious Marxist literary critic known to the West, using Marx's own economic analyses, produces similar ideas. Bergson's idea of "spatialization" is similar to (perhaps even responsible for) Georg Lukács's sense of "reification." Under capitalism, Lukács argues in "Reification and the Consciousness of the Proletariat," labor has become a commodity, specialized, rationalized and broken down into "abstract, equal and comparable" units—that is, made, like time itself under science, into discrete but quantitatively similar counters. Since, according to Lukács, "the

FAMILY, MACHINE AND PARADOX OF TIME

fragmentation of the object of production necessarily entails the fragmentation of the subject," man's basic attitudes toward the world undergo a transformation through capitalism and time is degraded to the dimension of space. Lukács then goes on to quote Marx's particularly powerful and passionate sentences (that bear requoting):

> "Through the subordination of man to the machine the situation arises in which men are effaced by their labour; in which the pendulum of the clock has become as accurate a measure of the relative activity of two workers as it is of the speed of two locomotives. Therefore, we should not say that one man's hour is worth another man's hour, but rather that one man during an hour is worth just as much as another man during an hour. Time is everything, man is nothing; he is at the most the incarnation of time. Quality no longer matters. Quantity alone decides everything: hour for hour, day for day...."[45]

In unexpectedly Bergsonian language, Lukács then concludes,

> Thus time sheds its qualitative, variable, flowing nature; it freezes into an exactly delimited, quantifiable continuum filled with quantifiable "things" (the reified, mechanically objectified "performance" of the worker, wholly separated from his total human personality): in short, it becomes space.[46]

The paradox of time, the collusion of time and the machine, time and history, time and the succession of children, and the linkage of names like Nietzsche and Marx, Bergson and Georg Lukács, D. H. Lawrence and T. S. Eliot, all offering similar analyses, or at least focusing on common problems, suggest that we are here touching one level of "solidarity" in Modernism, the level of basic attitudes.

5. *Time, Love and Industrial Management:* Women in Love

Tom Brangwen, who fills in many of the psychological character details of the paradox of time, is, however, minor when compared with Gerald Crich, the "suffering hero" of

Women in Love. The machinery that carried the younger Brangwen along was set in motion by the dominating will of Crich; the former was an organization man, the latter helped establish the modern managerial revolution. It is fair to praise Lawrence for being the "priest of love" (provided we appreciate, as his biographer does, his skill as a novelist). But such a visionary title must not keep us from seeing the remarkable correspondence and even fusion between his individual intuition and the larger social fact, the coherent power of his imagination. Frederick Winslow Taylor's *Principles of Scientific Management* and the figure of Henry Ford stand behind the supreme organizational drive of Crich. And when we consider the paradox of time, it is not an accident that this dynamic will is the very force that plunges him toward death and nothingness. Although never mentioned, as indicated above, the necessary background to *Women in Love* is World War I, where, in the words of Mann's Naphta, Western society seems to have been willing its own destruction.

Lawrence's novel captures the strained orneriness and bitchiness, the paradoxes of character and the atmosphere of decadence of that critical time. The first significant words heard from a Crich in the book (excepting casual salutations) is, "We are usually to time." To which Birkin—the attractive Alceste of the novel, whose being is fortunately better than his pronouncements—responds, "And I'm always late." (15) Unlike a similar exchange in the second scene of *Henry IV, Part One*, where Hal demands of Falstaff what business he could possibly have in asking the time of day, the time-prodigal seems not in the least endangered; it is the time-world hanging over the Criches that is threatening. Gerald is constantly in the position of defending institutions that his most ulterior will seeks to obliterate. A race or a nation, he asserts, is like a family and must have a commerical aspect: "You must make provision. And to make provision you have got to strive against other families." (22) And later, like Tom Brangwen, he commits himself to marriage as an institution (not necessarily to a relation with Gudrun): "It was a committing of himself in acceptance of the established world, he would accept the established order, in which he did not livingly believe, and then he would retreat to the underworld of his life." (345)

As with Gustav von Aschenbach there is a *Zweideutigkeit* to Gerald's intentions. And like Aschenbach, Gerald has a soldierly quality, that strained heroism that, in Mann's words, the times seemed to admire. As the favorite word of the former character was "*durchhalten*," that is, "persevere," so Gerald, too, cannot let go, but must see things through. This straight-backed power of will his mother fears, for Gerald is the most "wanting" of her children. (19) The soldierly quality of Gerald helps explain the relationship between Gerald and Rupert as one of alter-egos, and Rupert's love and admiration for Gerald's beautiful and soldierly face—"with a certain courage to be indifferent," (51) that is, careless of his own life and chances. It also helps explain Gerald's need for Rupert; he feels saved and made sufficient by Rupert's "odd mobility and changeableness that seemed to contain the quintessence of faith." (225) A similar relationship exists between the more open and experimental Hans Castorp, and his cousin Joachim, who is a soldier and, like Gerald, prefers, almost against his will, to stand and defend the citadel from its besieging powers. His death, to which we shall refer later, is clearly indicated by Mann to be an effect of this repression. When we think back to the Renaissance and its attitudes toward time, this soldierly discipline is not unaccountable, the very ethos of time requiring on the one side order and a kind of militancy vis-à-vis the hostile forces of the world: for Hal to redeem the time and to enter his father's world of history, it was necessary for him to arm himself against threatening external forces. In the nineteenth century, at least as Modernists perceived it, this armor began to crush the flesh it was intended to protect, just as function subsumed the man.

Curiously enough Rupert is the spokesman for this age of disintegration, this *fin de siècle* end of the *saeculum*. World War I is apocalyptic as well as decadent, and they are the *fleurs du mal* born at the end of an age, products of a dark river of dissolution.[47] The curiosity is, of course, that while Rupert is the spokesman, Gerald is the exponent, the figure—"a messenger, an omen of the universal dissolution." While Gerald defends the established order he has a better knowledge than Rupert of the deadliness of which the latter speaks. After all, he did kill his brother and bears the mark of Cain. While Rupert speaks of blowing it right down the "slopes of degeneration—mystic, universal degeneration," Gerald listens with a "faint, fine smile . . . as if, somewhere, he knew so much better than Birkin, all about this: as if his own knowledge were direct and personal, whereas Birkin's was a matter of observation and inference. . . ." (196) And, to be sure, although Rupert speaks of death, he enjoys the rejuvenation of the natural world. He makes love to Ursula for the first time in the almost sacred confines of Sherwood Forest, where the ancient wood offers comfort and protection. And he is able to leave the frozen Alps to return to the peopled cities of Italy. Gerald on the other hand knows the absolute blankness of indifference and non-being. Diving repeatedly for his drowned sister, he expresses his horror—and yet fascination—with the underwater world: "It's curious how much room there seems, a whole universe under there; and as cold as hell, you're as helpless as if your head was cut off." (176) Birkin sees two kinds of disintegration, that of the sun and that of the snow, fire and ice, the African beetle knowledge and the "frost-knowledge" of the northern races, of whom Gerald is the "messenger" and type. (246-247)

Of this race committed to historical continuity and the mastery of time, Gerald as "Industrial Magnate" is the supreme representative. Gerald carries this time-world to its farthest extent, to that point where it becomes the clearest example of what we mean by the paradox of time. The need to control time has evolved in his hands into a system of industrial organization so standardized that it actually approaches timelessness. Here we meet the crux of the novel, that is, the close association between the atmosphere of decadence and the world Gerald has managed to create, and, more importantly, the relationship between the system Gerald establishes and his terrible fate in love: that this arch-representative of the ultimate Western dynamic should have so fatal an involvement with Gudrun, and should be so incapable of detracking himself from what is obviously a line leading to personal death and oblivion. The paradox of time would indicate that this same need to lose himself was expressed in the "timeless" world he created, as it was in the underwater world he visited and the icy blankness where he ended. In short, the very dynamic of the West at its most extreme reveals a reversion to life at its most primitive:

> This was the sole idea, to turn upon the inanimate matter of the underground, and reduce it to his will. And for this fight with matter, one must have perfect instruments in perfect organization, a mechanism so subtle and harmonious in its workings that it represents the single mind of man, and by its relentless repetition of given moment, will accomplish a purpose irresistibly, inhumanly. It was this inhuman principle in the mechanism he wanted to construct that inspired Gerald with an almost religious exaltation. He, the man, could interpose a perfect, changeless, godlike medium between himself and the Matter he had to subjugate. There were two opposites, his will and the resistant Matter of the earth. And between these he could establish the very expression of his will, the incarnation of his power, a great and perfect machine, a system, an activity of pure order, pure mechanical repetition ad infinitum, hence eternal and infinite. He found his eternal and his infinite in the pure machine-principle of perfect co-ordination into one pure, complex, infinitely repeated motion, like the spinning of a wheel; but a productive spinning, as the revolving of the universe may be called a productive spinning, a productive repetition through eternity, to infinity. And this is the God-motion, this productive repetition ad infinitum. And Gerald was the God of the machine, Deus ex Machina. And the whole productive will of man was the Godhead.

FAMILY, MACHINE AND PARADOX OF TIME

> He had his life-work now, to extend over the earth a great and perfect system in which the will of man ran smooth and unthwarted, timeless, a Godhead in process. (220)

It is likely that in producing this prophetic passage Lawrence had in mind the real-life principles of Taylorism (as Lukács had, incidently, when he discussed "reification") and perhaps even their application by Ford. In a later essay, "Men Must Work and Women as Well," Lawrence shows the rationale of progress, from business to bigger business, and from job to job, to be the "plan of the universe laid down by the great magnates of industry like Mr. Ford."[48] Gerald's revolution is presented in the chapter entitled "Industrial Magnate." And Taylorism, as is well-known, was the guiding principle of the assembly line as utilized by Ford.

There are even more similarities in Gerald's scheme to the scientific principles enunciated by Frederick Winslow Taylor. One is a devotion to an efficiency that was pure and scientific. Another is the standardization of labor and of tools: "the relentless repetition of *given* movement." For this to be done there had to be created the roles of the middle men, those industrial managers who lay out the tasks for the workers and set up the machinery. Their presence is perhaps the clearest borrowing from Taylor:

> The working of the pits was thoroughly changed, all the control was taken out of the hands of the miners, the butty system was abolished. Everything was run on the most accurate and delicate scientific method, educated and expert men were in control everywhere, and miners were reduced to mere mechanical instruments. They had to work hard, much harder than before, the work was terrible and heartbreaking in its mechanicalness. (223)

Also, Lawrence adds, this "set of really clever engineers" who directed the labor, did not cost much. But it was their responsibility to see that specialized human traits were fitted to certain tasks, and that the most rudimentary physical motions were controlled and coordinated. The master then is the stopwatch, according to which the workers in Taylor's system were to be led by the manager, who would not only tell them when to work but also when they should rest. This supremacy of the stopwatch will have an important corollary in Gerald's relations with Gudrun.

Like the spinning of the wheel, this system would proceed fluently, with clockwork efficiency and harmony, and, according to Taylor, would reduce tensions between owner and worker. This point also Lawrence seems to adopt:

> [Gerald] had come to the conclusion that the essential secret of life was harmony . . . And he proceeded to put his philosophy into practice by forcing order into the established word, translating the mystic word harmony into the practical word organization.

Lawrence, however, indicates that this harmony in worker-management relations is some kind of sleight of hand, some deception that the workers have not quite caught on to. Gerald has "over-reached" them, and brought them to accept as the basis of all judgment and value the higher, inexorable logic of the mechanical rules of efficiency. (221)

The paradox of time involves paradoxes of character; that is why, in this study of time, our next chapter will be concerned mainly with Modernist character, and the fact that the Modernist's virtues must be measured against the qualities and fates of those stern upholders of the Western time-dynamic. The contrast of Gerald with Rupert Birkin presents itself from several sides. While Gerald is conventional and conservative in his loyalties he is actually subversive in his desires; while Rupert speaks of dissolution he has a rather healthy foundation to his being. Rupert seems changeable, mobile, even "selfless"; Gerald appears to be powerful in his person and massive in the direction of his will. Yet this drive of his will seems dedicated to a homogeneity, to a sameness (hence the repetitive quality of his "timeless" system), and, in the more disastrous personal equation, toward, as in Will Brangwen, a need for fusion and a dependency that is tantamount to loss of self. Hence his inability to let go of death, his need to assume burdens and to involve himself in a terrible masochistic relation with Gudrun. Rupert's selflessness actually indicates a sense of separateness, of independence, and as a consequence a stronger self. He is able to recognize his difference from the many objects that surround him, and to let go when he has to. Gerald, on the other hand, seems to need some confirmation of himself, which results in dependency and a loss of self. This loss of self is not to be confused with momentary forgetfulness of the self, with the capacity to become so absorbed in what is happening around one, that for a moment one is able to devote all one's energies to that moment. Such forgetfulness of self Lawrence finds highly desirable, and it is one of Rupert's qualities, while Gerald, like Gudrun, can never divest himself of that buzzing persistency of consciousness, can never lose track of himself. As a consequence, like Gudrun, he seeks oblivion. In fact, with Gudrun he seeks oblivion in his sexual experience with her, and through their trip to the Tyrolean Alps.

Gudrun is Gerald's ideal companion, her negative will to destruction perfectly matching his own need to yield himself up. When they arrive at the Tyrolean Alps, which provide, as in *The Magic Mountain*, a timeless décor—the correlative of their own needs—Gudrun's reaction is one of instant and fearful recognition. " 'My God, Jerry,' she said, turning to Gerald with sudden intimacy, 'you've done it now.' " (388) Yet there is some will in her that seeks out this locale, that is at home here, just as Gerald was at home in the homogeneous system he had established. Each finds in sameness an appealing "timelessness."

> Gudrun was driven by a strange desire. She wanted to plunge on and on, till she came to the end of the valley of snow. Then she wanted to climb the wall of white finality, climb over, into the peaks that sprung up like sharp petals in the heart of the frozen, mysterious navel of the world. She felt

that there, over the strange blind, terrible wall of rocky snow, there in the navel of the mystic world, among the final cluster of peaks, there, in the infolded navel of it all, was her consummation. If she could but come there alone, and pass into the infolded navel of eternal snow and of uprising, immortal peaks of snow and rock, she would be a oneness with all, she would be herself the eternal, infinite silence, the sleeping, timeless frozen, centre of the All. (400)

Timelessness, vastness, oneness—they are the products of what is finally Gudrun's destructive will toward isolation, and they stress the similarities between the industrial system Gerald has constructed and the emptiness in which he ends.

Throughout their relationship Gerald moves under bondage to his family and death. Rupert tries to redeem Gerald from this "mill-stone of beastly memories" that he has tied around his neck, but this potentially saving relationship is severed as the novel remorselessly proceeds and Gerald's lot is hopelessly cast with Gudrun. Their first sexual experience occurs against the backdrop of the painful, unyielding death of Gerald's father. Driven by a desperate need to find some release Gerald wanders through the night and surreptitiously enters Gudrun's house. In his relationship he seems to commit his well-being and power to her; this creature of drive and "go" becomes strangely enough a dependent; in Lawrence's description Gerald becomes as a child to Gudrun:

> He felt his limbs growing fuller and flexible with life, his body gained an unknown strength. He was man again, strong and rounded. And he was a child, so soothed and restored and full of gratitude.
>
> And she, she was the great bath of life, he worshipped her. Mother and substance of all of life she was. And he, child and man, received of her and was made whole. (337)

Gerald is as grateful to Gudrun "as an infant is at its mother's breast." (338)

Throughout this passage describing Gerald's relief and de-

FAMILY, MACHINE AND PARADOX OF TIME

pendency Gudrun is virtually ignored, until we are suddenly brought up short, "But Gudrun lay wide awake, destroyed into perfect consciousness." (338) And we sense that Gerald with his needs has put himself into the same situation of rejection that he experienced as an infant and child. Gudrun must wait out the hours of the night, not like a realized woman, but rather like a vigilant mother. Her accomplice in this wakeful and exhausting consciousness is the church clock striking the hours. In fact, emphasizing the destructive suitability of her own consciousness to Gerald's, and bringing together the larger social fact with the more personal psychic dynamics, is the constant association of Gudrun's own distracted mind and the world of the clock. Her own face is like the clock in her parlour, that grotesquely ogled an eye whenever the minute hand moved. (369) She was always supremely aware of clock faces wherever she might be or whatever she might be doing: "In vain she fluttered the leaves of books, or made statuettes in clay. She knew she was not really reading. She was not really working. She was watching the fingers twitch across the eternal, mechanical, monotonous clock-face of time." (457)[49] Curiously enough, this division of consciousness, this insufficient rallying of energies, reminds us of the divided world from which the humanistic educators first redeemed Gargantua; he, too, without any sense of time, might be reading a book, but his mind was in the kitchen. The super-developed time-world reverts to that which existed before the modern consciousness of time—but with a serious aggravation of tension and without any of the comic accomodativeness felt in Rabelais.

The total picture of Lawrence's imagination coheres when Gudrun's painful awareness of the clock, one that produces in her a "hard, metallic wakefullness" (407), turns on Gerald in language that unmistakably calls to mind the system he had introduced as industrial magnate, and its repetitive sameness. For almost three pages (455-458) of Gudrun's sustained internal monologue, Lawrence provides us with one of the most dramatic and effective passages on the dimensions of time in modern literature. Determined to break with Gerald and depart with the proto-Nazi artist Loerke for, of all places, Dresden, she imagines in fearful fancy what her life would have become at Shortlands in England:

> The thought of the mechanical succession of day following day, day following day, *ad infinitum*, was one of the things that made her heart palpitate with a real approach of madness. The terrible bondage of this tick-tack of time, this twitching of hands of the clock, this eternal repetition of hours and days—oh God, it was too awful to contemplate. And there was no escape from it, no escape.

Gerald cannot release her from this world of empty sameness and repetition since it is the world he has created. In its simple monotony, the paradox of time stands revealed: through uniformity time has become changeless extension, and this thought is maddening. The world that Gerald has produced, the world of magisterial industrial control, now, in the image of the clock, extends to their sex and causes revulsion:

> He, his body, his motion, his life—it was the same ticking, the same twitching across the dial, a horrible mechanical twitching forward over the face of the hours. What were his kisses, his embraces? She could hear their tick-tack, tick-tack.

She herself would like to be rocked to sleep from her own consciousness, and instead she must perform that function for Gerald. "Was she his mother?" she asks in angry desperation.

> So manly by day, yet all the while such a crying of infants in the night. Let them turn into mechanisms, let them. Let them become instruments, pure machines, pure will, that work like clock-work in perpetual repetition.

Like Lawrence's other powerful passage, so this one is imaginatively synthetic, bringing together and summarizing the materials of this study, the subjugation of the self to family and the machine, the will that becomes powerless by virtue of

FAMILY, MACHINE AND PARADOX OF TIME

its pathetic and undeviating needs, and the clock and the paradox of time.

The paradox of time, of which the dramatically realized fates of Gerald and Gudrun are the fullest expression in modern literature, can be placed in another perspective by the historical changes rung on the image of the clock. Dante in the early fourteenth century was delighted with the notion of the clock (at the time when the mechanical clock was in the process of development), and used it at the conclusion of *Paradiso*, X, as an example of the way that God brings together and harmonizes all of the pushing and divergent energies of the universe.[50] Later, in the seventeenth century, the clock became a model of the superbly unchanging physical laws of the world.[51] For the twentieth century the sheer triumph of time in history resulted in the death of history, in an excruciating sense of the trailing consequences of days, hours and minutes. The clock then came to represent not the driving energies of the world but rather a blank and empty face—that is, the triumph of space, or changeless extension. Such sameness, Modernists felt, was the ultimate product of the triumph of the *saeculum* and historical values, and of the linearity of time itself. As a consequence they sought for multiplicity, even multiple strata of existence. But before this could be effected some break-up of the former values was needed. This was done by depiction, at times painful and pathetic, of the devastating consequences of these values on those who embraced them fully and were, for whatever reason, unable to break their hold. It is with these negative examples that the first phase of Modernism had necessarily to concern itself.

CHAPTER III

Transformations

The world we have described in the preceding sections indicated nothing so much as a need for escape. Upon reading Schopenhauer's passionate discourse on the indestructibility of the soul, Thomas Buddenbrook experienced a great sense of liberation (short-lived though it was destined to be): "The walls of his native town, in which he had willfully and consciously shut himself up, opened out; they opened and disclosed to his view the entire world. . . ." (514/500) Ortega has described the feeling that occurs when we escape the narrow limits that circumstances (or our own wills) have imposed upon us: "We enjoy a delightful impression of having escaped from a hermetically sealed enclosure, of having regained freedom, of coming out once again under the stars into the world of reality, the world of the profound, the terrible, the unforeseeable, the inexhaustible, where everything is possible, the best and the worst." This kind of language—expressing a wide range of conflicting emotions and possibilities—will recur in Modernism; in fact, it probably forms its most important and typical stylistic trope.[1]

Frederick Karl, in his abundant biography of Joseph Conrad, quotes from a little-known letter to a newspaper where the novelist speaks most personally of his art, and in so doing uses terms that later novelists and poets would continue to use:

> The only legitimate basis of creative work lies in the scrupulous recognition of all the irreconcilable antagonisms that

make our life so enigmatic, so burdensome, so fascinating, so dangerous, so full of hope.[2]

Stephen Dedalus's own consciousness is brought to birth by his vision of the young girl at the seaside, "an envoy from the fair courts of life," who opened to him "in an instant of ecstasy the gates of all the ways of error and glory...." He was called "to live, to err, to fall, to triumph, to recreate life out of life.[3] T. S. Eliot, reviewing *Ulysses*, declared that it afforded him "all the surprise, delight, and terror I can require." To Arnold's belief that it is of undeniable advantage for a poet to deal with a beautiful world, Eliot retorted, "the essential advantage for a poet is not to have a beautiful world with which to deal: it is to be able to see beneath beauty and ugliness; to see the boredom, and the horror, and the glory."[4] Bernard, in his lengthy monologue in the final grand chapter of *The Waves*, declares his discontent with the neat outlines placed over existence: "I begin to long for some little language such as lovers use, broken words, inarticulate words, like the shuffling of feet on the pavement. I begin to seek some design more in accordance with those moments of humiliation and triumph that come now and then undeniably."[5]

There is much to be said about the importance of this trope, which is to be found everywhere in Modernism. Its first likely importance is the connection it establishes between the style of Modernism and its philosophical needs. If, as the preceding chapter demonstrated, the first (but not final) task of Modernism was to disrupt the temporal linearity that formed the basis of many nineteenth-century preoccupations (history, bourgeois continuity, scientific causality and progress), then this trope is a stylistic expression of that larger need. Rather than the "next step" Modernists looked to leaps of experience, to juxtapositions that could be startling and unexpected. The "next step" too often proved to be little different from the preceding and wearisome in its predictability. The Modernists introduced daring into their style as they did into their subject matters. Clearly corollary to this stylistic trope is the wide range of Modernist interests, extending from the sordid and subhuman, to the matter-of-fact, scientific or humorous, to the lyrical, the visionary and the mythic.

Not always mentioned in our analyses of Modernism is the emotional intensity that motivates this startling style and subject matter. For Eliot, nothing could be farther from the true nature of George Herbert's poetry than the nineteenth-century depiction of him as a country parson leading a pastoral existence of quiet contentment.[6] The appeal of Herbert's verse (and that of the other Metaphysicals) lay in its sense of struggle and religious passion, of man being stretched from hell to heaven. Some of these aspects of Modernism are summarized by I. A. Richards in an essay that should be better known, "Nineteen Hundred and Now," where he distinguished between the younger Modernists and their older contemporaries, Shaw, Bennett and Wells. D. H. Lawrence's descriptions of a life force seem to bear conviction, while Shaw's is only an "excogitated hypothesis." In *The Waste Land*, Eliot brings conflicting feelings into a "more balanced inclusiveness," and *Ulysses* may be characterized by its "robust acceptance of everything."[7]

As it reveals their emotional intensity, so this discrepancy of styles and subject matter shows their sense of adventure; the value they placed on variety, even uncertainty. If the predictable rules too rigorously then that which is unexpected, not willed or predetermined, assumes value. Surprise carries the imprint of authenticity.

Oddly enough, this need for stylistic freedom derives from the Modernist need to be faithful to the historical given of their time. In his review of *Ulysses*, Eliot distinguishes between criticism and poetry. In criticism it is easier to be a classicist, because then you are only responsible for what you desire, for what you would wish to be true: "In creation you are responsible for what you can do with material which you must simply accept."[8] By this view, Malcolm Bradbury concludes, "Modernism is not art's freedom but art's necessity."[9] But there is freedom as well. The freedom comes from breaking with the inherited world-picture, and rendering a picture more consonant with the experience of one's time. This is not so simple a task as it might seem. In Proust's extended novel, this change was presented as an essential conquest, involving the redemptive abrogation of the consciously directed will that sought to impose an all-too-customary form upon the artist's experience. Conrad summarizes this apparent paradox in the newspaper letter mentioned above: "It is only the writer's self-forgetful fidelity to his sensations that matter."[10] Oddly enough, Modernism, the most highly self-conscious of artistic movements, required the defeat of the conscious will and the definite ego so tied to restrictive conceptions of what was real. Only then would the true Modernist *disponibilité* emerge, that necessary openness to a wide range of experiences. This "readiness" befits the questing nature of Modernism, so exploratory in its search for new forms, idioms and subject matter.

This is the phase marked by transformations, where the "metamorphic impetus" of Modernism shows its full force.[11] In this chapter and the subsequent one dealing with the more positive phase of Modernist development, we shall be looking at two major areas, the complex central consciousness (in several of its facets) and the overall Modernist sensibility. In this section we shall see the emergence of a genuine contribution, the new typology of Modernism. This new character, or type, cannot help but be paradoxical. Despite his passivity he has remarkable inner reserves, detachment and sense of himself. Despite his inwardness he actually provides a window outward onto the complex happenings and shiftings of society. And despite his passive acquiescence to what is, he shows a remarkable freedom and comic variety—certainly not in controlling experience but by refusing to be controlled by one aspect of it. Behind all these multiple shadings there looms a new philosophy, one permitting, even requiring, the wide-ranging and multi-leveled zones of Modernist reference. And behind even this philosophy, perhaps, there lies a remarkable sense of the force of time, of the sheer passingness of things.

TRANSFORMATIONS

1. *The Complex Central Consciousness*

Of the same order as the criticisms of Graham Hough and Alan Bullock is Georg Lukács's belief that Modernism failed to evolve a stable typology.[12] Like theirs (either the belief that Modernism came up with no replacement for what it demolished, or that it did not represent a substantial spiritual change) so this charge questions the essential appeal and staying power of the Modernist movement. Since our concern is to mark the substantial importance and lasting impact of Modernism, we will show that just as there was a historical moment, a justifying condition and a philosophy to the first negative stage of Modernist development, so there evolved a clearly outlined and consistent character type as respondent to the new conditions of twentieth-century life.

If Modernists came to regard experience as multi-leveled and time not as a regularly flowing, sequential phenomenon, and if the evidence of human freedom was to be found in the capacity for supple transitions from one stratum of experience to another of a thoroughly different sort, and if these sudden startling jumps were to be juxtaposed in works of literature, then there are obvious implications for the Modernist hero, who would seem to require a register flexible and open enough to contain these experiences. Such a changed perception must bring about a new alignment of character types. In the Renaissance, with the discovery of time, the will and the ego emerged to play effective roles. The argument of time so powerfully present insisted that consciousness must be translated into action; in this transaction—from the aesthetic to the ethical, is one way it may be described—the will was a central agent. Such endeavor has as its end the preservation of the ego as an individual self with historical identity. Called to the lists, the reality-conscious Bolingbroke knows his name, "Harry of Hereford, Lancaster and Derby / Am I." The time-negligent Richard II finally knows not what name to call himself. Under the felt pressures of time, the emergent ego and the will are bulwarks against nothingness. In Modernist depiction, however, it is just those characters of will and ego who seem to seek oblivion. The very will power and singularity of commitment of such characters as Thomas Buddenbrook and Gustav von Aschenbach, of Will and the younger Brangwen, and Gerald Crich victimize them, binding them masochistically to an injurious relationship from which they cannot liberate themselves. Oddly enough, the more positive characterizations, those of Marcel in Proust's novel, Hans Castorp, Leopold Bloom, and Tiresias, seem to be marked by an absence of the will. They are not imposing upon experience a grid that does not fit.

For this new complex central consciousness, there are of course precedents in the literature of the second half of the nineteenth century. Flaubert's Frédéric Moreau (in *L'Éducation sentimentale*) and Stavrogin (in Dostoevsky's *Possessed*) are characters who prefigure the Modernist central consciousness. But, in the excellent phrase of Wylie Sypher, "Frédéric is a hero who cannot sustain his roles."[13] This distinguishes the precursor from the twentieth-century type, whose primary characteristic is the suitability of his traits to his role. If Wylie Sypher is right in perceiving an affiliation between Prufrock and Moreau, then we can see how these new central characters in Modernist works (Bloom, Tiresias, Marcel and Hans) represent a divergence from each.

What I mean becomes clearer when we compare Dostoevsky's Underground Man, who cultivates a mocking "passive awareness," with the more advanced of the Modernist heroes. Immediately, we see the difference in the orders. To be sure, Dostoevsky affirms that "a man of the nineteenth century must be, and is indeed morally bound to be, above all a characterless person; a man of character, on the other hand, a man of action, is mostly a fellow with a very circumscribed imagination." Yet, the Underground Man is pressured into positions of irrationality; the evidence of society—which he dimly intuits—has not yet given support to these intuitions. He concedes too much; he accepts society's characterization of his position as negligible. The man of order, who affirms that twice two is four, is also the realist who accepts nature's laws and sees no reason to bang his head against a stone wall. The Underground Man, however, wishes to affirm that twice two is five; there is a voluntarism in his assertions, as he doggedly insists on butting against the wall.[14] When we ponder the changed conditions of Modernist literature, we see that the charge against the early "negative" heroes (think only of such "realists" as Thomas Buddenbrook or Gerald Crich) is precisely that the persistence of their wills forces them into a destructive contest with stone walls. In Modernist literature the representatives of reality—in regard to which the Underground Man flaunts his inferiority—are themselves destroyed by their allegiances, which begin to appear irrational because lacking any capacity for change. Modernists were able to explain the Underground Man's complaints with much better reason. They were able to expand the domain of the argument, to lend it much better support in objective history. They move from marginality to centrality. This is another example of the solid basis in human experience that bestows confidence on the Modernist perspective, that brings together their insight into history and society with their positive creative energies. It also reveals the importance of their historical placement at an advanced stage of industrial development, where more of the liabilities involved with the paradox of time were apparent. As we have said before, the Renaissance "argument of time" has become the paradox of time.

Along with this reevaluation of the powerful nineteenth-century will, the attitude toward the conventional controlling ego undergoes drastic revision. The sharply defined identity has come to be regarded as an arbitrary and quite narrow holding action, one that merely gives the appearance of certainty, a façade of decisiveness. If it is true, as Lawrence frequently declared, that we live in a multiple universe, then any holds on permanence are mere postures. "Our ready-made individuality, our identity, is no more than an accidental cohesion in the flux of time."[15] Given such a view—and it is typically Modernist, so obsessed by the fugacity of things—the conventional ego can only be regarded as a set of blinders that compels one to disregard other areas of existence.

Rather than by concentration the Modernists could be typified by dispersal, geographic as well as psychic. The cosmopolitanism that the early Nietzsche deplored would become an identifying feature of the social backgrounds of the Modernists as it is of their characters and creations. Since this is a well-known fact of Modernism—the age and literature of exile, voluntary or involuntary—perhaps we can confine ourselves to a single illustration, the second volume of Joyce's letters, where the list of his residences covers eight pages— Paris, Trieste, Zürich and back again to Paris.[16] The basic disruption of historical values leads to a spatial fluidity, an international mixing that unsettles purely national identification. The break-up of the world of the fathers implies a loss of the fatherland's commanding position. The slogan of Franco's Spain, "Todo por la patria" does not hold much appeal for the expatriate Modern author (although, oddly and yet typically enough, the visions of the most transplanted were directed back to the persons and the places that they knew best of all: Joyce's Dublin, Eliot's Mississippi and Cape Ann, and one might even include Pound's admiration for the American founding fathers). There is a reason for this: successful liberation from historical values seems to require spatial removal. Thomas Buddenbrook relapses because his moment of vision is not followed by any departure. When, however, Hans Castorp leaves behind his *Vaterstadt* to travel to Davos, his physical separation announces his temporal alteration: "Space, like time, engenders forgetfulness; but it does so by setting us bodily free from our surroundings and giving us back our primitive, unattached state." (4/8)

Such ecumenicism feeds the broader vision of Modernist works, rescuing Modernism from the largely national preoccupations of nineteenth-century literature. For English literature, to George Orwell's way of thinking, the result was particularly salutary. Orwell wrote of Joseph Conrad that he was one of the non-English-born authors, "who in the present century civilized literature and brought it back into contact with Europe, from which it had almost been severed for a hundred years."[17] Works and characters began to assume a more international and mixed flavor (although the linguistic *pots-pourris* of *The Waste Land* or of Pound's *Cantos* no longer inspire that uncritical fervor they once did). Conrad wrote that all Europe contributed to the making of Kurtz, and he meant it spiritually as well as geographically. Thomas Mann could have said the same for his *Magic Mountain*: all Europe from the Caucasus to Spain (and even Mexico) exerted its influence on the open and susceptible German soul of Hans Castorp, the representative of his country's own ambivalent position *in der Mitte*.

This appreciation of a catholicity of background and of wide ranges of experience receives its embodiment in the central figures of each of the classic works of Modernism. For Joyce it became something of a critical principle of selection, determining his choice of the hero suited to overlay his modern epic. If the criterion is the variety of relations into which one enters, then Ulysses is a more fitting hero than Faust or Christ or even Hamlet. Ulysses was father, son, husband, lover, adventurer and homeseeker, the first gentleman of Europe and the inventor of the tank.[18] But beyond mere breadth of experience, Leopold Bloom joins with the other major characters—Marcel in the *Recherche*, Hans Castorp, Tiresias in *The Waste Land* (more a personage than a character, Eliot tells us), Rupert Birkin, in the sense we have already specified, and the ultimately transparent Jacob in *Jacob's Room*, or Clarissa Dalloway, Lily Briscoe, and the many facets shown in the characters in *The Waves* (but particularly in Bernard)—in their roles as reflective, passive, selfless and tolerant witnesses.[19] The creation of these complex central consciousnesses constitutes one of the major achievements of Modernism, an achievement that is epoch-making in several ways. In these characters and their new modes of being and perceiving, we were given the form of the intellect for roughly the next forty years of our culture—spanning more than two generations. We were given the form of twentieth-century man. A new type was thus created—*ein neuer Menschentypus*—in which to this day, although clearly some decline has set in and some changes were called for, we continue to find ourselves.[20] Joyce's use of Odysseus is then all the more pointed, since for Vico Homer's hero was similarly a new man, one who marked the transition from an heroic age to a time that was more democratic.[21]

The virtues of this "new man" must be understood in relation to what, by that curious process of reversal intrinsic to the paradox of time, the time-values emergent from the Renaissance had become. Gerald Crich's will to mastery had become mechanized, single-minded; this resulted, particularly in love, in a dogged pursuit of his own destruction (there are social implications as well), a refusal to buckle or to break, and finally, in the manner of a child, a simple yielding of himself to a woman who was rejecting him, who did not satisfy him. Total mastery of time seeks timelessness, and absolute will results in will-lessness.

Once this pattern is clarified other instances present themselves. In Lawrence, for example, the courage or incapacity to break off a bad relationship emerges as a basic theme. The older brother, William, in *Sons and Lovers*, becomes a negative example by virtue of his inability to break with Lily Western. Paul's break with Miriam or Clara, or Ursula's with Skrebensky, or even the departure of Aaron, become groping, yet vital signs of emotional well-being. This again explains why Modernism, in its initial stages, should be primarily concerned with negative examples, since the first step is one of avoidance, the refusal to make a misstep and the need to retrieve oneself from the expectations and needs of the forward-driving will. Gerald Crich, as a matter of fact, was trapped by his own need for mastery; his disastrous attachment was fed by an egotism that would not or could not admit failure.

Into this pattern fit the essential elements of the three main debilitating loves in Proust's great novel. His characters in love, Swann-Odette, Charlus-Morel, and Marcel-Albertine, show a remarkable willfulness (even inertia) in their attachments. In each case a man of brilliant yet squandered talents finds himself the prisoner of a lesser person. At first Swann toys with and is amused by Odette (he even has a more preferable rendezvous before his meetings with her), but when he misses her at the Verdurins' evening, and he finds some check and barrier to his total dominance of her, he becomes an impassioned (if titillated) prowler through the city (especially is this so when later he suspects she has another daytime lover). This entrapment does not occur because of the pleasure afforded. "All that is necessary," Proust reasons, "is that our taste for her should become exclusive." (I.177/I.231)[22] Torture enters love—a torture that enslaves when we need to "possess" the object of love. This new tantalizing passion at first seems to return to Swann the enthusiasm and interest in life that he had as an adolescent, even to that time when he thought himself an artist. But, and here Proust intercedes to mark an important difference, "ce n'était plus le même charme." Formerly, life had been enhanced by and found its virtue in many objects. Now it is only one object, Odette, who confers or possesses value. The need for possession has paradoxically resulted in the total subjugation of the lover to the object of love. Indeed, Swann in love seemed to become himself again, "mais à une autre," which Moncrieff correctly interprets as meaning, "but himself in thraldom to another." (I.183/I.239) The pattern is the same with the terrible infatuations of Charlus and of Marcel; in each case the object of the consuming attention is an inferior, who only assumes value when an obstacle is presented to exclusive possession.

To be sure, these men are not patrician industrialists, yet the connections between their imperious wills and Gerald Crich's industrial will are obvious—the same inertia in regard to a single object takes control of them all. In the case of Proust's characters they are further caught in the wave of nihilism and cynicism that is destroying the Guermantes set, that dissipates energy and commitment, talent and even taste and exposes them (particularly Swann and Charlus) to the malevolence of the petty Verdurins. Like Lawrence, Proust draws the connection between experiences in love and experiences in the larger society. We can understand then why the theme of the artist, given these emotional circumstances, should be so important for Modernists: it, too, is related to questions of will and self and multiplicity, or variety. Proust very clearly indicates that Swann and Charlus were, in their younger days, like Marcel, potential artists. In fact it is the very power of their imaginations—seeking to invest mundane objects with a special aura—that enslaves them. The artist manqué can love too much in life as well as in art, and the results of so doing are equally damaging. For example, the sheer will to be an artist (of the type that the Guermantes would appreciate) can only bring Marcel face to face with *le vide*, emptiness, which, as we have seen, has been the usual end-product of the will. (I.132-133/I.172-173) Imitation, as a consequence, can also only result in "barren uniformity," whereas the true artist (and here he is speaking of Bergotte, although the same can apply to Elstir) has an originality that is "incalculable and hence unrepeatable." (I.420/I.551) The variety of his effects reflects a separate and individual relationship to objects of experience; it lies in the "abundance of real and unexpected elements."

The same emptiness and uniformity occur when Marcel, like Swann and Charlus, pursues one of those mad demons of obsessive love: he suffers an impoverishment and reduction of vision similar to that of the barren imitator. Returning by automobile to see Albertine, Marcel is aware that the road, which once promised a view of the sea "pursuing as in the days when no living creature yet existed its lunatic, immemorial agitation," has changed: now it seems merely the same road of fixation that he had traveled in his infatuation with Mlle. de Stermaria or one not different from the Paris streets that he had paced in his anxiety over Mme. de Guermantes. "They assumed for me the profound monotony, the moral significance of a sort of ruled line that my character must follow." (II.292-293/II.1012) Fixation in love reduces everything to the sameness dictated by the controlling psychic pressures—no variety is allowed to enter this obsessive pursuit.

Which is the same as to say that the need to escape enthraldom, the search for variety, is, more positively, a love of freedom.

Later, Proust reflects that the same dynamic can be observed in regard to art. One can love Saint-Simon's *Mémoires* or the tales of the *Arabian Nights* too much, with the result that the more one adores the less success he has (another Modernist admonitory glance at the scholar). In the manner of his positive exemplar, Elstir, Marcel learns that "you can make a new version of what you love only by first renouncing it." One must not follow what one might wish to be true, but rather truth itself, the testimony of one's own experience, "qui ne vous demande pas vos préférences." As we have already seen, this conclusion has tremendous consequences for the content of modern art and its concern with the data of modern life. Eliot would say that one cannot choose to be a classic or a romantic: "At the moment when one writes, one is what one is, and the damage of a lifetime and of having been born into an unsettled society, cannot be repaired at the moment of composition."[23] The truth that is such an exigent (as well as redeeming) master for Marcel is similar to Eliot's, the historical given of one's own time and experience:

> And only if you faithfully follow this truth will you sometimes find that you have stumbled again upon what you renounced, find that, by forgetting these works themselves, you have written the *Arabian Nights* or the *Mémoires* of Saint-Simon of another age. (VII.268/III.1043-1044)

The genuine artist enjoys, then, historical and personal independence. Swann on the other hand can never approach history "critically" (in Nietzsche's sense) and Charlus, in enduring his many sufferings with Morel, quite consciously takes pleasure in identifying himself, in the manner of a Richard II, with the great *tristesses* of Balzac's homosexual characters. Whether Elstir, Bergotte or Berma, the artist becomes a model for Proust to counter the negative examples of Swann and Charlus. Whereas the mad lovers fall victim to the fixations of the will that result in a barren uniformity, the artist avoids the hazards of "imitation" by virtue of his individual response to multiple external objects. And, to anticipate somewhat, where Swann and Charlus (and incipiently Marcel) are undone by another kind of multiplicity, the swirl of parties, the lack of belief and the cynicism of the Guermantes way, the artist shows some kind of psychic reservoir that serves to separate his sense of himself from his harmful circumstances.

PARADOXICALLY, then, absence of the will in the Modernists' central creations is allied with the need to come into possession of some self-control, some separate identity and equanimity in relation to one's own will and that of others. A kind of stoic patience seems to be the quest and conquest of Modernism. "Teach me to sit still," is the prayer of *Ash Wednesday*; in *Four Quartets* even to hope would be to hope for the wrong thing; and in *Murder in the Cathedral* the final unlooked-for temptation is desire for martyrdom (that is, wishing or wanting to be assaulted so that one can reveal the qualities of the martyr). In *The Waste Land*, to return to the complex central consciousness, Tiresias is not a character, yet his suffering passivity reflects the city's many scenes of misery; the poem's voice finally asks, "Shall I at least set my lands in order?" So, too, in *The Magic Mountain* Hans Castorp is unformed and malleable, yet this very passivity is the means by which he transcends his own mediocrity; it is the perfectly suitable response to the "emptiness" of the times. As with Marcel, so with Hans, there is a justifiable nonchalance, even a saving laziness (and in Marcel's case, illness) that prevents them from committing their energies to goals and ideals that are ruinous. Marcel's lack of energy and of the wit and intelligence that are made much of in the Guermantes circle preserve him for the discovery of the psychic resources that might otherwise have been ignored.

In Hans, too, despite his passivity there is a sense in which his core is untouched by the polemical voices that encircle him. He listens, seems to consent, and yet follows his own life way. Hans Castorp is the unpromising hero from Medieval and Renaissance romance who becomes the national type. His nature is far from *einfach* (which in the standard English version is rendered as "unassuming"); rather than simple it seems complex. Castorp submits to Settembrini's harangues, but his mind can be elsewhere:

> [Settembrini] went on in this vein, and Hans Castorp listened without precisely following; first on account of his fatigue, and second because his attention was distracted by the proceedings of the lightheaded young folk on the steps. (114/121)

Corresponding to this distraction is the division that occurs between Hans's dream and waking worlds.

> Hans Castorp recalled how several times, in the extraordinary vivid dreams that visited his sleep in this place, he had taken umbrage at the dry and subtle smile curling the Italian's lip beneath the flowing moustache; how he had railed at him for a hand-organ man, and tried to shove him away because he was a disturbing influence. But that was in his dreams. . . . (149/158)

In his waking existence Hans is dominated by an openness and eagerness, *placet experiri*. But there is some offense beneath this experimental mode, the impertinence of the docility that tries all and accepts none fully. Clavdia Chauchat, late in the book and in Hans's development, rebukes (indulgently) this true independence:

> Even when you make admissions, there is always some impertinence about them. You are impertinent by nature—not only with me, but in general—God knows why. Your admiration, your very humility, is an impertinence. Don't think I can't see it. (595/629)

The Magic Mountain is a great pedagogic novel, but in the character of Hans Castorp experience transcends pedagogy. Hans carries with him his own psychic experiences, the adolescent attachment to Hippe, the schoolboy, that provides the pattern for his attachment to Clavdia Chauchat. In the Walpurgis Night episode he leaves behind the warning voice of Settembrini and makes his own way toward realizing the unconscious pressures of his love for Mme. Chauchat. When the appearance of Naphta turns Settembrini's monologue into dialectic, Hans follows his own need to retreat and dream, to rescue from the confusion his own nature, and dreams his "dream poem of humanity"—to which he declares his "verbriefte Rechte" ("prescriptive right"). He dreams in his own way a reconciliation of the Apollonian and the Dionysian, a dream that expresses the feeling of Greek tragedy. (494-496/521-522) The way of his experience is to mark, as Marcel did, the soundings of his own psyche. What involuntary memory and *moments bienheureux* are for Marcel, so unconscious reverie and dreams are for Hans: a means of safeguarding the self from unsatisfactory external identifications and discovering its psychic continuities with the individual's own past. Hence the importance of avoiding the "currents of action"—as Eliot affirms along with Bergson and Proust—lest they sweep away these moments of self-communication.

The very unassumingness of the new Modernist heroes corresponds to their sense of overwhelming change, their conviction that they are only one among many—a particularly poignant realization where woman is concerned. Unwilling to lie or boast, Hans must acknowledge to Peeperkorn that Clavdia was responsive to his feelings that Mardi Gras night. "But," he adds, "how much more so to yours. . . . And in all probability to many another. One has to face that. . . ." Peeperkorn gallantly stops Hans at that point: to pursue the argument would be common. (608-609/643-644) Nevertheless, it enlists the great and central argument of time in Modernism: openness and selflessness, the absence of will and ego, based upon an overwhelming sense of change and man's involvement in simple succession, actually effect a turnabout, a reversal, and preserve the individual's sense of self from any headlong flight to destruction that the more powerful and willful seem to risk.

This same resiliency combined paradoxically with a sense of a separate self serves Leopold Bloom when he encounters his own painful destiny. A middle-aged counterpart of Stephen—moving from identity to chaos as the younger man moves from confusion to definition—Bloom could very well play the Lear to Stephen's Hamlet. Transiency is universal:

> One born every second somewhere. Other dying every second. Since I fed the birds five minutes. Three hundred kicked the bucket. Other three hundred born, washing the blood off, all are washed in blood of the lamb, bawling maaaaaa. (162)

The next paragraph looks to cities and their constant dynamic of change, of ploughing under and building up, leaving Bloom with the conclusion, "No one is anything." This sense of flux, as it did for Lawrence, destroys the boundaries of the conventional ego. In the earlier Hades episode, where his father's suicide is revived for him, Bloom again thinks, "No more pain. Wake no more. Nobody owns." (98) The thought that nobody owns anything, that nobody is anything reminds us of Bloom's patron, the changeful Odysseus, who returned home and saved himself by being a "nobody." In fact, when he barks out his name he is in the greatest danger from the punishing forces of the universe. For Bloom, too, this passivity, this sense of himself as being caught up in larger, even universal forces, is a means of liberation and independence from his wife's own will and longing, about which he can do very little.

One of the bases of the Modernist character is this sense of separateness that allows for recognized realities. Thinking of the flirtatious beginning of the Blazes Boylan affair, Bloom tries mentally to stop what has happened. "Stop. Stop." But his own sense of reality intervenes, "If it was it was. Must." (165) It must be, he acknowledges, and we then learn that he and his wife have not had satisfactory relations since the death of their infant son some eleven years earlier. The tragic note of change enters as Bloom thinks of their earlier love and their present condition: "Me. And me now." (173) But unlike the great insistencies thrown up by Shakespeare's more willful heroes, Richard II, Lear and Antony, this radical fact of change is more easily (but not less painfully) accepted. The atmosphere of the piece and sense of the hero in *Ulysses* are closer to Shakespeare's last plays. Change is given a cosmic dimension in which man's own determinations count for little. "Can't bring back time. Had to be. Tell me all." (166) Curiously enough, Bloom's own expanded consciousness unsettles any tragic stance. His meditation upon change is followed by a remembered portion from Martha Clifford's letter, where she promises to tell him all. There is comedy in this self-reflection, as there is in the fact that Molly knows about his correspondence with Martha, and knows as well that Bloom knows about her and Boylan. The Modern consciousness inclines toward such multiple recognitions. In the Sirens episode, where Bloom must live through the hour of the rendezvous, he thinks about what marriage does to love, but also what hell there would be to pay if Molly found out about his correspondence with Martha (which she already suspects). In this instance he won't tell all; he sees no reason to inflict "useless pain." (275) What she does not know won't hurt her, he feels, but also the half-thought presents itself, "Sauce for the gander," which we as readers complete. In *Ulysses* a complex of forces present themselves that diffuse tragic grief—not the least of which is Bloom's consciousness of his own actions.

THUS, in a moral and ideological sense the complex central consciousness developed in Modernism represents a new type of positive hero. Lawrence can serve as summary for others when he shows the fatalistic movement of the highly directed will toward vastness, fusion and loss of self, and contrariwise, the survival capacities of those characters who have a combined sense of multiplicity as well as of their own separateness. If, as Arnold Hauser suggests, the flight from the more simply directed hero implies a flight from plot, we can see how this new type of hero has aesthetic implications as well.[24] The very "nothingness," the passivity and even transparency of the central hero permits him to be used as a telling device for otherness, for the rich presentation of the multiplicity of existence. Paradoxically (and paradoxes seem to abound in Modernism), the internalization of experience that seems so dominant in Modernist literature is a device for liberation outwards, permitting an opening out onto the many facets of the world. The passivity of these heroes, even the technique of internal monologue and stream of consciousness, makes more manifest the protean qualities of existence.

In Leopold Bloom, for instance, Joyce found a perfect instrument for registering the variety, the flux, the interpenetration, the simultaneity and the randomness of experience. Compared with the end-pieces of the Stephen and Molly sections, each in their own ways labyrinthine and cunning, Bloom, occupying the central bulk of the book, seems much more alive to the outer world. The rich, inquiring intellect of this wandering Jew-turned-canvasser in a modern city provides a range of curiosity and reflection that is remarkable. His schemes, his private life, his quick eye for what is happening in society and in business, his insuperable sense of libidinal intrigue, his quick associations and attempts to figure things out, his memories, all serve to give us a sense not only of Leopold Bloom but a reconstruction of Dublin life as well.

By its very nature as a passive recipient the complex central consciousness is highly useful in presenting others. Everyone feels free to impose himself and his ideas upon Hans Castorp. His unassumingness calls to mind the relatively naïve personae that both Dante and Chaucer chose to present the full richness of their times. Castorp's façade of docility and of malleability, his *einfach* nature, allows for the multitude of pedagogical influences that seek to alter him in their direction; that is, Hans's simplicity, compounded with a natural eagerness and curiosity, is the device that permits Mann to construct the complex intellectual life of pre- and post-war Europe. Similarly, the unassumingness of Marcel is the best key to the Thousand and

TRANSFORMATIONS

One Nights of Proust's Paris; his revelations come in moments of passivity and most acutely so when he is a voyeur. Even the great involuntary illuminations can be regarded as devices—they are the technical discoveries between whose supporting columns Proust is allowed to fill his novel with the day-to-day reflections, the adages and the humor that make it a great and comic chronicle. But the purest exploitation of this device is the personage of Tiresias, who is not a character, but what he sees, Eliot tells us, is the substance of the poem.[25] Oddly enough, the absence of will in the central character takes us beyond the narrower channels of action narrative. In the epic, the absence of the hero allows the pseudo-heroes to make their show; the sulk of Achilles permits the presentation of all the claimants to his role. And even the protean Odysseus, the nobody, enriched the repository of Western myth as a teller of tales. So, in Modernism, in the absence of a major character of will and of ego, we are provided with a mirror to a livelier, more varied world, where much more seems to happen.[26]

To be sure, Modernist literature is committed to the presentation of the rich and complex powers of inner reality: it is centripetal as well as centrifugal. Mrs. Ramsay presiding over a dinner party can move from a hell of fearful insecurity (the parental vision into chaos) and an anxious sense of nothingness to a heaven of achieved serenity—the truly momentous alterations that occur within one. Something indeed akin to the qualities of the "metaphysicals" resides in this Modernist range of speculative freedom and spiritual and emotional possibilities. Yet, in Virginia Woolf's work, this very internalization by virtue of the passive central consciousness opens out with zest onto the world. Clarissa Dalloway is another instrument for reflecting London street life (we must not forget that Virginia Woolf was an inveterate street-haunter):

> Such fools we are, she thought, crossing Victoria Street. For Heaven only knows why one loves it so, how one sees it so, making it up, building it round one, tumbling it, cre-

ating it every moment afresh; but the veriest frumps, the most dejected of miseries sitting on doorsteps (drink their downfall) do the same; can't be dealt with, she felt positive, by Acts of Parliament for that very reason: they love life. In people's eyes, in the swing, tramp, and trudge; in the bellow and the uproar; the carriages, motor cars, omnibuses, vans, sandwich men shuffling and swinging; brass bands; barrel organs; in the triumph and the jingle and the strange high singing of some aeroplane overhead was what she loved; life; London; this moment of June. (5)[27]

And yet, as a novel, *Mrs. Dalloway* is mainly concerned with the confirmations of the self that are arrived at by those with a sense of personal failure, like Clarissa Dalloway and Peter Walsh. They are offset by Sir William Bradshaw and Sally Seton Rosseter. The genius of *Mrs. Dalloway* is in its plotting, its lines that could be called arabesque, where individuals from one line will pick up a thread that has already been formed into a concavity and loop it into another, thus resuming and advancing the line of discourse.[28] In this regard, the inner conflict of Clarissa has already been reflected in and played out by her surrogates, Sir William and Septimus Warren Smith. In the famous psychologist we do not see the triumphant will and ego as self-destructive (as was the case with Thomas Buddenbrook and Gerald Crich), rather we see Bradshaw as victimizer of others, skillful in getting them under his thumb. Clarissa thinks, "Life is made intolerable; they make life intolerable, men like that." (281) From the story of Septimus's death that crosses her party she derives defiance; true, he was demented, badly so, but in his suicide she detects a human need to communicate, a reaching out through "corruption, lies and chatter." (280) This story of the young man, and also the example of the old woman across the courtyard turning on her own light, fill Clarissa with the simple courage of existence, and returns to her mind one of those many Shakespearean allusions that echo through Virginia Woolf's works: "Fear no more the heat of the sun." The Septimus-Sir William lines that converge at Clarissa's party, although different and physically unrelated to her own path through the novel, help us to understand the processes of her affirmation. They, together with Sally Seton Rosseter, once wild but now located at a place with children (like Anna Lensky Brangwen), help us to understand Peter Walsh. Sally has five sons, and Peter, whose career and marriage have run dry, has small prospects: "No sons, no daughters, no wife." (289)[29] And yet within this frame of modest failure, and the absence of any mark made on life, Peter achieves a sense of individual integrity, where his past life becomes real and is accepted not only as being necessary but also as being worthy. At this point Clarissa returns from her own private meditation, and with this reconciliation of private lives the novel ends. A masterpiece of poetic beauty, a modern *Libro del Cortegiano, Mrs. Dalloway* exemplifies the Modernist trait of achieving multiplicity by virtue of a seemingly passive hero while at the same time working toward a sense of personal unity and affirmation.

THE SPECULATIVE FREEDOM of the complex central consciousness obviously affords the range of experiences that Ortega called for and that Bergson had predicted. In this sense even the phrase "stream of consciousness" must not be understood as representing a single flow but rather divergent and different levels of experience. The river, like the sea, has many voices. An earlier (somewhat facetious) title of *The Waste Land* was to have been, "He Do the Police in Different Voices." Such ventriloquism points to the comic dimensions of Modernism. Most of the Modernists showed early signs of being comic writers—Mann writing for *Simplicissimus*, Proust composing his pastiches—they echoed, they mocked and they imitated, and this dimension is still powerful in their works. The centrality of the comic in Modernism has been affirmed by such critics as Valéry Larbaud and Ellmann on Joyce, Edmund Wilson (to be followed by J.-F. Revel and Roger Shattuck) on Proust, Mark van Doren and Erich Heller on Mann.[30] Almost inevitably, the Modernist sense of the multiplicity of

TRANSFORMATIONS

experience and their own intellectual separateness places them in ironic and comic positions.

If the stable ego is splintered one can then adopt many masks. Sensitive to the variability of human experience, Wallace Stevens wrote, "My opinions generally change even while I am in the act of experiencing them." And this is followed by the related thought: "There is a perfect rout of characters in every man—and every man is like an actor's trunk—full of strange creatures." Edmund Wilson wrote of T. S. Eliot that he was the original Possum, with a bag of many personae. Reflecting this multitude of personages, a variety of styles and of voices—Ulysses is the paramount example—replaces the normally single level of narrative exposition. This can induce a kind of playfulness in regard to style. Wallace Stevens wrote, "I like the coupling of the facetious and the sentimental."[31] Even with Thomas Mann, a touch of whimsy can attach to the ponderous dimensions of *The Magic Mountain* (the "perilous chapel" resonances of the sanatorium) as well as to the chronological foreshortenings in *Joseph and His Brothers*. Such distancing and variety render apt Mann's title as the "ironic German"; the artist himself as *homo ludens* is a *Schwindler*, a confidence man.

This enlargement of experience as well as the fragmented nature of the self brings out the casual comedy of existence, and communicates a sense of freedom. Yeats in "Easter 1916" shows the comfortable world of the eighteenth century, its easy skepticism, by thinking of a joke to tell a friend at the club while talking to one of those who would soon be hardened into a rock of ideological principle. Bloom in *Ulysses* trying to conceal and at the same time touch a letter from Martha Clifford (to see if there are any attachments) encounters C. P. McCoy. (72-74) As this conversation develops he is watching a woman across the street getting into a carriage. In this manifold encounter we hear McCoy, with Bloom responding inattentively and mechanically, but we know of Bloom's real interest across the street as well as his fantasies about the handsome woman's intentions. The number of things happening in this encounter comes close to approximating the actual dimensions of reality—the number of influences that the mind can bear at one time. Stephen Spender is right when he speaks of Modernism as a vision of the whole.[32]

Parties afford Proust the best opportunity for drawing these crossing bands of relationships—and they represent one of his major influences upon the novels of Virginia Woolf. At the Princesse de Guermantes's party we watch Marcel, who has just learned the truth about the Baron de Charlus, watch the Baron whose eyes are fixed upon the two sons of Mme. de Surgis. Showing a tragically fragmented consciousness, the Baron alters his gaze when he realizes that Marcel is watching him. Soon the Baron's nephew, Robert de Saint-Loup comes to Marcel's side and continues to propagate the myth about the wildly heterosexual activities of his uncle. Since Marcel knows the truth, he can only wonder about Robert's delusion (as the narrator speculates about the nephew's inheritance of his uncle's traits). Mme. de Surgis, who is the Duc de Guermantes's mistress, and hardly expects warm treatment from the normally acerbic Baron, the duke's brother, is surprised when he is cordial to her (not knowing that he is admiring in her the basic pattern for the fascinating lineaments of her sons). Having in the course of the conversation fed Saint-Loup's misconception and managed to "hook" the two sons, he then can strategically ignore them, and invite Mme. de Surgis and the narrator into another room. Knowing that Mme. de Saint-Euverte is within hearing, the Baron quite coarsely rails at the garden parties of his hapless victim. Her own fawning instincts make her an unattractive underdog—another type that Virginia Woolf learned from Proust and reembodied in the characters of Miss Kilman, with her Macintosh, in *Mrs. Dalloway* and Tansley in *To the Lighthouse*. Marcel returns to the card room to find Swann, and while talking to Swann continues to observe the Baron in conversation with the sons of Mme. de Surgis. He retires with Swann to hear the story of how both the Guermantes kept their Dreyfusard leanings to themselves out of fear of hurting one another, each thinking the other to be still a stout believer in the Army. The scene partially ends with the Baron's brother alluding to him as a "peculiar type" and then catching himself and making matters worse by trying to cover this unconscious slip. All of these crossed lines of perceptions and perspectives make for an expanding film of higher awarenesses, itself an attribute of comedy.[33]

In the Renaissance time was regarded as a principle of reality, a factor in the conversion from an aesthetic role to an ethical one. In Modernism this process was reversed; a new sense of time and of its human implications served to effect a partial change from the predominance of the ethical to a more conditional sense of values—beyond good and evil. At first these values were called "aesthetic," and Thomas Mann could point to Nietzsche and to Oscar Wilde, but, in fact, the ethical, if it is abrogated in Modernism, is not superseded by aestheticism but rather by an increased consciousness, by a fuller awareness of what is.

In Proust this is specifically the case in his awareness of Vinteuil. Along the Méséglise way, the way of the town and townsmen, the "provincial dogmatism" of his great-aunts, the way of known certainties, of common and settled experience, Vinteuil, the great composer, is an object of derision, as is the relationship between his daughter and her female friend. Marcel—and here his role as a passive, unpremeditating witness is the basis for revelation—is a hidden spectator to a wild lesbian bout between the two young women, climaxed by the friend's soiling M. Vinteuil's photograph. But somehow Marcel's role as an uninvolved witness allows him to pass beyond the immediate and expected moral reaction. He observes that the two women are trying too hard to be evil, that none of the coldness of calculated vice was present in their behavior. Later on, this insight is confirmed when he learns that it was the daughter's friend who saved for the world Vinteuil's almost undecipherable sheets of music, and through her personal association was able to translate them correctly. "Indecipherable they may have been, but they had nevertheless been in the end deciphered, by dint of patience, intelligence and respect by the only person who had lived sufficiently in Vinteuil's company to understand his method of working, to interpret his orchestral indications: Mlle. Vinteuil's friend." (I.122-127/ I.159-165)

In its reflective intelligence Proust's style can be characterized by its lack of literalism. Like Montaigne (with whom Revel frequently and rightly compares Proust) he has an awareness of the qualifications that time brings to our ideas and to our emotions.[34] Statements of conviction (perhaps those of Mme. Swann and Mme. Verdurin are the most vulnerable, but certainly not theirs alone) are not allowed to pass unscrutinized by the narrator, who turns them over in his mind and presents the reader with other possible motivations, or recalls different positions held in former times. Proust's arrangement of scenes, his need to render the totality of experience, is similarly aliteral. In fact, so pervasive is Proust's sense of the complex sheathings of vice and virtue, of foolishness and talent, that his sense of the comic, of that which is risible, is precisely Bergsonian. That is laughable which is mechanically repetitive. All of Proust's comic creations—and they are many and memorable—his grandmother's sisters, Flora and Céline, Norpois, Legrandin, Cottard, the "souffre-douleur" uncle of Bloch—are typified by a kind of social literal-mindedness, just that which, according to Bergson, it was the purpose of laughter to correct. A gift to Cottard that is obligingly deprecated by the giver will be so regarded by him. His punning is maladroit and out of context, as for example the mechanical way that he will complete a cliché if he hears the first part of the phrase in another sentence. If someone might use the phrase "sartorial elegance" he will chime in with "Andrea del . . ." And in the cases of the great-aunts even their cryptic aliteralism (their allusive compliments to Swann, whose real social accomplishments they refuse to acknowledge) are habitual and humorous. Legrandin's reflex action of subservience before any aristocrat (whom he professes to detest) bestows on his bodily actions the literal jerks and spasms of a Bergsonian marionette.

Yet, even here, the complexity of the Modernist vision differs somewhat from traditional comic practice, since Proust, so given in his style to eluding unitary formulations, acknowledges that Cottard is an instinctively brilliant pathologist. This sense of the striations of character even dissolves the comic, not sparing those who themselves laugh at Cottard or find him puzzling. Proust does not overlook the observation that the very contemporary fashion of the gentleman that Swann fills so gracefully, and from whose viewpoint he finds Cottard grotesque, is what ruins him and makes him the master of trivial considerations: for instance, his contentment with *petits faits* when discussing any work of art, or his greater failure of never hearing more than the little phrase of the Vinteuil sonata (an incuriosity contrasted with the heroic commitment of Bergotte, who rose from his deathbed in order to see a spot of Vermeer's *Street of Delft*, the essay concerning which artist Swann would never complete). And not unlike Cottard, he too shows some traces of a social literalism, most antipathetic to Proust's own views of personality. Swann dismisses out of hand the suggestion that possibly the old music master whom he knew in Combray might be Vinteuil, the composer of the sonata. His answer betrays the prejudices of social style: "If you had ever seen him for a moment you wouldn't put that question." The Modernists' sense of the contradictory levels of our being would lead them to focus on that very possibility.

Proust's style depends not only upon the changing perspectives of the multifarious party scenes (exemplified equally well by the matinée at Mme. de Villeparisis from *Guermantes Way* as by the soirée at the Princesse de Guermantes) but also upon bringing together in a total sense elements from separate planes of reality. The prime example of this would be his description of the events surrounding the death of Marcel's grandmother. (I.940 ff./ II.313 ff.) There indeed we are presented with *les donneés immédiates de la conscience*, with the expressed concern to reflect the data of modern life. Most apparent is the sublime and beautiful grief of Marcel's mother for the pending loss of her mother. But this level of sentiment is juxtaposed with the reaction of the maid-servant, Françoise, who has a blunter physical awareness of the closeness of death as well as the curiosity of one accustomed to wringing the necks of chickens while calling them filthy beasts. To say that these are contradictory reactions would be a mistake, since they exist on independent levels where each is valid. Unlike earlier works, where what is "high" is used to smile condescendingly at what is low (the last act of *A Midsummer Night's Dream*), or as might be more often the case, where the subplot is used to parody higher adventures, no attempt is made by Proust so to use these discrete reactions. Each does not comment upon the other; each is a "true" part of the total picture, where contradictions are not fused but simply brought side by side. We can call to mind the presence of the old hags in the inner temple of Mann's "dream-poem" of humanity (who at first do comment upon, and contradict, the more hopeful preliminary scenes, but who finally are seen—in opposition to Naphta's view—to represent a coexistent truth, which it is the duty of Mann as pessimistic humanist to represent), or look ahead—in material presented in a later section—to T. E. Hulme's discontinuous levels of experience.[35]

2. *Perspectivism and Relativity*

In discussing the crucial idea of the paradox of time, I had occasion to invoke the network of related ideas held by philosophers and other social critics of note. Here, too, after giving ample literary evidence of the dimensions of the complex central consciousness, I would like to indicate significant bands of connection with the philosophical thought of the period. This has two principal effects: (1) it establishes solidarities, the kind that are necessary if a movement is to prove durable and become an epoch; (2) it helps explain the remarkable creative confidence shown by the literary Modernists. That which they were promoting was not wayward, was not to be pushed aside or discounted, but was rather part of the vanguard of the intellectual developments of their day, supported by the most advanced scientific and philosophical thought.

Ortega gave another name to this new awareness in 1916 when he called it "perspectivismo"; he saw quite early its significance when he allied it with Einsteinian physics as being repudiations of the Newtonian world-view of an absolute space and time. In this association of literature and philosophy with the physical theories of relativity we are provided another common ground of relationships in Modernism.[36] The network is extensive and seems to be supported by two major cables: (1) the denial of an absolute reality and (2) the need to uphold the sense of individual truth in a complex of multiple truths.

Ortega fixes the time quite precisely at which he formulated "perspectivismo" as a philosophical theme. Since he began suggesting this theory as early as 1913, and gave it conscious thematic formulation in 1916 ("Verdad y Perspectivismo" in *Espectador*, I), Einstein's General Theory of Relativity published that same year lends "impressive confirmation" to his ideas.[37] Given his interests Ortega seems most fully to perceive the significance of Einstein's theories for the "theme of our time," its ramifications in life and thought (as his preface to the 1923 Spanish edition indicates). The Newtonian worldview, according to the Spanish philosopher, fails to take account of the fact that since there can be no absolute beholder, there can be no absolute space or time ("There is no absolute space because there is no absolute perspective").[38] Such a reality on which all observers agree can only be an abstraction. Modernism is moved to deny the possibility of such a privileged position. In *La Pensée et le mouvant*, Bergson writes that relativity substitutes an "ensemble de relations absolues" for a "système privilégié." (Each of the reactions to the death of Marcel's grandmother is, for instance, an "absolute" that is, exists without commentary upon itself or other, in an "ensemble" of relations. In fact, such a presentation can only exist where there is an absence of a "privileged" position, in relation to which deviations can be morally judged or comically abused.)[39] In translating Charles Mauron's essay "On Reading Einstein" for the 1930 *Criterion*, Eliot will find a similar phrase: since there is no one "observer-elect" there can be no single reality.[40] Such a possibility would further presuppose a simultaneous instant, an immediate "now" that is the same in all places. Einstein's theory would lead one to believe that this is impossible, and Alfred North Whitehead concurs: "classical scientific materialism ... presupposes a definite present instance at which all matter is simultaneously real. In the modern theory there is no such unique present instant. You can find a meaning for the notion of the simultaneous instant throughout all nature, but it will be a different meaning for different notions of temporality."[41]

Such consonance among major representatives of different forms of thought has specific importance for literature. Modernists had the strength of scientific inventors making known their new discoveries. Such a metaphor was used by Ortega in describing Proust, and by Eliot in marking the importance of Joyce's "mythic method," and by Pound in relating poetic technique as dependent upon discoveries or inventions (as in the sciences).[42] But the strength of Modernism lies even more with some of the basic tenets of the new theory of relativity. The complex central consciousness affirms both the separate reality of the self and the multiplicity of the world that it registers and reflects. Ortega, Whitehead and others evolved a similar view of things. It is a misconception of relativity to assume that it means all things are relative. This diminution of the individual perspective can only occur in a world-system that presupposes an absolute beholder—then all individual perspectives are in a depreciated sense of the term "subjective." Both Whitehead and Ortega are at pains to disprove this erroneous deduction. Rather, they would maintain that if there is no "observer-elect" then each perspective possesses a real relationship to the universe. That there is diversity does not reduce individual truth. Curtius, who is certainly following Ortega in his own arguments, quotes Proust, "L'univers

TRANSFORMATIONS

est vrai pour nous tous et dissemblable pour chacun."[43] This principle accounts for the strength of Modernism, its ability to present a rich variety of perspectives, all of which are "true," and none of which is victimized by any humbling disclaimers of "subjectivism." We have instead many visions of the world, each constituting a truthful position. Perspective, as Ortega advises us, is one of the component parts of reality ("La perspectiva es uno de los componentes de la realidad").[44] The effect of this revision is that it breaks up the assumption that real truth is of one form and of one language, and makes room for multiplicity. Appearances, those secondary qualities and impressions banished by scientific abstractionism, now become "objective qualities of the real." The world is really, according to Whitehead (and D. H. Lawrence in his many essays), a "manifold of prehensions"—that is, situations of relatedness existing between subjects and objects.[45] Rather than mind versus object we move to a network of mind-objects. Edmund Wilson, who was among the earliest critics to defend Modernism because of its similarities to the new theoretical physics, rightly finds in Proust this same kind of network of relationships.[46]

Modernism gives us what Whitehead found desirable: a fuller picture of the complex nature of reality. This commitment to the totality of the given—to those crossing bands of reflections and relationships—leads us to relativity's most fascinating dimension in Modernism, and that is the latter's need at once to create a world and to stand outside of it, and to have reflected in that world the fact that one is standing outside of it. For instance, the fault with normal logical and philosophical proofs is that once we utter the proof the condition of reality has altered by virtue of our consciousness that we are making a "proof," or "doing" philosophy; furthermore, a proof is by its very statement incomplete since it does not include one's consciousness that one is indeed making a proof. It no longer encompasses all of the known since it does not contain itself. This dilemma is the natural consequence of transcending the older subject-object dualism and is susceptible of very creative solutions.[47]

Given its overwhelming sense of change Modernism is suspicious of standpoints (in a section of the next chapter I shall call them "staying-points" in an emotionally related sense). Its expansive consciousness must always pass beyond itself and reflect the fact of its own reflecting. This accounts for what has been called the "reflexive" nature of Modernism, its sense of form turning back on itself as the panorama of multiplicity gives way to a circularity.[48] In this sense, of course, one of the more creative solutions is myth, where we are not led to some conclusive end but, as in *Finnegans Wake*, to resolutions that re-start, endings that re-commence. In its presentation of what is perennial and yet dynamic, myth seems to be a natural consequence of this phase of Modernism.

This insistent questioning of assumptions means that the dominant mode of Modernism could not be, in Lionel Trilling's sense of the word, sincerity.[49] Suspicious, as we said, of standpoints, Modernism must be constantly moving beyond itself, anxious and temporally disruptive. It is in contrast to this that the more stable philosophies of the past, Ortega tells us, have their appeal: "Their clear and simple schematic pattern, their ingenuous illusion of being discoveries of truth in its entirety, the confidence with which they rely on formulae which they imagine incontrovertible convey the impression of a closed circle, defined and definitive, where there are no more problems to solve and everything is satisfactorily determined."[50]

In the modern world the complex central consciousness occupies what Ortega called "the height of the times." It holds the commanding intellectual position: those who would transcend it must first pass through it, must first be in possession of its virtues and its strengths. Those ideologies that would deny it, whether communist or fascist, appear to be hopelessly retrograde, and those individuals who hanker back to a simpler emotional world, or a world more responsive to heroic will, are doomed to stagnation and barren repetitiveness. All

TRANSFORMATIONS

the more reason, then, that in this Modernist context we should make a controlling principle of development itself.

Erich Auerbach, himself a Modernist in his critical methods, describes the temptations that have existed in our century to deny the data of consciousness.

> The temptation to entrust oneself to a sect which solved all problems in a single formula, whose power of suggestion imposed solidarity, and which ostracized everything which would not fit and submit—this temptation was so great that, with many people, fascism hardly had to employ force when the time came for it to spread through the countries of old European culture, absorbing the smaller sects.[51]

From the Modernists discussed in this book, from the values and aesthetic modes of which their works are made up, it would not be possible to derive any code largely conformable to that of fascism. In fact, they are polar opposites.[52]

CHAPTER IV

The Modernist Sensibility

1. *Resources of Counter-Romanticism*

This description of the complex central consciousness, of its methods and of its resources, suggests concerns far different from those of Romanticism. In large points or in small, a character like Leopold Bloom, a poem like *The Waste Land*, the network of crossing bands of relationships, the close identification with modern physics and theories of relativity, the reflexiveness (spatialization, dehumanization, introversion) of the Modernist poem or novel—all represent major divergences from Romantic interests. How wrong it is for Northrop Frye to conclude (in an otherwise highly useful essay): "Anti-Romanticism . . . had no resources for becoming anything more than a post-Romantic movement."[1] In fact, its resources were enormous. This section, adding to the arguments that have already been made, will show what resources the counter-Romanticism of Modernism was able to draw upon.

The Moderns shared in the anti-Lockean and anti-Newtonian notions of the Romantics. But, unlike the Romantics, they had a philosophy (Bergson, Whitehead, Ortega) and a science (Einstein, Bohr, Mach and others) to support their positions. While Romanticism depended upon feeling, Modernism had recourse to analysis and expanded consciousness—that is, a larger frame of reference that could include the data of science. They were not constrained to adopt an antiscientific and antirational point of view. This is another way of suggesting that while both movements showed divided consciousness, the Romantics were motivated by a quest for unity (and this instinct in both Dostoevsky and Nietzsche is what makes them both precursors rather than full Moderns). The Moderns, on

THE MODERNIST SENSIBILITY

the other hand, were willing to accept and exploit the features of disunity. Just what Nietzsche condemned in modern society—its cosmopolitanism and fragmentation—the Moderns made into virtues in their works. For this reason, this second phase is crucial in the determination of Modernist sensibilities. The qualities and the characteristics that are shown in chapter 3 and here in chapter 4 are essential to their development.

Not only in the central consciousness of Modernist works but in the total register of their sensibilities we find a new complexity at work. A whole new range of experience, with new objects, new attitudes and different stylistic levels, is thus able to be presented in Modern literature. The image of the poet itself undergoes radical alteration. Assuming more of the ordinary dress of the twentieth century, the poet must divest himself of his priestly robes—his voice is no longer that of the magus uttering beliefs on a par with the religious. No longer "A weather-worn, marble Triton / Among the streams. . . ." (Eliot criticizes this remnant of the earlier Yeats in the essay commending Yeats's later development), the poet must come to inhabit a modern apartment.[2] According to Lawrence, his slide has been even more precipitous: he has come down off Pisgah in a somewhat unflattering position.[3] The bitter salt of deposition is tasted fully by Stephen in the first chapter of *Ulysses*. His flight to Paris has suffered an Icarian fall. He has even lost his national preeminence, and is no longer the poet-philosopher of his people. That role has been taken over by the medical student, Buck Mulligan, who speaks more to the interests of the old woman who brings the milk. To contrast this movement with Romanticism, we remember that Wordsworth, too, wrote of a descent in the Preface of 1802 ("the Poet must descend from this supposed height"), but that the height he spoke of was the height of Parnassus, of poets writing for other poets. If "Poetry is the image of man and nature" then the poet is not a specialist but rather a man addressing the perennial problems of mankind, those that affect us no matter what our profession. His language is inspired in defense of poetry: "Poetry is the breath and finer spirit of all knowledge; it is the impassioned expression which is in the countenance of all Science . . . the Poet is the rock of defence of human nature . . . he binds together by passion and knowledge the vast empire of human society. . . ."[4] The descent envisaged, even desired by Wordsworth, is from the presumed heights of professional specialization to universal experience. The differences with the Modernists are obvious. For this reason, as Ortega points out, the Romantics were essentially popular poets, while the Moderns were by their very natures anti-popular.[5] From this derives Stephen's deposition.

If the poet has many selves and commands many voices then the process of his art seems to demand change as well— he becomes less the creator and more the compositor who arranges into what he hopes is a functioning unity the various "givens" of experience. The new role of the poet is that of a medium, an amalgamator, and this applies as well to writers like Lawrence, Mann and Proust as it does to the more obvious cases of Joyce, Pound and Eliot. Lawrence, for example, had no compunctions about making his work a "collaborative" effort. Into *Sons and Lovers* he had incorporated narrative sections written by Jessie Chambers in 1911-1912 (she was the source for Miriam); she also annotated later manuscript versions of the novel. In fact, Lawrence's biographer explains that throughout his life Lawrence worked in close collaboration with women, using not only their verbal suggestions but their writings as well.[6] In *Dr. Faustus*, as Mann himself tells us, his quite conscious intent was to reproduce reality by his montage technique and this entailed taking over wholesale and verbatim documents and letters (see, for instance, Tillich's description of his days at Halle and the use Mann makes of it).[7] Proust's method of conceiving his characters was one of amalgamation: "He pieces together his recollections of persons, of incidents, churches, musical compositions, to compose his fictional creations."[8] Reflecting the Modernist commitment to the "given," Joyce's answer to the question, Why is Bloom portrayed as an Hungarian Jew? ("Because he was"), is forthright as well as famous. Ellmann has shown that Joyce's method was also one of literal composition, of patching together known elements from a variety of sources.[9] Rather than a creator, the Modern artist, according to Proust, is something of a translator, bringing together, relocating in a new whole, diverse elements of his experience.

According to Eliot's sense of the complexity and variety of modern life, new objects are to be regarded as suitable for the subject matter of literature. Eliot praises Dryden for his ability to write verse on subjects that are in themselves not high or noble, or while ostensibly mean are still instinct with universal importance (in his praise of Berma and of Elstir, Proust had a similar conception). Baudelaire is commended for the new objects he introduces to poetry and Swinburne is deficient because of their lack (James and Conrad in prose are correctives). Upon this issue there exists a broad consensus among Modernists. Their predominant need was to establish a new orientation to reality in their works and they did this in part by introducing matters and language that were down-to-earth, sexually frank and scientific. They were moved to bring into literature more of what was recognizably real to their existences. A new hard line takes possession of their works (of which Imagism is only one manifestation), a hard line that one would be tempted to call more aggressively positive, even virile, did it not entail so much defeat and suffering. James Joyce said that *The Waste Land* ended the idea of poetry for ladies.[10]

Modernists are fearful of vague superlatives, those questions and those statements that, as I. A. Richards claimed in *Science and Poetry*, seem calculated to assuage and reassure rather than to reflect the facts of being. In his *Adagia*, Wallace Stevens remarked, "Imagination applied to the whole world is vapid in comparison to imagination applied to detail."[11] Stephen Dedalus is akin to Ernest Hemingway when in *Ulysses* he declares, "I fear those big words which make us so unhappy." (32) The development is dramatically recapitulated by Bloom, "Hate. Love. Those are names. Rudy. Soon I am old." (285)

Specific facts of experience (the death of his son, his own isolation) make up more of reality than "names."

The solemn Mr. Kernan in the Hades episode of *Ulysses* represents what Richards has called the Magical view: " 'I am the resurrection and the life.' That touches a man's inmost heart." Mr. Bloom outwardly agrees but inwardly voices the more modern position: "Your heart perhaps but what price the fellow in the six feet by two with his toes to the daisies? No touching that. Seat of the affections. Broken heart. A pump after all. . . ." (104)[12] Joyce is on record as having uttered a similar thought. In relation to some love affair, which Frank Budgen located in proximity to the heart, Joyce replied, "The seat of the affections lies lower down I think."[13] In the Sirens episode—whose theme is Bloom's helplessness in the face of what is destined to happen (like Ulysses, he is fastened) and, at the same time, his resistance to the kind of emotional fusion and maudlinness represented by the barroom singing—Bloom once more refuses to be taken in. Of the Croppy Boy's Latin he thinks, "That holds them like birdlime." And his thoughts return to the rat scraping in the mortuary. (279)

If Bloom has a touch of the artist in him, it is a modern one: he is impatient with all that "gassing about what was it the pensive bosom of the silver effulgence." (159) He is closer to Stephen who, in the library permeated by the "tame essence of Wilde," (196) advocates a more virile conception of Hamlet than that offered by the representatives of nineteenth-century aestheticism. "The ideal is the actual become anaemic," Wallace Stevens wrote, and "the romantic is often pretty much the same thing." As he moves toward a positive identity in time—the reality of which he must affirm in the Proteus episode—Stephen does not believe that literature should be confined to "formless spiritual essences." (183) When a painter (one of the romantic sort, who later committed suicide) for whom Joyce was sitting, expressed the need to capture the poet's soul, Joyce replied, "Get the poet's soul out of your mind and see that you paint my cravat properly." T. E. Hulme, in the fragmentary *Cinders*, noted, "Philosophy is about people in clothes, not about the soul of man." Another fragment reads, "World as finite, and so no longer any refuge in infinities of grandeur."[14] Ortega, the thinker most adept at perceiving the moral and aesthetic implications of relativity, sees one of them as being "finitism," by which he means "a definite urge towards limitation, towards beauty of serene type, towards antipathy to vague superlatives, towards anti-romanticism."[15] The old injunction that the poet should look into his heart and write is not satisfactory for T. S. Eliot, whose poet must also consult his "cerebral cortex, the nervous system, and the digestive tracts."[16] Indeed, in the Mardi Gras episode of *The Magic Mountain*, Hans's language in love is grandly scientific: he would gladly embrace Clavdia's tibia, her fibula. And she upon departing leaves Hans with an x-ray negative of her lungs. Wildly, hermetically comic, still throughout Mann's work the interest in science and the use of scientific language lend a ballast of objectivity, of detached as well as ironic description to the passionate play of emotions.

2. *Points of Divergence*

The impact of Romanticism as a cultural epoch and a literary and aesthetic movement—in each case shattering and far-reaching—cannot be discounted. As Hugh Honour has concluded, "The influence of Romanticism has been so profound and so pervasive that no account can encompass it."[17] In so many areas, what we have been and what we are may be attributed to what was done then. And certainly in the large drifts and general directions of literary history there exists an unmistakable connection between Romanticism and Modernism. The tenor of T. S. Eliot's own "quest" poems was probably closer to that of the Romantics whom he deplored than to that of the Metaphysicals whom he emulated. If we think only of English poetry, and of Wordsworth in particular, his announced changes in poetic means—the avoidance of poetic diction and of personification, the endeavor to look steadily at his object and to avoid falsehoods of description, the revolutionary insistence on making poetry out of the common incidents of daily life and in the normal language of men—unquestionably played a major role in determining the conditions of modern literature. Furthermore, in the larger and more general patterns of culture and of thought, we see that the Romantic predicament was analogous to that of the Moderns. They both attempted to find personally satisfying imaginative ways for understanding their worlds. As Wordsworth's Preface, that magnificent statement of an innovator, makes clear, Romanticism was a call into the present. "To be a poet of the present time" is the great motivation inspiring Romantic and Modernist alike.[18]

However, the problem with pursuing such historical continuities and analogues is that they seem to deny the forthrightness of historical change and differences. Too often their implication is to belittle the genuine integrity and specific differences of the subsequent movement. They function at a level of generality that cannot sustain itself at the specific levels upon which literary appreciation and understanding depend. It is one thing to say that both Romanticism and Modernism have the "modernizing" impetus, that is, they are concerned to reveal the content of their current experience; it is another thing to say that because of this common inspiration they are therefore similar in their identities, or even that Modernism derives from Romanticism. The same argument of continuities could, for instance, be applied to Romanticism. When Wordsworth writes that his primary object in the *Lyrical Ballads* was to heighten the incidents of common life by tracing in them the "primary laws of our nature," one wonders how far he had come from the neoclassical code and, in particular, the concerns of Samuel Johnson.[19] One can further wonder how the *Prelude* could have been written without the example of Milton, and one can expand on the role of Milton's *Lycidas* in the argumentative discourse of other Romantic odes besides the more obvious case of *Ode to a Nightingale*. Such continuities and analogues are obviously real and shed light on genuine transactions of literary history. But their use should never encumber the historical newcomer—that is, they should not be used to discount (the Moderns are *only* doing what the Romantics did); nor should they be used to obstruct our perceptions of specific and original contributions.

As was the case of Romanticism in regard to its cultural past, so is the case of Modernism: while there seems to be a distinct formation in the background, in the actual working out of the literature a major change has occurred. If one were to follow a line of continuous development from Romanticism one could arrive at Tennyson or Thomas Hardy, but one could never arrive at Leopold Bloom or *The Waste Land*.[20] Despite historical indebtedness and beyond any unconscious assimilation, something new was being done. To slight that change is to diminish the stature of all innovators as well as to ignore the importance of discontinuity, mutation itself, in historical development.

Finally, what it comes down to is this: to overestimate the presence of Romanticism in the struggle of the Modern is to deny history itself. In meeting what may have been a similar predicament (although under vastly altered conditions), the Moderns had one component the Romantics could not have had—they had Romanticism itself. They not only shared in the fundamental reaction to the Enlightenment, but they had to contend with Romanticism as well. The Moderns had grown up in an atmosphere of late Romantic poetry and one of the requirements in the establishment of their own voices and styles was a separation from this inheritance. The reason Wallace Stevens emerges as a Modern is because he rejected the Keatsian mode, which he inherited in the late nineties, and became Wallace Stevens. How many of Joyce's chapters in *Ulysses* are explicitly combative of Romantic style and sentiment! In this sense, rather than post-Romantic the proper label to describe the Modernist relationship to Romanticism might be "Counter-Romantic."[21] In fact, it may be argued that Modernism can only be understood by means of such reaction. In any event, that is the way the Moderns understood themselves. Poetically, artistically, their historical point was to "unsay the Romantics," to try another response to the common conditions they may have known.[22] And, as Herbert Weisinger argued in a series of essays dealing with the Renaissance, essays that have become classics, the fact that the men of the Renaissance thought they were doing something different is itself objective evidence that they were different. Their intention is an ingredient of their consciousness.[23]

The Modernist point of departure frequently occasions a direct severance with Romanticism. Stephen, at the end of *A Portrait of the Artist as a Young Man*, does not wish to embrace the early Yeats's ideal of post-Romantic poetic beauty. He does not long to press in his arms the beauty that has long faded, but rather "the loveliness which has not yet come into the world." In that coeval work, *Sons and Lovers*, Lawrence must not only separate Paul Morel from the nineteenth-century ideal of continuity, he must also separate him from Miriam's Romantic ideals and tastes. By this act Lawrence shows the very tastes and achievements of Romanticism in the process of being superseded. In fact, and this is the essential point, Paul's Modernist character is defined by these divergences. Paul's tastes do not incline toward Miriam's favorites, such as Wordsworth, but rather to the French poets, Baudelaire and Verlaine (how similar to Eliot's own suggested alterations of the poetic map). The scene where he recites for her is a critical exposition of young Modernist tastes. Miriam finds that the lines from Wordsworth (both of which are slightly mangled—Lawrence's or Miriam's fault?) "nourished her heart," "these were like herself." What she derives from her reading is empathy and reassurance—qualities that Lionel Trilling figured among "sincerity," and that I. A. Richards dismissed from a modern poetry in need of becoming more like science. Paul's reaction to Baudelaire's intimately erotic "Le Balcon" is full-throated with passion and bitterness: "Tu te rappelleras la beauté des caresses." (208-209) This discrepancy in tastes is prototypal, marking the advent of the new Modernist allegiances.

Romantic poetry was dominated by a unity of feeling and a uniformity of style. However much such poetry might express disenchantment or alienation, Romantic poets in their imagery and thought suggest a substantial unity of experience and a basic accord between themselves and the world. Through a blessed mood or by change of heart, man senses himself to be one with the season, his being enhanced in Nature. He feels himself to be part of a larger process. "It is the first mild day of March," begins Wordsworth's poem, *Lines Written at a Small Distance from My House*, and sent to his sister as an invitation to give the day over to idleness:

> Love, now an universal birth,
> From heart to heart is stealing,
> From earth to man, from man to earth,
> —It is the hour of feeling.

In order for such unison to occur there must be a basic accord between man and Nature. Goethe affirmed that "human nature knows itself one with the world. Mankind can be sure that the outer world is an answering counterpoint to the sensations of its own inner world."[24] Wordsworth in his Preface declares this to be the poet's essential faith: "He considers man and nature as essentially adapted to each other, and the mind of man as naturally the mirror of the fairest and more interesting qualities of nature." To be sure, what is declared outright in the inspired prose of the 1802 Preface is shown to be the product of stages of growth in such poems as *Tintern Abbey*. While outgrowing his simple sensory reactions of youth, the poet's teacher and the anchor of his experience is still Nature, that in which he feels himself returned to himself, and that within which he senses the unity of all existence— that "sense sublime / Of something far more deeply interfused."[25]

Stylistically, such remarkable interfusion can only mean that image and object are also very concordant. For Wordsworth, the "Beauteous evening, calm and free" suggests a "Nun / Breathless with adoration." The human, the divine and the natural interpenetrate to suggest a sentiment of being in which man can find a spiritual peace and at-oneness. One can look at such satisfying verse another way and see that it is ill-equipped to picture true estrangement or complexity, discord or mere difference. Indeed, when we come to Modernism we find that such "natural supernaturalism" is precluded philosophically as well as stylistically, and that this is what I. A. Richards meant when he wrote of the "neutralisation" of nature (or what others meant when they utilized a variety of other phrases to describe the same phenomenon, "dehumanization," for example). The opening lines of *Prufrock* only too obviously ask to be contrasted with those of Wordsworth. In the early Modernist poem, alluded to most briefly in chapter 2, the evening is "spread out against the sky / Like a patient etherised upon a table." One is struck by jarring discrepancy—in fact, the effect of the coupling comes from the disappointment of an expectation— fostered by Romantic poetry—that the completion of the simile will be consonant; instead it is almost brutally discordant, suggesting the divergence between human emotions and needs and the facts of natural or social experience.[26]

Romantic poetry shows no startling juxtapositions of contradictory levels of experience. Wordsworth may have sought to alter the subject matter and the idiom of poetry by way of introducing common subjects in the normal language of men. But one can wonder if his essential stylistic faith is any different from that of preceding ages based upon a kind of natural correspondence. (In this regard it is tempting to say of Wordsworth what a French critic of Modernism said of Hugo, "Il n'a pas achevé la révolution qu'il a annoncée."[27] When Wordsworth introduced subjects from common life, his purpose was to show that they could yield matter as intense, as heroic and as tragic as subjects from a loftier plane of world history. Incidents of common life have the possibility of showing "the primary laws of our nature." Low and rustic life yields a better soil for the depiction of our "essential passions," and within such life "the passions of men are incorporated with the beautiful and permanent forms of nature." As with other Romantics, whether in painting or in literature, common life is made the subject of art in order to elevate it;

THE MODERNIST SENSIBILITY

the commonplace is imbued with a lofty significance, the ordinary with a mystery.[28]

If the everyday has its beauty (and the paintings of Turner or Constable showed it) this may be due to the essential Romantic belief that the Divine is in everything. Such belief explains the "microcosmic" possibilities of Romantic poetry, where the part reveals the whole. "To me the meanest flower that blows can give / Thoughts that do often lie too deep for tears." For the Moderns, however, common objects are found to be suitable for poetry (in fact they may be sought out desperately), but this is not necessarily with the attempt to elevate them, or to show them as heroic or tragic; it might merely be to show them as boring, or futile, or mean. The type of the "unattractive underdog" is exemplary here. Modernism represents a greater possibility for presenting things the way they might appear to the complex consciousness. For the Modernists, to involve the meanest flower with such thoughts smacks of egoistic projectionism, a refusal to let an object be what it simply is (and D. H. Lawrence has some harsh criticisms of Wordsworth on this particular point).

Such subjective projections are, however, intrinsic to Romantic philosophy and art: the world is what we perceive and half-create. The experience we bring to perception modifies the object of that perception:

> The Clouds that gather round the setting sun
> Do take a sober coloring from an eye
> That hath kept watch o'er man's mortality.

Man has the power to revise imaginatively simple "objectivism" and to bestow on things a happier feeling and color, or a greater significance. It lies within our resources to overcome the pathos of consciousness, creatively to mobilize and organize our lives. Consequently, Romantic sentiment depends to a large extent upon models of illumination, figures who restore faith, young children who come bearing great truths ("We Are Seven"), or old men who are instances of singular courage or devotion to duty. As we shall see, in Modernism there exist

THE MODERNIST SENSIBILITY

no such simple models of reverence, either from childhood or old age, none who seems immune to the changeful mode of complex human existence. Modernists were philosophically opposed to extracting these, as it were, "snapshots" from life, pictures of exemplary conduct by models who, in the singularity of their virtue, cannot sustain the emphasis placed upon them. Such models they regard as triumphs of willfulness. One picture of such bliss was used by Eliot (the section from "Two Voices" by Tennyson: "One walked between his wife and child, / With measured footfall firm and mild . . .") to contrast the Metaphysical and nineteenth-century sensibilities.[29] But this type of "picturing" is already present in Wordsworth:

> Behold the Child among his new-born blisses,
> A six years' Darling of a pigmy size!
> See, where 'mid work of his own hand he lies,
> Fretted by sallies of his mother's kisses,
> With light upon him from his father's eyes!

So burdened with fixed focus, it is practically impossible for such verse to survive modern scrutiny. The weight—the absence of variety, of different emotional scales, of contradiction or of simple change—is too heavy to bear without considerable squirming. Such discomfort is increased because we feel we are being solicited, asked to make too much of an investment in a passing scene.

The Romantics, such as Coleridge or Wordsworth, were themselves subject to doubt and alienation; their "greater lyrics" were largely based upon such experience.[30] Yet, the substance of their faith was such that the Romantics and their heirs retained a yearning for unity. Their poetry or fiction posits a need for it, and this is true from Rousseau through Dostoevsky, from Wordsworth and Coleridge to Tennyson and Hardy. Lionel Trilling wrote of Rousseau that "he speaks of himself as *une âme déchirée*. . . . But at the same time he aspired to be the 'honest soul' in its wholeness."[31] So, too, Dostoevsky's aim was fusion, to overcome the schism in the soul of Raskolnikov, to achieve a kind of universal brotherhood through selflessness. Modernists have tended to consider manifestations of this need as too much an act of the will (Mochulsky, for instance, has called Raskolnikov's conversion a "pious lie").[32] A common Romantic paradigm is one of a complex being, assaulted by doubt, looking with envy at the faith of simpler beings. The "Dear Child," of Wordsworth's "It Is a Beauteous Evening," does not know the poet's "solemn thought," but she does not need to, since she lies "in Abraham's bosom all the year . . . God being with thee when we know it not." In "The Oxen" Thomas Hardy is half-inclined to visit the stable, hoping the Christian folk myth of the oxen kneeling might in fact come true. Even his "Darkling Thrush" shows the continuation of Romantic longing for faith in the midst of almost complete disbelief.

This tendency may be profitably contrasted with the fourth of Eliot's *Preludes*, where the poet for once seems willing to offer his emotions, to instill with sentiment a squalid urban scene (as his character, Prufrock, seemed more willing to do):

> I am moved by fancies that are curled
> Around these images, and cling;
> The notion of some infinitely gentle
> Infinitely suffering thing.

Brought up against the reality, however, this emotion recoils upon itself and reissues in a kind of dark, sardonic humor:

> Wipe your hand across your mouth, and laugh;
> The worlds revolve like ancient women
> Gathering fuel in vacant lots.

Notice that Eliot did not write, "The world revolves," which might have been expected, but rather "The worlds revolve," as if indicating private hungers and separate circles that never merge, areas of experience that are totally alien to, and practically unincorporable into the framework of desire. This further reminds us of the old hags in Hans's dream: they mutter in the gutteral dialect of his native Hamburg. Modernism is committed to reflecting such "irreducible and stubborn facts,"

THE MODERNIST SENSIBILITY

such "irreconcilable antagonisms."[33] One can further think of that extremely promising American writer, Nathanael West, and particularly of his *Miss Lonelyhearts*, to see the fuller hold that this sense of discrepancy has on the Modern imagination.

For the touches of eternity Romantics may have felt by the ocean, Freud substituted modern analysis. Such "oceanic feeling" is probably a holdover from "an early stage in ego-feeling," when "the ego included everything" (a phrase, interestingly enough, that will be applied by Lawrence to Wordsworth).[34] Yet, it is precisely by the oceanic setting, in contrast to the privileged sense of oneness with nature that their forefathers had experienced, that Modernists show their own consciousness of alienation. "Oed' und leer das Meer" is the sense of emptiness experienced in *The Waste Land* instead of the feeling of sexual at-oneness. In *To the Lighthouse* the generation of the Ramsays, the heirs of "Dover Beach," had reached their personal synthesis. But in the critical, intervening "Time Passes" section, a new chasm occurs (perhaps the one that Mrs. Ramsay instinctively saw into, but suppressed) that separates man from Nature, and man from his past as well as from other men. "Now," and the temporal demarcation is emphatic, "the nights . . . are full of wind and destruction." The sea no longer affords the answering image to the human condition:

> Also the sea tosses itself and breaks itself, and should any sleeper fancying that he might find on the beach an answer to his doubts, a sharer of his solitude, throw off his bedclothes and go down by himself to walk on the sand, no image with semblance of serving and divine promptitude comes readily to hand bringing the night to order and making the world reflect the compass of the soul.

The human formula is lost as well, and any harmonization is broken in the discord:

> The hand dwindles in his hand; the voice bellows in his ear. Almost it would appear that it is useless in such confusion

to ask the night those questions as to what, and why, and wherefore, which tempt the sleeper from his bed to seek an answer. (193)

In the hardness of experience Modernism has been disabused of the "whence and whither" questions—they are the kind of "pseudo-statements," or questions seeking reassurance, that can have no place in the new scheme of poetry (as I. A. Richards described it in *Science and Poetry*, a work remarkably contemporaneous with this section of *To the Lighthouse*).[35]

In contrast to the former sentiment of fullness, such a universe induces a Sartrean feeling of nausea, emptiness, and vastness suggesting terror. In fact, two strands of modern philosophy seem to be involved in this second stage of Modernism. In describing the complex central consciousness and its relations to perspectivism we invoked the names of Ortega, Whitehead (even Bergson, Bradley, and we could have added William James). And in describing here the cosmic background against which the central consciousness defines itself, we bring in existentialism. So it is that in Virginia Woolf those who go down to the sea encounter an alien existence that is out of harmony with the happy play of children and the serenity of the seascape:

> There was the silent apparition of an ashen-coloured ship for instance, come, gone; there was a purplish stain upon the bland surface of the sea as if something had boiled and bled, invisibly, beneath. The intrusion into a scene calculated to stir the most comfortable conclusions stayed their pacing. It was difficult blandly to overlook them; to abolish their significance in the landscape; to continue, as one walked by the sea, to marvel how beauty outside mirrored beauty within. (*To the Lighthouse*, 201)

In *Kangaroo*, a novel that, while overshadowed by the tragic tracking of Gerald Crich's fate in *Women in Love*, is still important for its development of the Modernist consciousness beyond *Sons and Lovers* and *Aaron's Rod*, Richard Somers ex-

THE MODERNIST SENSIBILITY

periences the same lostness and emptiness. Here, too, despite Lawrence's own organicist position, the sea becomes menacing, hostile, and the imagery becomes scientific:

> Incredibly swift and far the flat rush flew at him, with foam like the hissing open mouths of snakes. In the nearness a wave broke white and high. Then, ugh! across the intervening gulf the great lurch and swish as the snakes rushed forward, in a hollow frost hissing at his boots. . . . A huge and cold passion swinging back and forth. Great waves of radium swooping with a down-curve and rushing up the shore. Then calling themselves back again, retreating to the mass. Then rushing with venomous radium-burning speed into the body of the land. (348)[36]

3. D. H. Lawrence: The Sense of "Otherness"

Two authors who normally in themselves and in the positions they represent may be regarded as polar opposites within Modernism are D. H. Lawrence and T. E. Hulme, the one more or less organicist and the other hierarchical. The same dichotomy might apply if we substitute T. S. Eliot for Hulme. Yet, as we have developed our argument it becomes more and more apparent that, particularly in regard to the break-up of historical values, there is not much that separates Eliot and Lawrence (and hence the late F. R. Leavis can see both as opponents of the techno-industrial culture). Indeed, the value of the particular paradigm, or *épistémè*, that I present, is that such polarities are undermined, and that a more basic substratum, or structure, is revealed—one showing such apparent opposites to be united at a fundamental core.

Especially, however, when we come to the complex central consciousness, is Lawrence, as a spokesman for Dionysiac culture (a simplistic attribution that does great injustice to Lawrence, or to anyone else for that matter), banished from the ranks of Modernism.[37] But this dismissal is overhasty and erroneous. First, it overlooks how closely related the break-up

THE MODERNIST SENSIBILITY

of the historical (covered in our first two chapters) is to the development of the complex central consciousness. The one grows out of the other. The preëminence of Lawrence in the one inclines him to active presence in the other. Secondly, specific evidence shows Lawrence to hold many of the thoughts and themes of the new Modernist counter-Romanticism. These are positions that he shares with other Modernists, most particularly, as we shall see in these next two sections, with T. E. Hulme.

Starting with his first major novel, *Sons and Lovers*, Lawrence contrasts the Romantic sentiment of Miriam Leivers with the Modernizing consciousness of Paul Morel. She finds daffodils "magnificent," but to Paul this is a "bit thick—they're pretty." (218) He is irritated by the ways in which she fondles things; and then follows with a series of harsh charges:

> Can you never like things without clutching them as if you wanted to pull the heart out of them. Why don't you have a bit more restraint or reserve, or something. . . . You wheedle the soul out of things. . . . You're always begging things to love you. . . . You absorb, absorb, as if you must fill yourself up with love, because you've got a shortage somewhere. (218)

Rather than wheedle, he shows a Modernist consciousness by his willingness to go "straight at" things. Indeed, to Miriam Paul seemed "too quick and almost scientific"—and yet his bouquets always had more "natural beauty" than hers. (237) Paul resists Miriam because he senses that what she wants from the flowers she also wants from him, "a sort of soul union." (277) He preaches the same in a letter to Miriam, "If people marry, they must live together as affectionate humans, who may be commonplace with each other without feeling awkward—not as two souls." (251) Already in Paul we hear an idea that will be sounded by Rupert in *Women in Love* and by Lawrence himself in *Education of the People*: the need for a separate identity even in lovers and the fear of fusion as a kind of terrible self-abandonment. There is some "shortage" in

Miriam, he cruelly tells her, that while wanting to merge with things seems to invalidate human identity and its own sufficiencies, as if denying any legitimate place and substance to the individual.[38]

Lawrence returns to these issues in an essay ". . . Love Was Once a Little Boy," which was first published in 1925. Awed before love as a great impersonal power, he still feels the need to defend the integrity of the individual self, particularly against an overly conscious love bent on anthropomorphization. (445)[39] His now-famous black cow Susan has her own will and nature; he can never enter into harmony with her. He has a relationship with her of smell and warmth and feel, "but as for her individuality being in balance with mine, one can only feel the great blank of the gulf." (447) This homely entree precedes an attack on Wordsworth's (and Romanticism's) violation of these differences. When Wordsworth, in contrast to the yokel, sees something far more deeply meant in the primrose, he is merely projecting his own ego onto nature. Lawrence agrees with Freudian analysis when he declares: "Ah William! The 'something more' that the primrose was to you, was yourself in the mirror." (448) The yokel at least saw a yellow primrose, but Wordsworth took from the primrose its own identity: "he doesn't allow it to call its soul its own. It must be identical with *his* soul. Because, by begging the question, there is but One Soul in the universe." (447)

Here, as in other Modernists, Romantic oneness comes into conflict with Modernist multiplicity based on otherness. To anthropomorphize in the Romantic way is to impose one's ego and will on the external world. Reinforcing the relationship between phases one and two of this study a clear correlation is drawn by Modernists between the bourgeois will and Romantic idealism, between the hard-driving aggressive will and the willful sentiment, or, stated another way, the discontinuity within history is paralleled by disunity with Nature. For Lawrence, each, industrialist and Romantic, desires a total possession, which can be tantamount to a total surrender and loss of self. The need to be master reveals the slave.[40]

THE MODERNIST SENSIBILITY

It is commonly held by Modernists that the Romantic ego, instead of preserving distinctions, blurs them and makes a mess. Ortega, in his *Dehumanization*, shows how this violates Modernist principles: "We shall yet see that all new art (like new science, new politics—new life, in sum) abhors nothing so much as blurred borderlines. To insist on neat distinctions is a symptom of mental honesty." (31) For T. E. Hulme, Romanticism was just "spilt religion." (118)[41] Similar thoughts and images are prominent in Lawrence. The concept of equality is an abstraction that tends to blot distinctions. Education's real aim is not equality but rather individualism: "If we break our own integrity, we become a squalid mess, like a jar of honey dropped and smashed." Anything that gushes or spills over or is otherwise sloppy is suspect. "We prefer abysses and maudlin self-abandon and self-sacrifice, the degeneration into a sort of slime and merge."[42]

While we might see in some of this a young man's attitude toward women and sex, the Modernists themselves regarded the firm lines of identity as a guard against annihilation. In *Aaron's Rod*, we are urged to give of ourselves, but the restraining clause is the greater: "but give thyself not away." (16l) If we yield up totally we can become a "guttering mess." In fact, as a recent critic has noted, the Romantic impulse to transcend form, to move beyond limit is to desire the ultimate freedom of death.[43] To merge with Universal Being is really an instinct for self-annihilation. Northrop Frye asserts that "in many Romantic poems, including Keats's nightingale ode, it is suggested that the final identification of and with reality may be or at least include death."[44] All of the Modernists, on the other hand, find something saving in limitation and self-possession. As a consequence they show little patience with martyrdom, nor, and this is striking, is there much celebration of the image of the dead, youthful poetic genius. If we recall their historical positions as second generation, that is, having behind them the example of Nietzsche, we can undertand their emphasis on survival. They enjoyed no cult of failure.[45] Lensky, Lydia's first husband in *The Rainbow*, martyred himself to his cause. A Polish revolutionary ("Very ardent and full of words"—45), he simply let himself go after the revolution had failed, as if there were nothing more to existence. Years later Lydia reflects and remonstrates (not without bitterness despite the passage of time): "He had failed in *his* work, so everything has failed. He stiffened and died." With hindsight she recited to her absorbed granddaughter (and hence the beneficiary of the admonitory address) what she ought to have said, " 'Don't be so bitter, don't die because this has failed. You are not the beginning and the end.' " Her final thoughts remind us of Gerald's mother's advice to her needful son, "We cannot take so much upon ourselves." (257) And this suspicion of martyrdom will be carried through by Lawrence to *The Man Who Died*.

Modernism, in disrupting the linear, moved toward multi-levels of experience, heights and depths. But in their appreciation of finitism, Modernists were quite wary of the cultivation of these profundities; more accurately, they were suspicious of the will that is intent on cultivating these emotional stresses. Miriam in *Sons and Lovers* "did not trust herself to support everyday life. She was prepared for the big things, and the deep things, like tragedy. It was the sufficiency of the small day-life she could not trust." (215-216) Nietzsche, with whom we opened this study and to whom we frequently refer, even here is something of a prophet. According to Foucault, "Il y a chez Nietzsche une critique de la profondeur idéale."[46] By this he means emotional profundity, depths of feeling, which Nietzsche felt were generally marks of obfuscation, or of resignation and defeat. In contrast to this, and the phenomenon is consistent throughout Modernism, the simple truth and easy superficiality of the Enlightenment personality are to be preferred. The Modernists placed a ban on pathos.[47] In *Aaron's Rod*, Lady Franks, while admitting to appreciating the music of Strauss and Stravinsky (a very odd linkage) dismisses the moderns:

"But my old things—ah, I don't think the moderns are so fine. They are not so deep. They haven't fathomed life so deeply."
Lady Franks sighed faintly.

Aaron's response is instinctively accurate (and Modernist): "They don't care for depths." (164)

And indeed when later Aaron plays his flute for the Marchesa it is like a breath of fresh air, an act of liberation from the heavy weight of required emotion:

> Oh, a horrible enchanted castle, with wet walls of emotions and ponderous chains, of feelings and ghastly atmosphere of must-be. She felt she had seen through the opening door a crack of sunshine, and thin, pure light outside air, outside, beyond this dank and beastly dungeon of feelings and moral necessity. (224)

She escapes on his light and agile notes from the enclosed rooms and heavy furniture of the nineteenth century. In fact, that this period was dank and damp occurred to both Virginia Woolf and T. E. Hulme. Hulme writes that for the Romantic, "Poetry that isn't damp is not poetry at all. They cannot see that accurate description is a legitimate object of verse. Verse to them always means the bringing in of some emotions that are grouped around the word infinite."[48] The conclusion of the eighteenth-century chapter of *Orlando* is famous. Growing clouds darken the gay lights of the city. "All was dark, all was doubt, all was confusion. The Eighteenth century was over; the Nineteenth century had begun."[49] And the following pages cover the penetration of this dampness into all aspects of nineteenth-century English life.

The sense of otherness in Modernists extends to the universe as well: they sense not only the blank gulf between themselves and black cow Susan, or between themselves and the ancient women gathering fuel, but between themselves and the larger otherness, the sheer blankness of space. In the same essay just quoted, Foucault, while denying correctly "ideal profundity" sees "limitless space" as the new arena of discourse initiated by Freud, Marx and Nietzsche.[50] Indeed in Modernism, the sense of the absolute blankness of empty space is the necessary stage in the development of its consciousness, and it is so, as we have seen, in two ways. First, it is the abyss of timelessness, as expressed by the paradox of time, toward which their wills and the temporal pressures of the developing West seemed to drive the very representatives of that Western dynamic (these formed the immense negative examples of chapters 1 and 2). This is corollary to the abyss of space toward which the Romantic ego had such yearning. Neither of these, however, is akin to the uses to which the Modernists put the discovery of vast and alien space in the formation of their consciousness. And this is the main point. This assertion by the Modernists of the "otherness" of existence is put to argumentative and methodological use. It is used to demolish the sense of humanistic or naturalistic at-oneness with Nature, and is the necessary backdrop to their realizations of separateness and of self. Such profound skepticism is a way-station, a point of transition in the course of their development, requiring a rearrangement of their intellectual baggage. Non-meaning is a stage on the way to the acquisition of new meanings.

Hemingway encountered the Nada of not even disbelief. T. E. Hulme, in the fragmentary *Cinders*, senses the presence of reality as the spaces between railroad tracks and the ash-heap at the foundation of the universe—all the non-human, non-meaning base upon which we construct and fabulate, and make our fictions and agreements to understand. *"Only in the fact of consciousness is there a unity in the world"* (a fragment he italicizes, and then adds, "Cf. Oxford Street at 2 A.M. All the mud, endless, except where bound together by the spectator"). Being a poet as well as a student of philosophy, he finds the confirmation of his ideas in genuine experience. Thus the sense of cinders fills him with "ennui, disgust, the sick moments—not an occasional lapse or disease, but the fundamental ennui and chaos out of which the world has been built.

... The sick disgusting moments are part of the fundamental cinders—primeval chaos—the dream of impossible chaos."[51] So, too, with Sartre, nausea follows the discovery of emptiness and, instead of the presumed fullness, the horrors of contingency. In *The Magic Mountain* the blank décor of the Alps effects the necessary dislocation required for Hans's own development.

Confronted by the dying Kangaroo's insistence that he love him, Richard Somers recoils from that need to feel what in fact he does not feel. In the process, love, humanity, the past and even thought itself become meaningless. Going down to the sea he finds none of the traditional solace, instead an increase of his quite literal alienation. An "octopus thing"—its utter differentness—imposes upon Somers a feeling of existential homelessness: "The fish has the vast ocean for home. And man has timelessness and nowhere." The outer indifference seems to call for an inner state of non-caring, of insouciance. Rather than talking and having feelings, "he wants to be still. And 'meaning' is the most meaningless of illusions. An outworn garment." Yet, such "soullessness" seems to be a necessary phase in the reordering of the older humanistic conception of life. "When a man loses his soul he knows what a small, weary bit of clockwork it was. Who dares to be soulless finds the new dimension of life." As the passage continues, this realization of the arbitrariness of existence extends to the ordering of human life, which takes on the mechanicalness of the clock: "Home to tea. The clicking of the clock. Tic-tac! Tic-tac! The clock. Home to tea. Just for clockwork's sake." And the philosophical reverie that follows again shows Lawrence's Modernist consciousness:

> No home, no tea. Insouciant carelessness. Eternal indifference. Perhaps it is only the great pause between carings. But it is only in this pause that one finds the meaninglessness of meanings—like old husks which speak dust. Only in this pause that one finds the meaninglessness of meanings, and the other dimension, the reality of timelessness and no-

where. Home to tea! Do you hear the clock tick? And yet there is timelessness and nowhere. And the clock means nothing with its ticking. And nothing is so meaningless as meanings. (340-341)[52]

4. T. E. Hulme: Discontinuous Levels of Existence

The philosophic frame—provided by a contemporary—that seems better than most to express the Modernist quarrel with Romanticism is T. E. Hulme's exposition of the three discontinuous levels of existence set out in "Humanism and the Religious Attitude." Relying upon Pascal, Hulme establishes three independent areas of experience: the inorganic—subject of the mathematical and physical sciences; the organic—subject of biology, psychology and history; and the religious and the ethical (5 ff. As they concern Eliot and Mann, such distinctions could be simplified to the natural, the human and the religious). Such vertical structuring seems to suit the needs of the complex central consciousness in its quest for freedom to handle the data of modern life, as well as its sense of the separate, noncontradictory and coexisting levels of life, and to fit Ortega's description of the world to which man must escape in order to encounter not uniform, linear experience, but rather different planes of reality.

Clearly Hulme's theory was derivative, and he was more the conveyor of ideas than the initiator, perhaps even the formulator of thoughts that were arrived at independently or held unconsciously by others. And while the various Modernists did not share all of Hulme's other ideas (and those presented here only in varying degrees and in their own ways), still his notion of the discontinuous levels of existence admirably suited the needs of Modernism, particularly after the break-up of the code of historical values. His schema not only shows us the intractability of the given but also the relativity of the human and the historical (and hence the need for a complex central consciousness), with all of its possibilities for transformation and metamorphosis. It further allows, as we shall see, for the larger awarenesses and culminations of the next development of Modernism.

Following Worringer (whose *Abstraktion und Einfühlung* he knew; in fact, he quotes from it extensively in his essay, "Modern Art and Its Philosophy"), Hulme is at one with Nietzsche and other Modernists in seeing the time since the Renaissance as a single, continuous age.[53] The Renaissance initiated several errors that only reached their full maturity in the Romantic nineteenth century. One of these was the idea of human perfectability and the other that of the integrity of human personality.

Hulme entertained the idea of a kind of secular original sin, a sense of human limitation. The Renaissance, however, committed the error of introducing the idea of man's goodness and of his potentialities and possibilities.(33) Thus the idea of perfectability was removed from a vertical hierarchy, leading to the religious, and instead placed lengthwise at the end of a temporal process of development. In short, existence became progressive and divinity was lodged in history. We have already looked at the end of this development and some of the early Modernist reactions in chapter 1. But here we notice that in Hulme's theory this kind of "divine immanence" also degenerated into the vague aspirations, the hunger for an infinity of emotions that were identifiable with Romanticism.

Supremely middle-class, humanism channeled all experience into the middle-level of existence, reducing it to a single evolutionary line, and removing its basic dualistic tensions. Hulme's accusations are precisely the charges that Naphta levels at Settembrini (indicating that Mann's perception of the crisis of humanism was indeed integral to Anglo-American as well as to continental literature): "Doesn't your monism bore you? ... Dualism, antithesis, is the moving, the passionate, the dialectic principle of all Spirit. All monism is tedious.... You don't want even Absolute Spirit. You only want to have spirit synonymous with democratic progress." (*The Magic Mountain*, 374/396) Such thoughts in Mann are not accidental, since

Naphta too has benefited from his inventor's reading of Worringer, among others.

Hulme correctly acknowledges that humanism served the historical purpose of saving the human from the encroachments of the mechanistic; it eluded materialism. But when it tried to anthropomorphize the divine it transgressed the distinction between the historical-organic and the religious (distinctions that we have seen to be so important to characters like Stephen Dedalus or Ursula Brangwen, particularly in their insistence on the separation of the procreative and the religious) and made what was in fact a historical process and relative coterminous with divinity and of absolute value.

Along with progress Hulme regarded the other erroneous humanistic bequest as being personality. The "substantial unity of the soul" is no longer a valid belief; instead literature testifies to its disunity—the concomitant of the historical discontinuity traced in the preceding chapter.[54] In Proust a renowned pathologist can be a social buffoon; a Baudelaire can stand hat-in-hand before a Sainte-Beuve, who has obviously treated him shabbily.[55] Proust's recollection that "on ne peut à la fois avoir le ciel et être riche," is the Shem-Shaun duality that Yeats made into one of his most compelling epigrams, "the intellect of man is forced to choose / Perfection of the life or of the work." At the same time that the Verdurins venomously turn on the Baron de Charlus, they take pains to provide funds for the dying Saniette. And Proust must conclude, "So I am brought up against the difficulty of presenting a permanent image as well as of a character as of societies and passions." We are not fixed entities, Proust declares, but "plusieurs personnes superposées," like the heavens of the catholic theology.[56] This application of discontinuity to personality can be best summarized by Eliot's admiration for Pascal, in whom he found the mathematician, the *honnête homme* and the religious fideist. And even after his conversion, he can still speak admiringly of that distinguished line of French moralists, Montaigne, Pascal and LaRochefoucauld: "In the honesty with which they face the *données* of the actual world this French tradition has a unique quality in European literature...."[57]

Some of Worringer's other ideas were echoed and independently confirmed by other Modernists—always with some modification. Joseph Frank, writing only of English letters, has recognized the centrality of his role: Worringer "exercised a strong influence on Hulme and through Hulme, by way of Eliot, probably on the whole of modern English criticism."[58] When we read of Ortega's "dehumanization," or I. A. Richard's "neutralisation" of nature, or Frank's later conception of "spatialization," or the ideas of the "introverted" or "reflexive" novel, then we can see how ready writers were to receive Worringer's ideas. His distinction between abstraction and empathy may be seen in modern art, with its renewed appreciation of geometrical and abstract forms, as well as its rejection of the aesthetic of empathy, of art as a theatre of "self-enjoyment," or self-projection.

These aesthetic conclusions are, as Worringer and Hulme explain, based upon philosophical ideas that in Modernism derive from a primary sense of separation and alienation from Nature. Romantic empathy, on the other hand, rests upon a sense of at-oneness, or concord, and of common interest—the "matrix version of Nature."[59] The usefulness of the paradox of time, described in the preceding chapter, is here shown, since it helps to explain this new alienation from Nature. Where Romantic values imply an immanence, Worringer finds in pre-Renaissance art a sense of transcendence, and a dualism that is inspired by a discontent with the conditions of man's natural state. Basically, this sensed diminishment of nature and of natural powers is caused by an overpowering dread of vast, empty space. "Dread of space" is one of the causes Worringer presents to explain the coincidence of the religious and the geometrical in primitive art and in the more sophisticated Eastern art—the human form is as nothing in contrast to the enormous incomprehensible forces. The paradox of time—the notion that the triumph of time leads to the spatialization of

THE MODERNIST SENSIBILITY

experience—fits with Worringer's ideas and helps explain the Modernist alienation from humanistic Western culture.

Hulme is thus something of a crossroads for continental and Anglo-American lines of Modernism. He introduced and translated Georges Sorel's *Réflexions sur la violence*, and made, as we have seen, full use of Worringer's idea—both writers entering into the delineation of Naphta's ideas in *The Magic Mountain*. Moreover, as has been recently shown, Hulme's major influence on the thought of T. S. Eliot occurred as early as 1915-1916.[60] Fully representative of the complications of Modernism itself (some of these complications will be followed in the next chapter), Hulme also helped introduce Bergson's ideas to England. In all of this he was fulfilling the honorable role of intellectual transmitter ("propagandist" if you will), and England its historical role of importer. Yet, beyond this, in the vehemence of his personality and the sharp, contentious scrupulousness of his intellect, Hulme managed to react to and reflect upon the changes that were overtaking the modern world. The contradictions of his personality and of his thought, as an astute reader, Miriam Hansen, has noted, were themselves "meaningful."[61]

5. *Suspicion of "Staying-Points"*

In "The Crown," that essay of 1915 so valuable for an understanding of Lawrence's fiction and to which we repeatedly turn, the great sin is "this tying the knot in Time, this anchoring the ark of eternal truth upon the waters. . . . In Time and in Eternity, all is flux. . . . We come and we go."[62] If, as we saw in regard to our ways of knowing, there are no fixed standpoints, neither are there in relation to emotional commitments any secure "staying-points." Modernists experience extreme reluctance to invest with any special significance the natural processes of existence, as if to "stay" them, in a snapshot, as it were, would be an act of willful sentimentality contravening the natural changeableness of things. As a consequence, Modernism plays havoc with many of the pieties of

THE MODERNIST SENSIBILITY

nineteenth-century public belief. Here, as usual, Nietzsche is prophetic, a man rising out of his time to express the needs of the coming time:

> Not to remain stuck to a person—not even the most loved—every person is a prison, also a nook. Not to remain stuck to a fatherland—not even if it suffers most and needs help most—it is less difficult to sever one's heart from a victorious fatherland. Not to remain stuck in some pity. . . . Not to remain stuck to science. . . . Not to remain stuck to one's own detachment. Not to remain stuck to our own virtues and become as a whole the victim of some detail in us, such as our hospitality, which is the danger of dangers for superior and rich souls who spend themselves ravishly, almost indifferently. . . . One must know how *to conserve oneself*: the hardest test of independence.[63]

Nietzsche himself emphasizes the phrase "to conserve oneself. . . ." In Modernism that seems to be the greatest struggle, primarily because the most acceptable and conventional positions (those they were working to overthrow) were precisely the positions that concealed the greatest harm. Gerald Crich, Thomas Buddenbrook, and many others, fell precisely because they undertook to shoulder the burdens and pieties of their society. Those who were saved were more passive witnesses, who, paradoxically, maintained a securer sense of their separate selves. Lawrence's great fear was to be lost in fusion. To conserve oneself one had to avoid the great phrases of the nineteenth century—and here Romanticism, Victorianism and Realism are all, as Ortega has reminded us, of the same family.[64]

For Virginia Woolf in *Orlando*, the damp that seeped into the compartments of life forced that century to bundle itself up in great phrases.

> In a desperate effort to snuggle their feelings into some sort of warmth one subterfuge was tried after another. Love,

birth, and death were all swaddled in a variety of fine phrases.[65]

John Morley, writing of *Death, Heaven and the Victorians*, registers "those high-sounding Victorian passwords . . . that chime like bells, combining to form irreproachable sentiment."[66] But Modernists, like King Lear, will cry, "Off, off you lendings," as they attempt to come into contact with a reality that had been muffled, or swaddled. *Youth, old age, childhood, children, relationships within the family* (particularly those involving the mother), *death*—these preserves of emotional commitment are vigorously scrutinized in Modernism with a scrupulosity that is at times terrifying. If this were not done, they would constitute areas of safety, staying-points, that the Modernists' sense of change as well as their fear of consciously willed emotions render suspect.

If the link with Nature is broken in Modernism, it is broken in youth. Few things separate Modernism from nineteenth-century values as effectively as its honest depiction of troubled young people, young people who are troubled not because of any exclusion or deprivation but because their aims and ambitions run counter to prevalent values. The nostalgic bourgeois notions of youth as (1) a period of great unity and intimacy with nature or (2) a period of freedom, when one sowed his wild oats, are equally repugnant to the Modernist consciousness. Adrian Leverkühn, in Mann's *Dr. Faustus*, that composite picture of the growth of the twentieth-century artist, denies these falsified conceptions: "I do not find that youth stands on a particularly intimate footing with nature. Rather its attitude toward her is shy and reserved, actually strange *(fremd)*. . . . The young one is by no means disposed to see and enjoy nature. His eye is directed inwards, mentally conditioned, disinclined to the senses. . . ."[67] For the Modernist, whether it be Stephen Dedalus, Paul Morel, Adrian Leverkühn, or the "drowned Phoenician sailor" of *The Waste Land*, there exists no unity either with nature or with natural generation; the child is not father of the man, nor son of the father, either, but rather the stages are separated by rupture and discontinuity.

Robert Musil has written, "My father was younger than I."[68] Stephen, too, feels himself cut off from his father and his cronies and their nostalgic self-indulgence:

> An abyss of fortune or of temperament sundered him from them. His mind seemed older than theirs. . . . No life or youth stirred him as it had stirred in them. (346)

Indeed, in relation to his immediate family he stood in the "mystical kinship of fosterage; foster child and foster brother." (349) Yet, there is as well, alongside this alienation, tremendous hope and vision in Stephen, responsiveness to scenes and to language, and an inner consistency (the sense of his own developing form, entelechy) that is at odds with his external world. The difficulties that he and the other young Modernists encounter and generate are the difficulties of the young Modern struggling to transform a not-yet-born second nature into a commonly accepted first nature. This was the problem Nietzsche foresaw. And it is the same problem that Musil expressed in *Young Torless*:

> For there is, in the development of every fine moral energy, such an early point where it weakens the soul whose most daring experience it will perhaps be one day—just as if it had first to send down roots, gropingly, to disturb the ground that they will afterwards hold together; and it is for this reason that boys with a great future ahead of them usually go through a period abounding in humiliation. (29-30)

Modernism shared in the aggressive twentieth-century emphasis on youth, the new "ideology of youth."[69] But while being a part of this general tendency, Modernism differed radically from it. Glorification of youth represented no new change of values; what it represented was a newly emergent sector of society demanding its rights. In fact, its retrograde function can be seen in the ease with which its energies were diverted to the purposes of the Fascists and the Nazis. If Modernism is a youth movement, it is so in Ortega's sense of *dehumanization*, wherein he means not a humanistic sense of energy and at-oneness, but rather an introverted concern with the mind's play of perception. The point is that Stephen is as alienated from his cohorts as he is from his predecessors. He was at school "proud, sensitive and suspicious." (340)

None of the young Modernists sits well among the elders. Particularly is this so when they would serve as teachers. "We resent teachers," is Bernard's conclusion in *The Waves*. (305) Old Crane, the headmaster, earlier aroused his suspicion: "I love tremendous and sonorous words. But his words are too hearty to be true. Yet he is by this time convinced of their truth." (196) In the Nestor episode of *Ulysses*, Deasy advises Stephen to put money in his purse. The voice of history and of Empire has simply become Iago-like in its formulae. Sir William in *Aaron's Rod* places his confidence in God and his bank account. Norpois in Proust's *Recherche* is a more Delphic Nestor only because he is part of the super-subtle diplomatic corps—but his knowledge is just as remote. "Is this old wisdom," Stephen asks himself, as Deasy fails to comprehend that not only the Jews but we all have sinned against the light. "He awaits to hear from me." (35) Lawrence is, as usual, more emphatic: against the German phase, *Weisheit der Alten*, he protests, "Nineteenth-century lies!"[70] In that painful and farcical meeting between Rupert Birkin and Ursula's father, the two men are immediately at odds. Baffled and annoyed by Rupert's answers and questions, it is the older man who is on the verge of breaking (throughout this novel, *Women in Love*, Will Brangwen is angry and bitter, lacking because of his own unrealized marriage). Birkin wonders:

> How could he be the parent of Ursula, when he was not created himself? He was not a parent. A slip of living flesh had been transmitted through him, but the spirit had not come from him. The spirit had not come from any ancestor, it had come out of the unknown. A child is the child of the mystery, or it is uncreated. (248)

THE MODERNIST SENSIBILITY

Knowledge itself, not being linear and progressive, cannot be handed down from generation to generation—the fruits of experience benefitting those who come after. Since old experience does not apply to new conditions, even old age itself is not immune to the shocks of existence—the Modernist sense of sudden and radical change forecloses even that clearing. Lily Briscoe in *To the Lighthouse* wonders, "Could it be, even for elderly people, that this was life?—startling, unexpected, unknown?" (268) D. H. Lawrence in his *Education of the People* declares, "We are a million things which we don't know we are. Now and again we make new and shocking discoveries in ourselves...."[71] These passages are quite similar to lines from "East Coker," that part of *Four Quartets* most expressive of historical disillusionment, and where, as a consequence, both the order of experience and the wisdom of old age are unsettled: "Every moment is a new and shocking / Valuation of all we have been."[72] The knowledge derived from experience is then of only limited value, for it imposes patterns that are quickly outmoded. There can be no periods of calm security in existence:

> In the middle, not only in the middle of the way
> But all the way, in a dark wood . . .

If this is so, the historical validity of the ancestral voices must then collapse: "Do not let me hear of the wisdom of old men, but rather of their folly. . . ."

When history suffers a dislocation the means of continuity suffer. Progeny, formerly a source of identity, had for some time ceased to be the great theme that had preoccupied many of the Renaissance writers: it returned to the silence from which it had emerged in the early Renaissance.[73] Without fatherhood, the role of the father is necessarily diminished. As we have seen in chapter 2, section 3, rebellion against the domineering will of the father was not essential to the assertion of the Modern. In fact, Modernists grew up in an atmosphere more marked psychologically by the absence of the father than by his presence. They moved in a vacuum of acknowledged

THE MODERNIST SENSIBILITY

authority. For this reason, perhaps, some of them sought hardline interpretations of the world, firm distinctions, even philosophical hierarchies (tending, perhaps, in some, toward social hierarchies). Their works may be regarded as attempted solutions to this break-up of the world of the fathers.

Robert Wohl, in his valuable study, *The Generation of 1914*, sees this change in the relations of fathers and children as the expression of deeper shifts in the social structures of the industrializing countries of Europe:

> Young men began to feel the dominance of their fathers as oppressive and to denounce it as illegitimate not because their fathers were harsher or less affectionate than before but because fathers could no longer guarantee their sons a smooth entry into the society outside the home. In a period of rapid social and economic change the skills and patterns of behavior that had served the father well often appeared useless to the son, especially if he belonged to the middle strata of society most caught up in the maelstrom of modernization.[74]

This is a sociological interpretation that suits well with the evidence of literary Modernism. The fathers were outmoded, not only in their professions, but in their ways of thinking, their emotional needs and responses. Here, as in other parts of our theme, we come up against the conclusion that Modernists spoke for and struggled to establish a new order of consciousness. Their culture in crisis was to be sure a crisis of social change, but it was also a crisis of attitudes. The mid-Victorians lived through greater social changes, but there is no indication that they sought to alter the thought patterns of Romanticism. The Modernists, however, sought to counter the social change they were experiencing with new ways of thinking.

Along with that of the father, the roles of children and mothers were submitted to serious revision. In the nineteenth century, as has been pointed out, the family became the refuge and sanctuary from the increasingly aggressive outside world.[75]

THE MODERNIST SENSIBILITY

Privacy, domesticity, emotional investment in the conjugal family itself—all were centered around mother and child, emotional enclave and preserve, which the father protected from the rougher intrusions of society.[76] Ariès locates these changes at least as far back as the eighteenth century:

> The modern family ... cuts itself off from the world and opposes to society the isolated group of parents and children. All the energy of the group is expended on helping the children to rise in the world and without any collective ambition: the children rather than the family.

A new sensibility inheres in the family—should we call it Romantic? "The child was irreplaceable; his death irreparable." "Nobody would now dare to seek consolation for losing a child in the hope of having another, as parents could have admitted doing only a century before." Again looking at the later eighteenth-century sensibility (and again quoting Ariès), "In his correspondence with his wife, General de Martange treats everything much more seriously. His is already the gravity of the nineteenth century, applied to both little things and big: Victorian gravity."[77]

In much of the nineteenth-century literature children and childhood figure prominently. Schiller showed the Romantic sensibility when he "linked animals and plants with children, peasants and primitive people, all inspiring a kind of love and 'respectful emotion' simply because they were natural."[78] For Blake and Wordsworth children represent imaginative wholeness, untainted by atomistic thought. "Heaven lies about us in our infancy." As we become adults we lose "that visionary gleam." Peter Coveney, whose *The Image of Childhood* is the fullest study of the subject in nineteenth-century literature, regards Dickens as heir to the Romantic poets.[79] He writes of a "common nineteenth-century sensibility" and the "continuity between the romantic and the mid-Victorian." (162) Dickens' children are sources of near-ethereal innocence and beauty victimized by the forces of industrialism, by adult cunning, or

155

by the rigors of an iron discipline. They are children not allowed to know what childhood is.

In contrast to the extended preëminence of the child in Romantic poetry and Victorian fiction the sheer numerical appearances and relative importance of the child in Modernist literature are negligible. And while there are some instances, they have usually nowhere near the same characteristics as the children of the nineteenth century. The new children are not possessors of any special moral sensitivity. They are quite "realistically" presented. Coveney has concluded,

> The child would no longer be used for a romantic "message," or as the vehicle for self-pity, indulgent pathos or escape. If he were "impure," malicious, cruel, tender, kind, painfully sensitive—and most often an amalgam of all these qualities—then he would be presented in his reality. (306)

While Coveney especially looks to the presence of Freudian thought in order to explain this change, we can see that this new presentation of children fits into the larger patterns of Modernist thought, such as their concern with the given of experience, the need to present the fuller picture of things, their ban on pathos, and, most particularly, their suspicion of consciously willed emotion. But most importantly we must understand that the role of children in Modernist literature is dominated by one fact: the struggle of the young adult to assert his nascent consciousness. As a consequence, there can be no condescension to children. They are part of the same mystery, debate and struggle; they are on the same level, perhaps even antagonists in the same contest.

As Joseph K. is mounting the stairs for his interrogation by the inscrutable Court of Inquiry, he passes by some children playing on the staircase and thinks to himself, "If I ever come here again . . . I must either bring some sweets to cajole them with or else a stick to beat them."[80] He awaits until a marble stops rolling, thus allowing two children to hold him by his pants legs. They have the "pinched faces of adult rogues."

THE MODERNIST SENSIBILITY

Rather than adults wishing to become as the little children, children are like adults: they bear the same vices.

This comes very clear in the strangely ugly episode of *The Rainbow* (396-405), where little Vernon Williams serves as a remarkable contrast with the children of Dickens. Repulsive morally as well as physically, he carries on with a whining, cowardly, fawning, clever defiance. He poses a serious threat to Ursula's control over her class (a disciplinary role she has little taste for). Fully determined not to let him insidiously wrest the class from her, she thrashes him, most viciously, when he attacks her like a cornered rodent. While my language is lurid, such is Lawrence's depiction of this case of irreducible knavishness, for which there seems to be no possibility of social amelioration, or for which no law or governmental action seems to be responsible. This is confirmed when the boy's mother visits the school and shows the same physical and moral attributes, the same sickly, repulsive pallor, the same cowardly insinuation.

The Modernist difference is not only with Victorian sentimentality but also with its origins in Romanticism. Not only children but childhood, itself, loses its Romantic associations. This is especially apparent in the poem most thought to resemble the Romantic preoccupations with childhood, T. S. Eliot's *Four Quartets*. Two episodes—the children in the rose garden in *Burnt Norton*, and the need to consolidate adult experience with childhood, itself, in the remarkably satisfying final verse paragraph of *Little Gidding*—seem to reestablish Romantic associations. Yet, if we look more closely, we see that each bears the imprint of Modernism. Whereas the relationship of child to adult in Wordsworth's *Intimations* ode is one of organic growth, harmonious development like the rings of a tree, in Eliot's major statement the connection is marked by grimness, isolation, disruption, that is, it comes from the Modern:

> Sudden in a shaft of sunlight
> Even while the dust moves

> There rises the hidden laughter
> Of children in the foliage
> Quick now, here, now, always—
> Ridiculous the waste sad time
> Stretching before and after.

In the sudden, inexplicableness of its manifestation, the laughter of the children is far from natural. It stands as a revelatory moment in an otherwise bleak world, one possessing very little fruitfulness. No gradual ripening, or mature growth, but rather a spiritual desert is suggested into which there intervenes a sudden source of grace. If that is the case it is hardly possible that what is commonly called Nature can have by itself a restorative function or can heal the breach in the human psyche and its development.

The hearth and the home had become the acknowledged anchors in a changeful society, and everything depended upon the mother, who was the center of the home. She raised the children, was responsible for their moral education, and was herself the paragon of virtues. All sentiment was invested in this relationship. In fact the mother was a far greater emotional presence in Modernist works than the father, and separation from her involvement is a major travail on the road to Modernist consciousness. For while it was an emotional preserve, the role of the mother involved a larger dominion—she endorsed the means of continuity, marriage and children. With reproduction inevitably went production of goods, and with the surplus of goods went the demands of Empire. No wonder then that when Stephen resists his mother's request that he make his Easter duty, he is resisting a chain of related duties and encumbrances. To escape the nets of religion, language and nationality is to fly above the earthbound mother and seek the more ideal father.

In her own sacrificial and relegated position the mother stands for a kind of self-surrender. When Gerald curls up pathetically in his bed of snow and "lets go," he is in effect yielding himself up to a vast mother. Yearnings for a womb-like warmth

THE MODERNIST SENSIBILITY

and oblivion, yearnings for timelessness—in effect, the triumph of space—seem to be associated with the mother. Erik Erikson's psychohistorical study of Maxim Gorki traces the development of the modern consciousness in that Russian's liberation from the self-abandonment to the mother, where the need for timelessness is reinforced by the vast space.[81] Mother Russia. And Joyce in *Finnegans Wake* puns triply when he refers to "Mother Spacies," indicating not only the feminine principle of space but also the continuity of the species that is the mother's other concern. Hence the last Siren call that Paul Morel in *Sons and Lovers* must overcome is that of his mother. Alone after her death he senses the vastness and the terror of the immense night. "There was no Time, only Space." His mother was now intermingled with that vastness, and he wanted her to be alongside of him. " 'Mother!' he whispered—'mother!' " While inclining toward such personal immersion, he nevertheless gains control of himself. "But no, he would not give in." With clenched fists, and jaw set fast, he moves toward the city, the traditional locus of time. "He would not take the direction, to the darkness, to follow her." (419-420) This choice is prototypally a Modernist choice.

Death in Modernist literature is frequently a central event, particularly the death of the mother. Since she indeed held together the family's emotional and domestic life, her loss sent the family reeling. The deaths of Mrs. Morel, of Mrs. Dedalus, of Mrs. Ramsay—and even here we can add the centrality of the death of Marcel's grandmother—were all so overwhelming as to traumatize the family and debilitate the survivors (effects against which the struggling sons, or daughters, had to aspire). This should provide some lead to the fact that in Modernism we find changed attitudes toward death.

Alexander Welsh, whose study of *The City in Dickens* is actually a gathering of nineteenth-century attitudes to many of the themes touched on here, inclines to link the novels of his period with twentieth-century novels at this point. They are each, he maintains, "more concerned with the style of dying than with the transcendent meaning of death."[82] Yet, if the

THE MODERNIST SENSIBILITY

Victorian novel brings death into the hearth, if its aim is to domesticate death, and if publicly the Victorians themselves were much given to great displays of emotion, then it is obvious that these fictional means and attitudes cannot be much like those present in the works of Modernism. To domesticate death is to rob it of its sting by bringing it within the processes of continuity and establishing feelings of unity with Nature. For these and other reasons, John Morley in his *Death, Heaven and the Victorians* concludes, ". . . it was Romanticism that largely determined the nature and form of early Victorian emotion."[83] Furthermore, death is even given ethical implications and justified, since memory of the dead may be the source of good deeds by the living.

None of these extenuations seems to hold for Modernist writers. Far from reinforcing the links of continuity or emotional at-oneness with Nature, death seems to scar existence badly. The infant death of Rudy (as well as the suicide of Bloom's father) seems to have provoked a malaise in the declining marriage of Molly and Leopold Bloom. Death in Virginia Woolf's novels, from *Jacob's Room* onward, seems to open a glimpse into the abyss, an experience of nothingness (and we recall from the Quentin Bell biography that Virginia's own recurrent bouts with madness were precipitated by deaths of those close to her). The deaths of the mothers devastated many young Modernist heroes and heroines. Nor is this true of mothers alone. Extra meaning is attached to the death of the bright young men, the knights at arms, the brothers, whose deaths seem to reflect the terrible loss of the young élite in World War I. The losses of Andrew and Percival in Woolf's novels remove sustaining poles of expectation from existence. And the meaning of Joachim Ziemssen's death in *The Magic Mountain* is similar. While the last section of the novel moves in support of a renewed sense of temporal objectivity, of the reality of external event, the death of Joachim strengthens Hans's own temporal indifference, his own resistance to the time-economy of the bourgeois world, since it was his cousin's zeal for duty that brought him more surely to his death.

THE MODERNIST SENSIBILITY

This traumatic impact of death is even more evident when Peeperkorn commits suicide. The death of Peeperkorn, whose semi-fabulous personality seemed powerful enough to transcend the harsh dialectic of Settembrini and Naphta, is like the death of Nature itself, and accordingly a deep depression seems to take hold of the sanatorium, a depression that shows the advent of World War I. In the Modernist authors, the presentation and uses of death are part of the antipathy to continuity and the sensed unity with Nature. It throws the survivor out of an orderly, reliable existence and forces him to rearrange his life (one might say he passes from sincerity to authenticity)—not his financial life, his fortune, or his legacy (curiously none of these practical matters is of concern following Modernist deaths)—but his emotional life, his hold on existence.

Furthermore, just as a break with the conventional attitudes of time is the necessary point of Modernist departure, so an encounter with death is part of the Modernist spiritual itinerary. Before the Thunder speaks, Phlebas the Phoenician must drown—a symbolic death to the world. The Proteus episode of *Ulysses*, where Stephen develops the sense of his own identity and form, or entelechy, has, like *The Waste Land*, Shakespeare's *Tempest* in reserve, as well as Milton's *Lycidas*; it too is marked by a drowning. And the parallel episode of Bloom's story, as it were the prelude to his day, is the Hades section.

In this regard, Hans Castorp—certainly the most engaging and encompassing of the young Modernist heroes, especially when expressing his passion for Clavdia, whose presence has transformed him into a great philosopher—is representative of the spirit of Modernism. "There are two paths of life," he informs Mme. Chauchat, "the one is the regular one, direct, honest." And the other, answers this knight from the past of medieval adventure, this heir of Luther, carried by the spirit of Dostoevsky, this voice of the northern Modernist renaissance, whose ways of metaphysical freedom are those of twentieth-century Modernist man, "The other is bad, it leads through death—that is the *spiritual* way." ("und das ist der geniale

Weg.") This finally confirms the role of death in Modernist literature as being indeed transcendent, a way through which the developing Modernist hero must pass if he is to achieve his fuller being.

If this is so, it is virtually impossible for death to be ignored in Modernist literature. Yet, Phillipe Ariès' study, *Western Attitudes Toward Death*, has traced the process whereby in contrast to the nineteenth-century's familiarization (or domestication) of death, the twentieth century, particularly in the countries of northwestern Europe and America, sought to reduce its momentousness, even to banish it.[84] And Geoffrey Gorer's well-known study, *Death, Grief and Mourning in Contemporary Britain*, has even contrasted the fortunes of death with those of sex, and found them reversed in the nineteenth and twentieth centuries. Whereas the Victorians celebrated death and seemed to conceal sex, the moderns, for their part, seemed to place death under ban and made public displays of sex.[85]

In regard to both of these areas, the banishment and the attenuation of death, Modernists diverge from the tendencies of their society. When the question turns to public grief and mourning, however, then Modernism seems to be in accord with its society. "They did not court sorrow," is Quentin Bell's apt summary of the responses of Virginia Woolf and her friends to deaths in their circle.[86] After the undertakers had come to dress Paul's mother, he left the house and played cards at a friend's house. Very instrumental in the prosecution's effective case against Meursault in Camus' *L'Étranger* is the fact that he declined to see his mother's body, smoked cigarettes, slept and had drunk *café au lait*. Since the Modernist line is somewhat hard-bitten and tough-skinned (at least in appearance), the absence of manifestations of grief is part of the recognition of certain *données* of mortal existence. Such finitism does not contribute to displays of mourning. The refusal to mourn, or to participate in the rituals of grief, might represent a basic act of modesty, an expression of humility before those facts of experience about which nothing can be done, facts of imper-

THE MODERNIST SENSIBILITY

manence in which the Modernists knew themselves to be included.

Ariès attributes this change in the custom of mourning, as he does the apparent banishment of death, to the need for happiness. And yet, judging from the works of Modernism (to be sure, the responses of an élite, but an élite whose reactions in other matters have indeed initiated the directions of future change), this need for happiness does not seem to be a sufficient explanation. In Mann's *Magic Mountain* the "Walpurgis Nacht" section is preceded by the "Dance of Death": his saturnalia are rooted in death, as, of course, is the spirit of carnival itself. *Di doman non c'è certezza*, the Medicean carnival song, was incorporated into Shakespeare's *Twelfth Night*. But there are other reasons, those, too, expressed in the new, Modernist sensibility. Modernists were keenly sensitive to the willfulness of emotional self-abandonment. In "Death and Love," that painful chapter of *Women in Love*, Gerald's mother, fearing his emotional needfulness (and converted into a frank-speaking prophetess by her knowledge of the lies she had lived), bitterly tells him, "Let the dead bury the dead—don't go bury yourself along with them—that's what I tell you. I know you well enough." (319-320) In some ways, it might appear that the Modernist attitude toward death is a return to the greater casualness of the eighteenth century. Indeed, the same proverb is urged by Settembrini against Hans Castorp's early preoccupation with death. (308/I.326) However, the tone does not suggest a return to the eighteenth-century pursuit of happiness. It grows out of a more strongly felt tension, an ever-present danger from which they must save themselves, the fear of being swallowed, of pitching oneself into the abyss, of unconsciously willing one's own annihilation. This is the struggle behind Stephen's attitudes. Rather than be a "Ghoul. Chewer of corpses," Stephen, in his desperate struggle to save himself must deny his dead mother, "No, mother. Let me be and let me live." (10)[87] So threatened has the need to conserve oneself become that such a response is the expression of a true struggle.

CHAPTER V

"The Songs That I Sing"

> My beloved, the songs that I sing are not mine, no, no, I tell you they are not mine.
> William Blake to his wife, as quoted by James Joyce in his essay, "Blake."

If today we can now recognize the need and even the desirability of a protean consciousness, and can gauge the supple strength supporting its apparent indecisiveness, its true suitability and responsiveness to the complexities of the modern world, it is because we first had in the literature of Modernism, particularly in what I call its complex central consciousness, a full picture of the virtues (as well as some of the vices) of this consciousness revealed in the new type of literary figure. Indeed, judging from some of the changes in attitudes that were brought about by Modernism (and that were shown in section 5 of the preceding chapter), there is little that has happened in the developing personal and social attitudes of our century that would have come as a surprise to an alert reader of the high Modernists.

Yet, the greatness of Modernism, somewhat in the manner of Renaissance humanism, was shown in the capacity of its chief representatives for self-transformation—their ability to take a mood or manner, a style or a train of thought to its appropriate end, to let it fulfill its function, and consequently reveal other needs and other possibilities. This capacity—also protean—is intrinsic to the developmental genius of Modernism. So, while stressing the importance of the new complexity and the new sensibility, we must still measure the distance that Modernists travelled from it. Their directions took them by way of deracination to a rediscovery of roots that were appro-

"THE SONGS THAT I SING"

priate for them. If in the previous two chapters we traced the remarkable centrifugality of the Moderns, their avowed, purposeful avoidance of connection or of continuity, in this chapter we shall look at their rediscovered connections. Such are the complications of Modernism, enjoying the complexities of consciousness, and yet searching for, requiring a deeper sense of self. As it gave us the consciousness and sensibility of a new type of man, so it provided the "sense of being for a new era."[1]

The introduction to this study has already indicated the complex nature of Modernism in the apparently contradictory attitudes of Baudelaire and of Nietzsche, in Thomas Mann's description of Schopenhauer as containing the characteristics of a Voltaire and of a Jacob Boehme, and in T. E. Hulme's call for an imagistic hard line while at the same time possessing the Bergsonian sense of a more fundamental self, one that breaks through the surface in moments of extreme tension.[2] In the same way, Nietzsche had prescribed as antidotes to the infection of history the *unhistorisch* and the *überhistorisch*. The former's way is that of utter forgetfulness of the past and immersion in the interests of the present. The latter also looks to the present (that is, it shares in the same disillusionment with history), but a present in which all phenomena, past as well as present, are gathered ("past and present are one and the same, typically alike in all their diversity and forming together a picture of eternally present imperishable types of unchangeable value and significance"). If the material of the previous two chapters approximates to some degree what Nietzsche had in mind by the "unhistorical," the material of these next two chapters is even closer to the "supra-historical," that "which turns the eyes from the process of becoming to that which gives existence an eternal and stable character—to art and religion."[3] What is special for Nietzsche—and for Modernism—is the insistence on the validity of each of these ways and their common origins in the break-up of the historical.

Lending support to the developmental thesis of this study, Thomas Mann, in his own essays and letters of the thirties, is convinced that myth is chronologically the later stage. In "Freud and the Future" (1936), he declares that "while in the life of the human race the mythical is an early and primitive stage, in the life of the individual it is a late and mature one."[4] In a letter to Karl Kerenyi, he writes more personally, "My interest in matters of religious history and myth came only late, an inclination of mature years that was not at all present in my youth."[5]

Mann goes on to explain the appeal of the mythic as not only depending upon a sense of larger happenings but also upon an identification with them, that is, the self is enhanced and even vindicated by its identification with a larger coherence. What is gained by the mythical is an "insight into the higher truth depicted in the actual; a smiling knowledge of the eternal, the ever-being and the authentic; a knowledge of the schema in which and according to which the supposed individual lives, unaware, in his naïve belief in himself as unique in space and time, of the extent to which his life is but a formula and a repetition and his path marked out for him by those who trod it before him."[6] In a similar way, for his *Four Quartets* Eliot chose as its epigraph the Heraclitean idea that the Logos is all-ruling while the masses live as if they had lives of their own. Out of the crisis of the historical, the fragmentation of consciousness, Modernists were intent on discovering and sensing those larger patterns and designs whose perception enhances the individual life.

This same transcendence of mere individualism is a vibrant faith for D. H. Lawrence, both in relation to history and to the cosmos, and it is also clear that his approach to the mythic—however basic it was to his quest—was a later expression of his work. Writing in 1929, Lawrence indicated how much an earlier manuscript version of Frederick Carter's *Dragon of the Apocalypse* had meant to him.[7] It effected a "release of imagination." "For the first time I strode forth into the grand fields of the sky." He was granted "sudden release into the great sky of the old world, the sky of the zodiac." He was one with the old Chaldean stargazers; the Bible was brought back in its "living conditions." The mythic—and Lawrence uses references to the zodiac and to myth interchangeably, both having the same effect—seems to provide the same kind of escape as well as the same kind of reintegration required by Modernists. Zodiacal figures bestow approachable form on the cosmic vastness. This third phase reestablishes connections that had first been falsified and then severed: "The sense of astronomical space merely paralyses me. But the sense of the living astrological heavens gives me an extension of my being."

In whatever the area, essay or fiction or poetry, and in relation to whatever subject, history or myth, the past or the ever-present, we find in these Modernist masters a largeness of thought that is based upon the creative participation of the self in its past and its myths. Events are not discrete in themselves, but, like hieroglyphs, allude to deeper processes. Crossings and conjunctions occur, shadowings and more basic patterns that those who are only pursuing external facts and events do not see. Occasionally this kind of interpretative largesse leads to an inspired prophetism. D.H. Lawrence, as his biographer reports, was not taken in by the Armistice.[8] Ravingly but accurately he predicted that the end of World War I just prepared the way for another war. He was remarkably sensitive to the survival of the ancient Germanic past, and writing in 1924 saw Germany retreating from the positive center of Europe (from the Socratic Enlightenment culture of France that Nietzsche deplored) to its other pole of Asiatic origins (this was just a few months before *The Magic Mountain* was published).[9]

This sense of largeness, of the continuation of the past into the present, this capacity of the modern-day Lawrence to look at Germany and feel the same ominous unpredictability as did a Roman soldier at the frontier two millennia earlier, this "standing-in-the-place-of" shows an expansiveness beyond the consciousness of phase two. We recall Lawrence's critique of Futurism that it lacked naïveté (and Eliot's assessment that Imagism performed essentially a "critical" function).[10] Perhaps what both are saying is that these avant-garde movements never transcended technique, never sought or introduced that sense of wonder. Lawrence describes this sense of wonder in relation to the nonconformist hymns that permeated his childhood; and, as was the case with Proust's childhood books, one source of intense pleasure derives from the rediscovery of a "pocket" of pleasure that had been left untouched, as it were, in his memory:

> To me the word Galilee has a wonderful sound. The lake of Galilee! I don't want to know where it is. I never want to go to Palestine. Galilee is one of those lovely, glamorous worlds, not places, that exist in the golden haze of a child's half-formed imagination. And in my man's imagination it is just the same. It has been left untouched. With regard to the hymns which had such a profound influence on my childish consciousness, there has been no crystallizing out, no dwindling into actuality, no hardening into the commonplace. They are the same to my man's experience as they were to me nearly forty years ago.[11]

"Wonder" is the word in the "Air-raid" section of *Little Gidding*, when Eliot meets his own poetic tradition: "The wonder that I feel is easy."

This phase of Modernism will show much that is grand and luminous, cosmic extensions, personal projections of mythic and historical proportions, recoveries of the self. And yet, as we indicated at the end of chapter 3, the critical stage of development is that of the complex central consciousness. By that we mean that the discovery of the mythic and the self can only occur through the preceding stage; it can only occur in the context of the virtues there exhibited. The extraordinary has the ordinary for its setting. An entry in Virginia Woolf's journal of 1926 makes this clear:

> Arnold Bennett says that the horror of marriage lies in its "dailiness." All acuteness of relationship is rubbed away by this. The truth is more like this: life—say 4 days out of 7—becomes automatic; but on the 5th day a bead of sensation

"THE SONGS THAT I SING"

(between husband and wife) forms which is all the fuller and more sensitive because of the automatic customary unconscious days on either side. This is to say the year is marked by moments of great intensity. Hardy's "moments of vision." How can a relationship endure for any length of time except under these conditions.

This extract makes explicit what will be one of the major arguments of this chapter: in Modernism extraordinary vision is dependent upon the ordinary out of which it grows (it cannot exist in defiance of it). The mythical, the visionary may not be willed phenomena; they are part of the same involuntariness that was characteristic of the literary type met in the preceding phase.[12]

1. *From Discontinuities to Myth*

With the full flowering of the mythic a new and different phase of creative solidarity is encountered in Modernism. This is evident in Eliot's work, for instance, when we move from *The Waste Land*, and such related and contemporaneous essays as those on "The Metaphysical Poets" and "Andrew Marvell," to "Marina" and *Four Quartets*, and their obvious critical pendant, *The Use of Poetry and the Use of Criticism*. A similar sort of gradation is seen when we mark the distance between *Ulysses* and *Finnegans Wake*, or *Jacob's Room* and *The Waves*, and between either *Aaron's Rod* or *Kangaroo* and *The Plumed Serpent* or *Apocalypse*. Another letter from Mann to Kerenyi is useful since it recognizes at once the obvious anticipations and interrelations but also makes clear distinctions. In *The Magic Mountain*, Mann writes, the mythic interests were in the background, but they occupy the foreground of *Joseph and His Brothers;* in fact, they are the "expressed subject" of the work. In other words, he continues, "the 'Sanatorium novel' is the link between the realistic youthful work *Buddenbrooks* and the manifestly mythological works of [his] now approaching sixtieth year."[13] In the second phase, where consciousness predominates, the Modernists utilized the mythic method, the biplanar manipulation of a paradigm with contemporary events. In the third phase they show a mythic awareness, they move from the outside, so to speak, toward the inside of myth and seem to be writing from its very source.

In terms of imagery, if in the preceding chapters we dealt with the consciousness that amalgamates discrepant experience, in the third we are more aware of the unconscious substratum from which these images derive their source as well as their meaning. A passage from *The Use of Poetry and the Use of Criticism*, Eliot's Norton lectures at Harvard University, shows what I mean. Speaking of images that seem "saturated" with personal meaning and appeal for certain authors, that seem to come from some depth of being, and as such acquire a density of meaning, he can only wonder about their origin: "Why, for all of us, out of all that we have heard, seen, felt in a lifetime, do certain images recur, charged with emotion rather than others." He then lists some five images, a few of which have reappeared in his own poetry (notably in "The Journey of the Magi"), and concludes: "Such memories may have symbolic value, but of what we cannot tell, for they come to represent the depths of feeling into which we cannot peer."[14] While the origin and even meaning of these important remnants are hard to uncover (Eliot treats them with his typical modest skepticism), still it is clear that poetry is dependent upon, at its source, allowing such imagery to well up into consciousness and expression. In a footnote to the printed text the reader is referred to an article entitled "Le Symbolisme et l'âme primitive." Poetry, Eliot declares, "may make us from time to time a little more aware of the deeper unnamed feelings which form the substratum of our being, to which we rarely penetrate; for our lives are mostly a constant evasion of ourselves, and an evasion of the visible and sensible world." (155)

In a similar vein, Virginia Woolf always sought to write from what she called a "central feeling," in which the apparently disjunctive surface images have their roots. The painter,

"THE SONGS THAT I SING"

Lily Briscoe, in *To the Lighthouse* opens herself to the same kind of rhythm that was bearing her in its current:

> Certainly she was losing consciousness of outer things. And as she lost consciousness of outer things, and her name and her personality and her appearance, and whether Mr. Carmichael was there or not, her mind kept throwing up from its depths, scenes, and names, and sayings, and memories and ideas, like a fountain spurting over that glaring hideously difficult white space, while she modelled it with greens and blues. (238)

As this argument has suggested, to mark the gradations of Modernist development is also to suggest the interpenetrations, the dynamics of growth, the way, for instance, one phase prepares the road for the subsequent, the way "perspectivismo" is related to the perceptual constructivism of Stevens's later poetry. Of particular interest is the way that the complex central consciousness itself is a step on the way to the mythic. Eliot's "auditory imagination"—expounded in *The Uses of Poetry and the Uses of Criticism*—while new in formulation seems to be a further understanding on his part of some of the more enduring efforts of his earlier poetry, the strange and haunting rhythms, the probings beyond conscious sense, the reaching out toward a more profound area of the self and its associations. The Heraclitean epigram could just as well have been used above *The Waste Land*, it too showing the vast, almost instinctive movements amidst the well-trod itineraries of city life, the Logos of their patternings contrasted, as in the "Fire Sermon," with their deluded individual consciousnesses. In a valuable essay, Robert Langbaum indicates that the very fragmentation upon which the poem is based is a new method of characterization that, reacting against the nineteenth-century belief in the individual ego, is actually working toward the archetypal.[15] That is, what we have called the complex central consciousness and its reflections, the discontinuous self, brings us much closer to the collective self of myth.

These same London streets provide for Virginia Woolf the

discontinuities that merge into larger vistas and associations. The utter fragmentation of the city has produced a temporal dislocation to the effect that her street-haunting tends to jump over times, to see the mysterious, the instinctive, to feel ancient rhythms in daily comings and goings. The hordes crossing Waterloo Bridge in *Jacob's Room* to catch the nonstop to Surbiton are not impelled by reason; and the procession from the Surrey to the Strand and from the Strand to the Surrey side must have been going on for centuries:

> But what century have we reached? Has this procession from the Surrey side to the Strand gone on forever? That old man has been crossing the Bridge these six hundred years, for he is drunk, or blind with misery, and tied round with old clouts of clothing such as pilgrims might have worn. He shuffles on. No one stands still. It seems as if we marched to the sound of music; perhaps the wind and the river; perhaps these same drums and trumpets—the ecstasy and hubbub of the soul.[16]

Almost in the process of formation we can detect in Virginia Woolf city scenes becoming isolated from their immediate surroundings and forming connections with emotions that are perennial. The instability of immediate identification lends to the creatures of the streets associations thrown far back in time. The woman singing an old love song opposite the Regent's Park tube station is not immediately given an identifiable form in Peter Walsh's perception; rather we gather her presence by a series of notations and gleanings.

> A sound interrupted him; a frail quivering sound, a voice bubbling up without direction, vigour, beginning or end, running weakly and shrilly and with an absence of all human meaning into
>
> > ee um fah um so
> > foo swee too eem oo—

"THE SONGS THAT I SING"

the voice of no age or sex, the voice of an ancient spouting from the earth; which issued ... from a tall quivering shape, like a funnel, like a rusty pump, like a wind-beaten tree for ever barren of leaves which lets the wind run up and down its branches singing

> ee um fah um so
> foo swee too eem oo

and rocks and creaks and moans in the eternal breeze.

And for two more pages Virginia Woolf travels back and forward with this woman—"through all ages—when the pavement was grass, when it was swamp, through the age of tusk and mammoth, through the age of silent sunrise"—and her love song, which has echoed for millions of years. The figure of her dead lover has lost its sharpness; she probably now only detects a "looming shape, a shadow shape, to which, with the bird-like freshness of the very aged, she still twittered." And it is only that lover she addresses (however much her hand was ready for coins), so that "all peering inquisitive eyes seemed blotted out, and the passing generations—the pavement was crowded with bustling middle-class people—vanished like leaves, to be trodden under, to be soaked and steeped and made mould by that eternal spring." This lyrical poem in the city's midst attests to Modernism's transcendence of consciousness and its important formal reflexive forms; yet it also shows how necessary are the disruption of the busy middle-class values and the resulting fragmentary consciousness for this discovery of enduring human properties.[17]

Even in the classic Modernist works of the twenties, *The Magic Mountain* and *Ulysses*, we see the same preparations for the mythic. Gradually in *The Magic Mountain*, Hans Castorp, leaving the orderly time of the city and the seasons and the human constructions of order, comes to live, like Lawrence, in a more zodiacal sphere. The Sixth Book of this great novel, that culminates in the mythic and frankly Jungian dream-poem of the "Snow" chapter, commences with a new temporal orientation for Hans. The break-up of the middle way of ordering experience has intensified his rapports with the subhuman as well as the supra-human, or, rather, his sense of the human now must be taken to encompass these larger dimensions. "Evenings he gazed at the stars," Mann tells us and his "mental furniture" began to be composed of references to the "primitive heavenly signs"—much to Joachim's surprise and some disgust. But Hans, with his remarkable openness, finds all these new coordinates of his experience to be "great." "Imagine, they have been found employed as ceiling decoration in an Egyptian temple—and a temple of Aphrodite, to boot—not far from Thebes. They were known to the Chaldeans too, the Chaldeans, if you please, those Arabic-Semitic old necromancers, who were so well versed in astrology and soothsaying." (369/391) Obviously, when after completing *The Magic Mountain* Mann started work on *Joseph and His Brothers*, the ground was already well prepared.

The journey to the mythic in the earlier book culminates in the vision Hans dreams while perilously dozing during a snowstorm. Yet this is not an ordinary dream; he dreams of places to which he has never been, the Mediterranean, Naples, and Sicily and Greece, places which he has never visited, and yet in his dream he *remembers* them. His dream returns him spiritually to the classical—the triumph of the human form over the irrational—that has been so threatened by the allurements and wisdom from the East, and he experiences it precisely as a *re*-cognition: "as though in his heart he had always cherished a picture of this spacious, sunny bliss." And when the humanistic frame is enlarged to include the Greeks and the irrational, the terror amidst the serenity, Hans wonders where this dream came from:

> Where did I get the beautiful bay with the islands, where the temple precincts, whither the eyes of that charming boy pointed me, as he stood there alone? Now I know that it is not out of single souls that we dream. We dream anony-

mously and communally, if each after his fashion. The great soul of which we are a part may dream through us, in our manner of dreaming, its own secret dreams, of its youth, its hope, its joy and peace—and its blood-sacrifice. (495/521)

Such vision, independent from either Settembrini's rhetoric or Naphta's poison, yet taking something from each (for instance the phrase "anonymously and communally" complies with Naphta's description of the makings of medieval art), represents Mann's own consciousness—through Hans—of the particular vision of the Modern. And interestingly enough this affirmation of the mythic is also based upon an affirmation of the self, and Hans's right to dream that dream and to place it as the way of the Modern alongside the other visions that have historically determined man's values. "It is meet and proper, I hereby declare that I have a prescriptive right to lie here and dream these dreams."

The Nausicaa episode of *Ulysses* is one of the finest in the book not because of the fairly obvious ways the romanticized yearnings are undercut by unregenerate realities, but rather because these somewhat coarse ironies are themselves transcended by Bloom's own dawning mythic consciousness. He shows his own sensitivity to larger instinctive and involuntary movements, menstruation, magnetism, the flights of bats and the draw that the sea has for sailors. A powerful reality that consciousness itself is swept up into—but in Bloom's case, never submerged—takes possession of the mood of the piece so that it is more than an account of a middle-aged man and a virgin. And yet there is a connection between the two, since the larger configurations are, unlike Gerty's prettified coyness, rooted in realities (much as the mythic sense in Hans's dream includes the concealed terrors)."How many women in Dublin have it today? Martha, she. Something in the air. That's the moon." (361) Such growth of speculative meditation leads Bloom to recognize the convergences in his own personal history. He wooed in June:

"THE SONGS THAT I SING"

The year returns. History repeats itself. Ye crags and peaks I'm with you once again. Life, love, voyage round your own little world. And now?

The Viconian world is already present in Joyce's work. Bloom thinks back to his and Molly's moments of ecstasy on the hill of Howth (although there was a lot more calculation in Molly's part): "Where I come in. All that old hill has seen. Names change: that's all." Further meditations lead to more personal coincidences. He finds it curious that both he and Molly were each the only children in their families. "So it returns. Think you're escaping and run into yourself. Longest way round is the shortest way home." (376) Such reflections join up with Stephen's, in the "Scylla and Charybdis" and "Nighttown" chapters—again suggesting the rapprochement between the two figures. We walk through all our protean selves, Stephen concludes, "but always meeting ourselves." (210) "Self which itself was ineluctably pre-conditioned to become." (494) This illustrates once again the extent to which the mythic and other larger awareness are part of a renewed sense of the self.

2. *Involuntariness and a More Authentic Self*

The process of rendering up the conventional self for the sake of a "truer" self is, in Modernism, frequently a painful one, occasioned by moments of extreme emotional intensity. The desired break-through requires a break-up, or even at times, a break-down. Both Eliot and Mann spoke of the association of periods of creativity with sickness, Eliot in particular having the composition of *The Waste Land* in mind, large sections of which were written when the poet was recuperating in Switzerland. In the essay, "The Philosophy of Intensive Manifolds," T. E. Hulme gives the argument temporal significance when he finds that the conventional ego, whose realm is daily action, exists extensively, that is, on a linear plane. Only in moments of great tension does the inner self "break through" this outer crust. Eliot's sense of inspiration is admittedly negative since its purpose seems to be the almost involuntary breakdown of strong habitual barriers. We are so committed to the evasive actions of ordinary existence that an extraordinary event is required before at long last and almost against our will a true record reemerges.

In the experience of identity Modernists almost consistently reduce the role of the conscious will. Instead, they value that which seems to come unbidden, which surprises and seems to take hold of one in an undeniable manner. In fact, with all of the writers covered in this study the token of the revelation's authenticity is its involuntariness—that being the second thread running throughout this chapter dealing with the reintegration of the self with the larger forces of the universe.

Obviously there is a relation between the passive type of phase two and this higher involuntariness. In *Orlando* Virginia Woolf shows how the former is the natural ground of the latter. If we exist in multiple time, that is, if we are part of a cultural break-up, then we must have multiple selves to deal with the shards of existence. Problems develop from the simple desire for unity, when the "conscious self, which is uppermost and the power to desire, wishes to be nothing but one self." The simple fact is that this "Captain self, the Key self, which amalgamates and controls them all," does not come on call. The conscious self can call "Orlando" again and again without results; it was only "when she had ceased to call 'Orlando' and was deep in thoughts of something else that the Orlando whom she had called came of its own accord...."[18] In Modernism the selves that come on call are correspondents of consciousness and multiple in nature; they are hardly calculated to transcend fragmentation and to produce the conviction of identity.

We are further indebted to Virginia Woolf, in the diary passage quoted earlier in this chapter, for making explicit another feature of Modernism's experience of the extraordinary. We not only see that this sense of higher significance follows upon involvement in the ordinary, it is even dependent upon and caused by a fidelity to the ordinary. The moments of great intensity in married life are such because of the "automatic customary unconscious days on either side." The same honest abiding within the ordinary routines of daily life, the unwillingness to force meanings or to covet emotional depths, the waiting without hope or love, means that when such significances do occur their validity is uncontested, plain and patent to experience.

In *A Sketch of My Life* Mann recounts the way his major works—*Buddenbrooks, Death in Venice* and *The Magic Mountain*—all seemed to have their own head and take their own way, independent of his first intention. "Things," he concludes, "have a will of their own, and shape themselves accordingly." All Modernism is a lying-in-wait for such manifestations. Working on *Death in Venice* ("as always, it was a long-drawn-out job"), he "had at moments the clearest feeling of transcendence, a sovereign sense of being borne up, such as [he] had never before experienced."[19] The appeal of such experiences Mann himself makes clear; it lies in the perception of an order in what had seemed arbitrary, the sense of a texture in what had appeared to be diffuse, and finally in the sense of a coherent self that is more basic than the simple determinations of the ego. It is in this sense of wonder that phase three transcends phase two, and yet together they are joined by the continuing thread of involuntariness.

Like Mann and other Modernists, Lawrence was sensitive to those aspects of a story that seem to come by themselves. Clifford Chatterley's incapacitation Lawrence could not alter: "The story came as it did, by itself, so I left it alone. Whether we call it symbolism or not, it is, in the sense of its happening, inevitable."[20] In the essay ". . . Love was Once a Little Boy" Lawrence derides nineteenth-century freedom as the ethic of a slave: "I have no life, no real power, unless it will come to me."[21] Lawrence was fascinated by power, but in each case he regards it as a derived, not a directed force: "True power never belongs to us. It is given us, from the beyond." Power is a blessing that, like Joseph's in Mann's retelling of the Biblical account, comes from beyond and from below. "The real power comes into us from beyond. Life enters us from behind, where we are sightless, and from below, where we do not understand."[22] We need, then, Lawrence wrote in a letter of February, 1915, to relinquish our conscious selves and egos for the sake of these greater blessings.[23] This act of relinquishment is almost of necessity traumatic. Thus it was with Ursula at the end of *The Rainbow*. What was happening to her was the product of forces within her that were yet beyond her own consciousness and will. Rupert Birkin in *Women in Love* undergoes the same dissolution of the self and is saved thereby (with the aid of an ugly blow to the head by Hermione). Life requires such death to the egoistic will: "The near touch of death may be a release into life; if only it will break the egoistic will, and release the other flow." But, Lawrence continues in "The Crown," if the survivor credits his success to his own powers, then he will remain defeated and barren. "If, however, a man says, 'I fell! But the unseen goodness helped me, when I struggled for life, and so I was saved'—then this man will go on in life unimprisoned, the channels of his heart open, and passion still flowing through him."[24]

While having little patience with emergent evolution, Modernism had plenty for emergent revelation and consciousness. Beyond the scientific, the objective, the hard-edged, the classical line (dry and precise), even the discontinuous—all so critical for the Modernist consciousness—the greatest of the Moderns proceeded to a higher poetry of the psyche and of the self. Not only the conditions of their society, but the conditions of their writing made this extremely difficult. The very artistic values suggested in phase two—the dissolution of character and of event, the multiple and reflexive perspectivism, the requirements of complexity, the tendencies toward comedy and irony, the opposition to standpoints and even emotional staying-points—all are reflective of a philosophy of change and destructive of stability and identity. For these reasons, as Proust explains, the moments of illumination must come from outside, must be as unavoidable and undeniable as

"THE SONGS THAT I SING"

lightning, and not susceptible to the tamperings of consciousness.

In writing, then, a certain naïveté is also admired by Proust, particularly that involvement that does not impose a structure, but allows it to reveal itself in the themes that the artist almost unconsciously pursues. So, the most valued parts of Michelet's works are the prefaces, where he takes cognizance of what his work has been. And Wagner, who putting together scraps, suddenly discovers that he has written a tetralogy, is like Balzac, who, casting over his work the eye of a father, adds the final and most sublime stroke when he decides to have his characters reappear and form a cycle. This unity is to be preferred since it is ulterior and not artificial; since it is the product of a "single and transcendent design" of which the author may have been only subconsciously aware, a design that manifested itself:

> Not factitious, perhaps indeed all the more real for being ulterior, for being born of a moment of enthusiasm when it is discovered to exist among fragments which need only to be joined together. A unity that has been unaware of itself, therefore vital and not logical, that has not banned variety, chilled execution. (II.491/III.161)

Bernard in *The Waves* is definitely speaking in a Proustian manner when he expresses his fatigue with the "neat designs" of stories; the designs he now seeks are the kind that assert themselves "undeniably."

Like Spenser's allegorical world, Proust's Parisian nights are phantasmal. There are the false and destructive phantoms of an obsessive love, and the imaginary ones of the next party. Proust learned well that great Tolstoyan theme of parties and death. The law of the salon is the *Realpolitik* of live bodies: the dead contribute nothing. The Guermantes' plans are discomfited by the pending death of their cousin, Amanien; the death of the once loyal Dechambre is too painful for Mme. Verdurin, hence there must be no mention of it so that the party can go on; similarly with the Princess Sherbatoff, and,

"THE SONGS THAT I SING"

of course, the most exasperating episode—that relating to Swann and the ballet of the "red slippers." But in the midst of these frankly comic contretemps (and more painful because they are only that), along the way of the Guermantes' dinner, the soireé at the Princesse de Guermantes, the Verdurin gathering at Raspelière, a true phantom reappears, whose impact is profound and verifiable by virtue of its belatedness as well as its involuntary nature. The memory of his dead grandmother overcomes Marcel to such an extent that he even rejects two invitations. But more seriously she emerges like some guardian protectress who returns to him his own identity. She causes a "felt discrepancy" that separates the individual from the objects outside of him. Bending over to unbuckle his boots, Marcel *experiences* the return of his grandmother as she had once come to his aid.

> The person who came to my rescue, who saved me from barrenness of spirit, was the same who, years before, in a moment of identical distress and loneliness, in a moment when I was no longer in any way myself, had come in, and had restored me to myself, for that person was myself and more than myself.

But this experience is also a painful one. The revenant brings back to Marcel's mind thoughtless acts of sadism and other unkindnesses. And the very fact of her return makes finally realizable the truth that she is indeed dead, "perdue pour toujours." But this experience of finality is one that is never admitted along the Guermantes way, endlessly caught in the casual comedy of existence, and it seems to be a hopeful sign for Marcel's later separation from the deadly currents of his society:

> This painful and, at the moment, incomprehensible impression, I knew—not, forsooth, whether I should one day distill a grain of truth from it—but that if I ever should succeed in extracting that grain of truth, it could only be from it, from so singular, so spontaneous an impression, which

> had been neither traced by my intellect nor attenuated by my pusillanimity, but which death itself, the sudden revelation of death, had, like a stroke of lightning, carved upon me, along a supernatural, inhuman channel, a two-fold and mysterious furrow. (II.116/II.759)

He finally experiences a reality that he had not anticipated and that he cannot, by cowardice, dissipate. And yet, these almost "objective," impersonal, and terrible or grand signals of a powerful reality are only realized when, somehow, the conscious intelligence has relaxed its guard or the normal involvement in the external world has been abrogated—when one, in Eliot's words, "resigns" his normal world, so as to be able to recover the self in the grips of significance, even if that significance be crossed by terrors.

And finally the reaffirmation of a more positive identity takes place in that marvelous series of occurrences prior to the Princesse de Guermantes' matinée. These were anticipated by the Vinteuil septet that Marcel had heard at the Verdurins' party years earlier, where Charlus was so cruelly destroyed. Despite the composer's deliberate attempts to introduce similarities between his pieces, these were artificial and as nothing in comparison with the deeper identities that he could in no way conceal since they were involuntary, the mark and sign of his genius, establishing his identity, or, as Proust adds, providing "the permanence of the elements that compose his soul." Given the context of constant and universal change, such proof is dearly needed. And this is what the similar involuntariness of the accidental recollections contributes.

> For the truths which the intellect apprehends directly in the world of full and unimpeded light have something less profound, less necessary than those which life communicates to us against our will in an impression which is material because it enters through the senses but yet has meaning which it is possible for us to extract.

The essential mark of these great revelations is "that [he] was not free to choose them, that such as they were they were given to [him]." (VII.138-139/III.878-879) This involuntariness is a mark of their authenticity, as well as of the real existence of their recipient.[25]

If it were not Shakespearean—and in the mood of the final romances—T. S. Eliot's "Marina" would be Proustian in the sense of laying hold of and allowing to emerge from that area where dreams and memories cross reality images that confirm and even redeem the self. Like Shakespeare's last plays the atmosphere of this poem is magical and mythic, and miraculous in its sense of recovery. And like us, Eliot, in a lecture of 1937, was at a loss for words to account for the appeal of *Pericles*, which he called a "great" play. In fact, only recently has criticism devoted itself to the vogue of these last plays and the close association of their revival with Modernism.[26] In an earlier age, where plot and conflicts of character were central to critical discussion, it was inevitable that the last plays would be regarded as evidence of Shakespeare's failing powers. In the twentieth century, however, where the older dimensions of plot, character and even narrative continuity have been superseded, and necessarily so, there is a better disposition to appreciate the "important and very serious recurrences of mood and theme" in Shakespeare's last plays, read as a separate group.[27] The quoted words come from Eliot's 1930 introduction to G. Wilson Knight's *The Wheel of Fire* (which then included the famous essay, "Myth and Miracle" later republished in *The Crown of Life*), and testifies to that poet's very creative use of interpretative and scholarly works. Both Knight's and Colin Still's discussions of the last plays suited Eliot's needs to attend to the figure in the carpet, the larger design "which reveals itself gradually."[28]

For Eliot *Pericles* is the "perfect example of the 'ultra-dramatic,' a dramatic action of beings who are more than human. . . . It is the speech of creatures who are more than human, or rather, seen, in a light more than that of day."[29] Eliot's language, like ours, gropes for "ultra" words since only they, in expository prose, seem able to indicate the staggering suggestivity of these plays. But in "Marina," named after the young heroine born, lost and recovered at sea (it is interesting in this regard that Eliot perceives the "saturated" image which lay in the depths of Shakespeare's memory as rising "like Anadyomene from the sea"),[30] Eliot does succeed in capturing some of the qualities of the rich, post-tragic dimension of the play. Although slighted (except by Elizabeth Drew, Donald Davie, and John F. Lynen),[31] "Marina" is easily one of the finest of Eliot's smaller poems, and forms the connection between the "time of tension" in *Ash Wednesday* and the more secure *Four Quartets*. Here Eliot does seem to summon up images that come from some special terrain (similar to Proust's *domaine inconnu*), a world of "sub-terrene and sub-marine music," which we normally deny or ignore, and to reestablish connection with a lost but never dead sea of the self (similar to the childhood memories at the beginning of *Burnt Norton* and the end of *Little Gidding*):

> Whispers and small laughter between leaves and
>   hurrying feet
> Under sleep where all waters meet.[32]

To reconvene at these waters is to undergo a kind of psychic cleansing, where what has been done and ruined in the past is looked at in another light.

This is the use of the epigram to the poem. In the light of the Modernist rejection of progeny and those more natural means of continuity the choice of epigram is revealing, since it comes at the point when Hercules has just wakened to the fact that in his madness he had killed his children. As a figure he complies with the poet's own sense of failure in the natural world. But from the wreckage of the past a form emerges that forces another recognition. A boat, imperfectly made years before and now weather-worn, becomes an article of self-identification, a part of his own nature and necessities, with a spiritual depth that is his and yet beyond his intention: he made it "unknowing, half conscious, unknown, my own." The general sense of natural waste (a poignant, personal note from Eliot's biography) summarized in the lines from Hercules as well as the pattern of estrangement prevalent in the last plays is now recompensed in a kind of spiritual renewal for which the symbol is the recovery of Marina herself. What in the Elizabethan world amounted to a miraculous recovery of familial wholeness, is, in the Modernist imagination, equated with the revival of the self in an equally rich, miraculous and mythic context. Somehow the poet has come to look at his own life and work as having their own controlling purpose and psychic depth, and this recognition is now responsible for a new wave of commitment, hope and creativity:

This form, this face, this life
Living to live in a world of time beyond me; let me
Resign my life for this life, my speech for that unspoken,
The awakened, lips parted, the hope, the new ships.

3. *The Road Taken: Wallace Stevens and Romantic Reassessments*

Concern with the psychic sources of imagery—the basis of personal myths—should indicate that the stage of reintegration may be evidenced by suggestions other than those of universal myth. Wallace Stevens, for instance, can hardly be called a "mythic" poet, and yet his own verse after the long period separating *Harmonium* from *Ideas of Order* seems to partake of many of the same qualities as those of the other Modernists. His example allows us not only to enlarge the scope of our considerations but to engage once again the argument of Romanticism.

In a letter of 1940 Stevens wrote, "About the time when I personally began to feel around for a 'new romanticism,' I might naturally have been expected to start a new cycle. Instead of doing so, I began to feel that I was on the edge: that I wanted to get to the center: that I was isolated and that I wanted to share the common life."³³ This need "to find the center" may be seen as an attempt to establish a felt communion with life similar to the efforts of the other Modernists who utilized grander mythic conceptions. Stevens' poetry beginning with the volume of the mid-thirties asserts a new validity in the role and power of the imagination, and indeed his verse is marked by a more cohesive lyrical-meditative quality. His years of silence, of establishing himself in his profession, of buying a house, of having a family, evidently served him well in locating him more centrally in his own life (it certainly did not detract from the imaginative freshness of his later poems).

Indeed, the life that he affirms is the life of the imagination. "If we live in the mind, we live with the imagination." And this imagination is not fanciful, it is actually constitutive, or, better, constructive, of the world we inhabit. In "The Noble Rider and the Sounds of Words," Stevens declared, "What makes the poet the potent figure that he is . . . is that he creates the world to which we return incessantly and without knowing it and that he gives to life the supreme fictions without which we are unable to conceive it."³⁴ The sentence makes a unity of Stevens's later career, linking "The Idea of Order at Key West" with "Notes Toward a Supreme Fiction" and the other poems of his rich and extended final phase.

The background to the pivotal poem is again the sea, and again, as in the earlier Modernist point of departure, "A sea that was not ours . . . Inhuman." Nor does the sea yield itself to allegories of meaning, to affective human projection. The sea, the veritable ocean, "was not a mask." Yet the singer constructed an order to the sea. She was the single artificer, the maker. Her auditors "knew that there never was a world for her / Except the one she sang and, singing, made." Our perception orders the world by delimiting and selecting, so that turning again to the sea after her song what is seen is what the singer chose to have seen. And in the splendid final lines that return us to Wordsworth's *Intimations* ode (although its more immediate source is doubtless Yeats's "Sailing to Byzantium") the exercise in epistemology suggests a core to being:

"THE SONGS THAT I SING"

The maker's rage to order words of the sea,
Words of the fragrant portals, dimly-starred,
And of ourselves and of our origins,
In ghostlier demarcations, keener sounds.[35]

The return to "origins," previously banished from a Modernist poetic determined to eradicate the "whence and whither" questions in the interest of neutralizing nature, is once again valid, but only after the most laborious of struggles and the most intricate of routes.

Stevens's development allows us once more to raise the question of Romanticism, which is most keenly relevant for this section. He has been the central figure in the post-Modernist revisionary thinking of the relationship between Romanticism and Modernism. In my previous chapter I intentionally gave a view of Romanticism that confirmed the counter-Romanticism of the Modernists. That was more or less a consensus view of Romanticism held in varying degrees by a large number of older Romantic scholars. This view of Romanticism has been challenged in the last ten years by another, perhaps more refined and intriguing, view (although not for that reason truer or more accurate), best represented by two writers, Harold Bloom and George Bornstein.[36] They spurn the view of Romanticism that would have it desiring a restored unity with Nature (Bloom even calls Romantic poetry "antinatural"). Its real aim, they hold, was to overcome nature by the power of mind, imagination (this view incidentally is not too new, since even older masters of Romanticism, say, the late Douglas Bush, followed Wordsworth's development beyond Nature to the growth of the "philosophic mind").

Rather than having Romanticism represent a displacement from a supernatural to a natural frame of reference, Bornstein would substitute the word "imaginative" for "natural." Romantic poetry is the poetry of mind in dialogue with itself. The Romantic poet turned not from society to nature but from society to the natural development within himself that results in his own liberated creativity. According to Harold

Bloom, this development is trifold, moving from an attack of the Promethean will on the external world, through a crisis of inner withdrawal and solipsism, to "the Real Man, Imagination." Romantic poetry dramatizes this development. Stressing the continuities of nineteenth- and twentieth-century poetry, Bornstein sees the poems' contents as being projections of psychic activities—the "speaker" may be a "principle of mind." It is in this sense—and Wallace Stevens is the prëeminent example—that the Modernists are carrying on Romantic tradition.[37]

Yet even this "best case" argument of Romantic continuity presents difficulties. One is hard put to identify any major Modernist work as being in any unironic sense an "act of the mind," where its forces represent a "principle of mind." Bornstein alludes to Prufrock and his lingering in the chambers of the sea, but of course that anti-hero is rejected as an ineffectual and outmoded figure of nineteenth-century derivation.[38] If Joyce, Lawrence, Eliot or Mann are any indication, the primary Modernist impetus is to "go on" and to "go out" to meet the forces of their worlds. Even the so-called "introverted" novel can only be understood as allowing this window onto a rich and complex external world. Modernism is marked by a philosophical neorealism, as evidenced by the relevancy of Whitehead for the "complex central consciousness." This applies to Proust as well, whose *Recherche* in its reflexiveness might be considered a poem of the act of the mind, did it not communicate so much about a society that Proust knew so well.

For his part, Bloom's monomyth refuses to allow to the Moderns what he does to the Romantics. His language is sweeping: Joyce and Stevens are "in later Romantic tradition." "Late Romantics as various as Eliot, Proust, and Shaw. . . ." Yeats, "the very last of the High Romantics."[39] Yet, Wordsworth showed an "uncanny originality, the most astonishing break with tradition in the language."[40] With this last judgment, a bit more modulated, I would agree. But I would also allow some of the same powers of originality, at least some historical innovation, to Eliot or Joyce. Bloom's work, as this evident one-sidedness confirms, is more happily programmatic than descriptive. But the call for a revival of Romanticism should not deny the existence of Modernism. Indeed, how could one possibly engineer such a creative realignment, if there had not been something in need of realignment, a counter-Romantic critical aberration that had intervened?

Moreover, what Bloom is willing to admit in regard to Freud and psychoanalysis he is unwilling to admit in regard to Freud's literary equivalents, the Moderns.[41] Against Romantic fusion and projectionism, as we saw, Freud invoked the famous "reality principle," a force of separation and of ego-maintenance that Conrad most effectively exemplified in the character of Marlow in *The Heart of Darkness*, who is weighted by the pathos of consciousness that so shadows Freud's work. Bloom's third phase of Imagination was intended to overcome the rational solipsism of the bruised and retreated interiority. And, indeed, one can see something of the same courageous overcoming of wary withdrawal in the second and third phases of Modernism. But if one admits the existence of a powerful Freudian argument that is counter-Romantic, is there not equally admissible an allied—and remarkably so—Modernist argument that is also counter-Romantic?

Even with Wallace Stevens, who most fully seems to embody the principles of Romantic continuity as described in the newer revisionist thinking, one can register serious objections to denying in him the imprint of the Modern. These objections derive from Modernism's particular development and from the principles of development itself. It should give some pause to notice that Wallace Stevens's development is remarkable in its similarity, both in kind and period, to that of other Modernists. Sometime before his poetry, his journals began showing new methods of perception, new needs in language, and sensibility.[42] *Harmonium*, the harvest of what was begun in the pre-War years, appeared in 1923, the full season of Modernism. The next efforts of fuller, more integrated imagination coincide with other Modernist works that show greater concern with myth and—as we have seen in the statements of T. S. Eliot and Virginia Woolf—images that have their coherence in the psyche, images that seem to impose themselves "undeniably."

In the process of development itself, it is inevitable that early phases should have their larger effect. One continues to take with him the road he has travelled, as subsequent phases bear the impression of the earlier ones. So that even if Wallace Stevens's last phase is similar, or analogous, to Romantic solutions, it still shows its origins in his Modernist development. The road taken has made all the difference—and that is what we mean by history. The Modernist point of departure, that was in various ways marked by severance with nineteenth-century poetics, philosophy and sensibility, continued to persist, recurring in later works. This is the crucial importance of establishing a point of departure. As a prior example we offered Eliot's *Four Quartets*, where even the remarkable moments of recollections of childhood are registered against a backdrop of alienation and discontinuity. The later phase cannot separate itself from what was intricate with the growth of its own sensibility. "Look now, here, now, always," cannot be a Romantic formulation (even less so the concluding lines to *Burnt Norton*, where the "waste, sad time" separating these moments of illumination is "ridiculous").

Wallace Stevens's later poems are no different. They have borne with them the road they have travelled and continue to show its effects. For instance, many earlier comments in and out of his poems are explicitly anti-Romantic, that is, Romantic meant as a specific form for another period of time. Even after his turn to a "new romanticism" Stevens continued to maintain this viewpoint.

> ... the imagination as metaphysics will survive logical positivism unscathed. At the same time, we feel, and with the sharpest possible intelligence, that it is not worthy to survive if it is to be identified with the romantic. The imagi-

nation is one of the great human powers. The romantic belittles it. The imagination is the liberty of the mind. The romantic is a failure to make use of that liberty. It is to the imagination what sentimentality is to feeling. It is a failure of the imagination precisely as sentimentality is a failure of feeling.[43]

Even if Wallace Stevens is speaking here of the debased later version of romantic character and feeling and not the so-called high Romantics, nevertheless the point is clear. Debasement is the inevitable consequence of the failure to evolve a new sensibility. Debasement itself is a cry for change. And nowhere perhaps does Stevens show his links with the other Moderns more than in his insistence on sheer historical change, and the need for the imagination to respond afresh to changed circumstances.

CHAPTER VI

Three Major Works

In the previous chapter we have seen how the argument of genetic development, one of the main avenues of approach in this study, has had distinct critical yield. This argument serves a similar usefulness when we approach one of the major historical problems of Modernism: namely, should discussions of Modernism terminate with those great years of the 1920s, or is indeed the full course of Modernism only realized when the enormous and intriguing works of the thirties are considered? To my mind, as I have already indicated, one of the few, yet major, defects of the excellent anthology of essays edited by Bradbury and McFarlane is precisely its editors' refusal to go beyond 1930. Using Nietzsche as our guide, can we not say that the urge toward the mythopoetic is implicit in the very beginnings of Modernism, it being the ultimate literary purpose toward which the disruption of the historical aspired, discernible, for Nietzsche, in the common genesis of both the unhistorical and the supra-historical? Such teleology is frowned upon, of course, even within the relatively narrow dimensions of a limited historical movement. However, the argument receives greater support from historical development, as well, particularly when we discover that the later works are of a piece with essential issues raised in earlier works. The initiating conditions of Modernism, present in the points of departure, persist in the later major statements, even though they are there more fully exploited and even though other concerns are introduced along with them.

In this sense the point of departure has proved to be a us-

THREE MAJOR WORKS

able idea both early and late. It served as a principle according to which the young Modernists took cognizance of their own emergence, thus bearing a different emphasis than the simple chronological and continuous idea of a beginning. Furthermore, it is repeated in later works when the Modernists wish to recapitulate essential stages, or critical features, of their own growth.

1. *Four Quartets*

Discovery of a shaping spirit in the self amounts to a pattern of vindication and is the basis of hopefulness in the Modernist writers. In Stephen's Aristotelian language this is the "entelechy," the basic form whose potential is being realized in time. It persists through multiplicity, and even multiple selves, and emerges to predominate and give legitimacy to the activities of the individual. Along with the context of ordinariness, and the remarkably consistent factor of involuntariness, the discovery of the self is the distinguishing feature of this new phase of Modernism, and in the major works of three of the Modernists with which we are now concerned, *Four Quartets*, *Joseph and His Brothers*, and *Finnegans Wake* this self is projected onto the larger screens of history and of myth. We have even come to speak of personal myths, or of myths of personal consciousness. Harry Levin has pointed out the paradox in this usage, "a paradoxical disparity between one person's powers of self-expression and an underlying framework of transmitted belief." But he also goes on to show that these diverse elements have converged in Modernism (a convergence that has made most fruitful recent discussions of autobiography and self-portraiture).[1] In *T. S. Eliot: The Design of His Poetry*, still, because of its framing argument, one of the more useful books on Eliot, Elizabeth Drew shows how congenial was Jungian thought to this kind of aesthetics. Discussing a passage where Jung describes the particular emotional intensity with which certain mythic situations can affect us, Miss Drew writes, "It is as if the individual were agent and interpreter of something which is as it were shaping *him*

193

and being shaped *by* him in a reciprocal action. . . . In such cases it is as if the individual were himself caught up in the world of myth, made living instead of legendary, and with the content of its conscious and unconscious material revealed gradually as a creative process." In such circumstances, "the individual has the power to collaborate consciously in the design."[2] Ever since Nietzsche this resolution would seem to be an important one for Modernists.

The motif of *Four Quartets* is that of the adventure-quest transformed into a spiritual adventure. The language and directions of the journey persist residually: "Go, go, go, said the bird. . . ." (*BN*, I)[3] "In that open field / If you do not come too close, if you do not come too close. . . ." (*EC*, I) "If you came this way. . . ." Hence the importance of place names as titles of the separate sections, Burnt Norton, East Coker, Little Gidding, and the rocks off the coast of Cape Ann in Massachusetts called The Dry Salvages. So, too, *Prufrock* begins with an invitation to a journey, "Let us go then you and I. . . ." but it is a journey that is unrealized, representing no change of a spiritual nature, its pathos residing in its temporal sameness. *Four Quartets*, like *The Waste Land*, superimposes the Christianized death-to-life vegetative myth upon the journey motif. As a consequence, despite the specificity of place and its broad geographic dispersion, the poem requires an inner journey. The "you" that is addressed is a general and indeterminate one, implying that while these places have meaning for Eliot other places would serve the same general pattern for his reader:

> If you came this way,
> Taking the route you would be likely to take
> From the place you would be likely to come from. . . .
>
> (*LG*, I)

What is critical is not space, then, but time. The spiritual quest is a temporal journey: into our first world "the last of earth left to discover / Is that which was the beginning." (*LG*, V) And the first step is the liberation from the dimensions of past and future, a specifically coupled phrase that recurs at least ten times in the poem. Dislocation of historical continuity is the elementary act that Prufrock was unable to perform, and it shows how close must be the connection between Eliot the Modernist poet and religious quester, as well as the connection between this later poem and the poet's earlier concerns.

As in *The Magic Mountain*, spiritual discovery is dependent upon temporal disjunction. The pilgrimage to Little Gidding occurs during a "midwinter spring." The blossom of snow upon the hedge is not in "the scheme of generation," and this springtime of the soul is not part of "time's covenant." In fact, given the preconditions of Modernism, any covenant between man and nature must be broken. What, in fact, is summer, "the unimaginable / Zero summer?" (*LG*, I) At its outset the poem confronts us with temporal interpenetration and simultaneity:

> Time present and time past
> Are both perhaps present in time future,
> And time future contained in time past.
> (*BN*, I)

If this is so, and all time is "eternally present," we must further confront the conclusion that "all time is unredeemable." Here Eliot is using the root phrase "redeem" in a strictly secular sense, the sense of one's taking account of his past life and wishing things had been done better or differently. But such playing with "what might have been" is a blind alley that produces no negotiable self. For Eliot genuine alteration can only commence by the identification of the self with its limited past, and with death itself.

> We die with the dying:
> See, they depart, and we go with them.
> We are born with the dead:
> See, they return, and bring us with them.
> (*LG*, V)

To recognize that "in my beginning is my end," means a circumscription of the possible, an establishment of limits and a kind of death that is the termination of the wild hopes encouraged by the prospects of linear time—it leads to the possibility that "in my end is my beginning."

In Modernism adventure has been internalized. The securities that each of the Modernists would break away from are the securities of the past-future continuum. Although the bird urges us to "go, go, go,"—to follow our lives back to the moments of greatest meaning—Eliot recognizes that "human kind / Cannot bear very much reality." (*BN*, I) What prevents this journey is adherence to the dimensions of past and future,

> ... the enchainment of past and future
> Woven in the weakness of the changing body
> Protects mankind from heaven and damnation
> Which flesh cannot endure.
>
> (*BN*, II)

This commitment to the dimensions of past and future is not, however, as comfortable as it would seem. "Enchainment" indicates what we have already seen in the experiences of Thomas Buddenbrook, Ursula Brangwen, Stephen Dedalus and Jacob Flanders—the linkages of history have taken on something of the prison house. Determinism seems to be the product of temporal linearity:

> ... the world moves
> In appetency, on its metalled ways
> Of time past and time future
> (*BN*, III)

The restrictiveness of the railroad track as well as the blind forward impulse of will and desire limit the movement of the soul and prevent the kind of perception that can only occur when one enjoys some distance from the currents of action. Another product is anxiety, that of

> anxious worried women
> Lying awake, calculating the future,

Trying to unweave, unwind, unravel
And piece together the past and the future,
Between midnight and dawn, when the past is all deception
The future futureless. . . .

(*DS*, I)

    Separation from the liabilities enjoined by past and future occurs by stages. The first and most noticeable action involves the experience of space—the emptiness of soullessness and non-meaning. As we have seen there are two varieties of this experience: the first, the experience of spatialization, the product of the triumph of time and what is meant by the paradox of time; the second, the more fruitful experience outlined in the fourth chapter that is the necessary background to growth beyond the historical and the linear—the "dread of space" that broke up the unison of man with nature and helped create the "tiered" understanding of experience. In the third movements of *Burnt Norton* and *East Coker*, the first dealing more with metaphysics and the second with personal history, these two kinds of experiences are explicitly contrasted. (*The Dry Salvages*, given its prospect of the sea, is almost totally concerned with the second kind of alienation.) Here the twilight world of the subway—the tunnel that leads to no light—is marked off from the true dark night of the soul. Through the underground move the time-ridden inhabitants of the time-kept city; their darkness is actually a product of their involvement with time past and time future, allowing neither fulfillment nor horror—those expressions of extremes so indicative of freedom and authenticity for Modernists—"neither plenitude nor vacancy."

    This darkness is the product of travel. In order to experience the darkness of God one must descend lower into the world of internal darkness, an experience requiring the adjournment of the individual will. "I said to my soul, be still, and let the dark come upon you / Which shall be the darkness of God." (*EC*, III) Hope would be hope for the wrong thing, love would be love of the wrong thing; one must wait, even, without thought. The Modernist suspicion of the will that tries to provoke a solution, that seeks emotion or sainthood coincides with Eliot's own religious motives. The language of travel infiltrates the process:

> In order to arrive at what you are not
> You must go through the way in which you are not.
> And what you do not know is the only thing you know
> And what you own is what you do not own
> And where you are is where you are not.
>
> (*EC*, III)

Only through dispossession—the spiritual "agony / Of death and birth"—can the moments of illumination that once occurred be recaptured.

As in Proust, so in *Burnt Norton*, this epiphanic manifestation is sudden, involuntary, timeless, overwhelmingly undeniable in its force, and modest in its circumstances. Such experiences form the basis of discontent with the ordinary world and provide patterns of recovery; that is, they indicate alternate models to the standardization of experience.

The later *Quartets* in tone and statement suggest the need to extend these moments, to incorporate them somehow into the larger dimensions of history. To such hints and guesses, Eliot adds—in clear expansion beyond *Burnt Norton*—"prayer, observance, discipline, thought and action." (*DS*, V) Yet, this commitment is quite consciously separated from the possibilities of the saint. By his utter and continuous death to himself the saint constantly lives at the intersection point of time and the timeless. He suffers a true death to life. "For most of us," Eliot repeats twice, so graced an existence is not possible.

> For most of us, there is only the unattended
> Moment, the moment in and out of time,
> The distraction fit. . . .
>
> (*DS*, V)

Yet Eliot's own journey stops short of that of the saint. In perhaps the most crucial phrases of the poem, he describes his own life purpose as involving a "temporal reversion," that is,

THREE MAJOR WORKS

a return to the dimension of time and of history where he will cultivate the "life of significant soil." Formerly, of course, the soil was the harbor of dung and death, but now it yields significance. His meaning of course is that he will follow his calling as a poet, a poet devoted to time and history but one who nevertheless benefits from a religious ground of experience. His vision of the rose—the symbol for significant soil—is never too far from the yew tree, which I gropingly take to represent the saint's sheer and abiding death to this world.

This clear statement of purpose, at the end of *The Dry Salvages*, the darkest of the *Quartets*, returns once again to human history—not to the familial past of *East Coker* but rather to Eliot's chosen past, that of the fashioners of his mind and of the seventeenth-century religious community of Little Gidding. This is a history with texture—much more intimately connected with his own spiritual being. Consequently there is something to Hugh Kenner's insight that the "Air-raid" section of *Little Gidding* is a dramatic version of "Tradition and the Individual Talent."[4] In an atmosphere both strange and rich, at an intersection point where consciousness and unconsciousness seem to merge, Eliot hears himself playing out the encounter between Dante and his mentor, Brunetto Latini, in *Inferno* XV—a canto that Eliot tells us he responded to even before understanding it. (*LG*, II) This sudden apparition on a city street ("où le spectre en plein jour raccroche le passant"—interestingly enough Eliot quotes these lines in the 1950 essay, "What Dante Means to Me," where he also discusses his use of Canto XV in *Little Gidding*) has an intimate connection with Eliot's own psyche. There is something mysterious and unaccountably not quite conscious, as with the boat in "Marina," in this emergence of a dead master whom the poet had "known, forgotten, half recalled / Both one and many." The boat and the dead master seem to be products of some shaping purpose in Eliot's own psyche, his own emergent sense of himself as a poet. The dead master is in fact a fluid crystallization, under the aegis of Dante, of all the men of letters ("a familiar compound ghost") whose work and utterances have become involved with Eliot's own. The apparition's message is ethical, as he outlines the gifts reserved for age (we recall Eliot's praise of the later Yeats, a figure not absent from this lineup) and the real consequences in time of what had formerly been thought to have been worthy. No wonder then that this presentation of man as a creature of change and error should have been derived from the *Inferno* and not from the greater interview with another poetic father, Cacciaguida, in the *Paradiso* (in the same essay mentioned above Eliot quite deliberately omits the *Paradiso* as a possible parallel with this section, instead he only mentions the *Inferno* and the *Purgatorio*).

Purgatorial to be sure is his reference to the "refining fire" that only can redeem the error-prone "exasperated spirit." That is, like most of us, and perhaps serving as a spokesman for the twentieth century, Eliot cannot proceed as far as Paradise. In effect saying what had already been said at the end of *East Coker*, he keeps his dimensions earth-bound and temporal but transformed by pattern and given meaning. The figure's final words of hope—"where you must move in measure, like a dancer"—are of a piece with the perception of pattern, that is, the means of deriving significance from time. Such meaning requires what could be called "just vision," representing a combination of love and consciousness, but which perception the individual cannot reach until his own motives are purified. Thus it is that the paradisal vision, which is a constant presence for the saint, of which in fact he is the living embodiment, can serve as a guide for the human involvement with history. What prevents this just vision is adherence to the dimensions of linear time and will, which it was the necessary first step of Modernism to disrupt.

This vision into pattern shares something with the work of art, where beginnings and endings seem to merge, and the end is seen in the beginning and the beginning in the end. Like a work of art, pattern renders purpose and coherence to things, and above all significance. This moment of vision further requires distance and detachment, stillness and silence. For Eliot it is only such vision that bestows meaning on time, that gives it significance. A passage from the seventh section of "Choruses from *The Rock*" suggests the same:

> A moment in time but time was made through
>   that moment:
> for without the meaning there is no time,
> and that moment of time gave the meaning.

In *The Waste Land* the need of the young man of "A Game of Chess" was to break through icy silence to compassionate speech; in *Four Quartets* the need is to achieve stillness and silence so that the Logos can be heard.

The particular historical focus of this vision is the period of the English Civil War, that period so critical, in Eliot's estimation, for the future directions of England, and one from which so many of the old animosities and political divisions continue to hold force. (*LG*, III) Oppositions are reconciled as Eliot regards the men involved in that historical action somewhat from the viewpoint of God. All had their roles to play, all were "touched by a common genius." In fact, the participants in the antagonism are, like all dualisms, mutually defining and complementary, as each side completes, whether it be Erasmus-Luther, Roundhead-Cavalier, the horizon of the other: they are "united in the strife which divided them." The rose of just vision now enfolds all the offending parties:

> These men, and those who opposed them
> And those whom they opposed
> Accept the constitution of silence
> And are folded in a single party.

The rose had been organic and it perished in elemental flux; it had been an historical flag, combative and partisan, and it too faded; now as a visible sign of just vision it seems to join the religious level of experience to the temporal, or historical, and in its way to redeem time.

> History may be servitude,
> History may be freedom. See, now they vanish,
> The faces and the places with the self which, as it could,
>   loved them,
> To become renewed, transfigured in another pattern.

Through the vision of the rose, redemption in history and time is brought about, but not through the means of historical values and temporal continuity—the essential problem for the Modernist. "A people without history / Is not redeemed from time, for history is a pattern / Of timeless moments." (*LG*, V)[5]

Undeniably Eliot is the poet of history, even of backward vision, and some would say that an essential ingredient to his charitable vision is that its objects are deceased and no longer threatening. Yet *Four Quartets* seems to summarize so much of the Modernist literary experience, to express its most basic motifs, particularly the need for spiritual adventure. "Old men should be explorers."

> We shall not cease from exploration
> And the end of all our exploring
> Will be to arrive where we started
> And know the place for the first time.

The meaning of the poem is not "deadness" or the past, but the necessary encounter at almost every moment with the existential newness of experience, and the conviction that the sentient human life is one of risk. While vision is directed at history, and the personal quest returns us to what was at the beginning, still in *Four Quartets* a sense of excitement has been returned to time. It is no longer worn smooth, muffled, or swaddled:

> And any action
> Is a step to the block, to the fire, down the sea's throat
> Or to an illegible stone: and that is where we start.
>   (*LG*, V)

The attitude that typifies *Four Quartets* can best be called one of "readiness"—the phrase so important for Job, which Petrarch adopted in his own time of troubles, and which Shakespeare then used to summarize the spiritual conquest of his own tragic hero.[6]

2. *Joseph and His Brothers*

The very subject matter of *Joseph and His Brothers* is the mythic thought-patterns of its protagonists. Their mental habits give to the present a transparency through which shine the prototypes of the past. Cosmological patterns support their sense of repetition and renewal. "Association of thought" controlled Jacob's entire inner life. "Wherever he went, his soul was played upon by chords and correspondences, diverted and led away into far-reaching considerations, which mingled past and to come in the present moment . . . it might almost be said that in Jacob's world intellectual value and significance . . . depended upon the copious flow of mythical association of ideas and their power to permeate the moment." (I.94/ I.67)[7] As a consequence, then, the well whose association with Joseph is so troubling is not just the well, it is a pit, the abyss, the underworld of death and destruction, in which the Adon is dismembered. To this way of thought time is terribly foreshortened.

Even the sullen brothers, who hardly possess the same skill at reading several levels of meaning into events, are restrained from outrightly killing Joseph by their consciousness that they would thus be fulfilling the Cain-Abel pattern (although Mann speculates that, at least in Reuben's case, other considerations were active). This same sense of imitation and succession is always present in Joseph's mind—he understands his own exile in Egypt as the equivalent of that which Jacob endured laboring for Laban. And Mann adds, in a passage that could be derived from any of his essays,

It is uncanny to see the mixture of free will and guidance in the phenomenon of imitation. In the end it is hard to tell whether it is the individual or the destiny that actually follows the pattern and insists upon the repetition. The inward and the outward play into each other, and materialize apparently without act of will into the event which was from all time bound up with and one with the individual. For we move in the footsteps of others, and all life is but the pouring of the present into the forms of the myth. (III.178/II.614)

This certainly supports the first Heraclitean epigraph from *Four Quartets*, and in its admission to partnership of the individual with the form, it suggests the second as well, "The way up and the way down are one and the same." As the young Pharaoh Amenhotep, very given to this kind of speculation, and thus finding some congeniality in Joseph, explains to his mother:

Our being is only the meeting-place between not-being and ever-being; our temporal only the medium of the eternal. And yet not only that. For we must ask ... whether the temporal, the individual, and the particular get more worth and value from the eternal, or the eternal more from the particular and temporal. (IV.122/III.1074)

Only through time is time conquered, but only through the enduring patterns does the temporal emerge and receive form.

In all of these double speculations, of course, Joseph plays a double role. He receives Eliezer's identification with the mythic journey of the house steward with a nod of forbearance and with a smile of indulgent scepticism, and of the two, Mann informs us, the smile was the truer revelation of attitude. An inner distance separates Joseph from identification with the myths of his tribe, just as temporal distance separates Mann the author and his readers. In fact Joseph's own playful skill and good humor at weaving these tales is the counterpart of Mann's own attitude. In a letter of 1935 to his French translator, Louise Servicien, Mann explains that Joseph is "an *ar-*

tistic personality living in a religious sphere."[8] But in addition to his smiling artful consciousness, this dreamer and reader of dreams is also a great and successful public man. And it is this aspect that casts some shadow over an otherwise brilliant and engaging personality. Joseph is a "user." He was "less spiritual and more shrewdly calculating" than Jacob—although that double master of pulling the wool over others' eyes was hardly in a position to object strenuously. Nevertheless Joseph still believed in the role of higher associations and meanings in the patterns of life—"he seriously held that a life and activity without the hallmark of higher reality, which does not base itself upon the traditionally sacred and support itself thereupon, nor is able to mirror itself in anything heavenly and recognize itself therein, is no life or activity at all. He was convinced that nothing in the lower world would know how to happen or be thought of, without its starry prototype and counterpart; and the great certainty guiding his life was belief in the unity of the dual, in the fact of the revolving sphere, the exchangeability of above and below, one turning into the other and gods becoming men and men gods." All of this in its context was as it should be. "What was after all not quite as it should be, but seemed more like a degenerate deviation from the significant and admirable type, was Joseph's inclination to draw advantage from the general prepossession in his favour and consciously to impose himself upon those about him" (II.218/ I.434-435)

What Joseph had done quite consciously was to derive from his background two religious concepts and secularize them for his own purposes. The first would be the idea of the promise, the pact and covenant between God and Abraham's people that, in the midst of exile, lent great confidence and hope for the future. The other could be called the quest for the Highest. Abraham's conception of Godhead could only be one suitable to his own dignified idea of his worth; as a consequence, the worship of images, elements or the planets can only be scorned by one devoted to the Highest above all. In Joseph's personal rise the religious pursuit of the All Highest became an ascent toward the Pharaoh himself. All the rest, the Ishmaelite trader, Mont-Kaw, Potiphar and Potiphar's wife, and Mai-Sachme were only means toward that end. The beauty of the book and its implied criticism of Joseph's self-confidence and high hopes is the way he uses and regards many of these admirable people only as stepping stones. This is the rebuke implicit in Joseph's double-dealings.

Mann even works out a defense of Potiphar's wife, that frustrated Lady Chatterley of the novelistic third volume. There are many reasons for Joseph's chastity and they are good ones: his unwillingness to bare himself, to forget himself, his backgrounds and his future. Like an Aeneas in relation to Dido he could not allow her to possess his future. But this does not then condone the double game he plays with her—that by being in her presence and speaking of household matters he is really educating her. Behind it all is the satisfaction of male dominance—that he, the sunken one, the swaddled Osiris, will break through the bindings with his male sex. Joseph not even quite unconsciously complies with her subservience, so that when he returns to the empty house (except for her) early from the public festival, justifying his behavior on proverbial grounds of good husbandry, he is really provoking the last and desperate struggle. And in it, although consciously holding himself aloof, like Osiris, his flesh responds, and Meni, like the vulture women, tears at his garments because of his erection. This remarkable reading of the great story shows Joseph's virginity to be of the professional sort, and the embarrassments of motive to be of the kind that normally, if furtively, attend the arduous climb of any great man.

Mann expresses these doubts about Joseph in a letter to Harry Slochower. Indeed, there is a good deal of Mann in Joseph—but this does not exclude "a good deal of skeptical criticism of the 'Great Man,' who is represented at once as a miracle and as a 'public misfortune'. . . . After all, what we have here, is a German Great Man—and they are the most questionable." Mann then goes on to the most telling issue, and one that in its terrifying self-candor, gives a glimpse into one of the highest points of aesthetic realization that his book affords: astonishingly enough, and in its subtle, uninsistent classical manner, the criticism of Joseph is self-criticism. The portrayal of Joseph's questionable character is the point at which Mann identifies with his hero and shows the solidarity of creation and author, of self and the myth. In this same letter he continues, "The criticism is partly from within the affinity, and thus becomes a kind of intensified self-criticism."[9] On one level Joseph's double nature is equivalent to artistic schizophrenia, whereby a writer may be involved with people, to be sure, while always being aware of their usefulness to his own higher purposes. The Joseph legend fits this realization. But there is another affinity as well. During the writing of the last two volumes of his tetralogy, from 1933 on, Mann was himself an exile, making use of the friendship and opportunities offered by his host countries, and, in the case of his American residence, relying on people from whom he felt distant (perhaps even secretly scorning them), a German Great Man, most of whose private thoughts were devoted to the restoration of himself and his true country of Europe. Such connections and frank revelations are told in his Joseph story. And it is unquestionably these personal identifications that give substance to the historical Joseph.

These shadows that flicker over Joseph's career and suggest the ambiguous dimensions of his personality and role do by no means eclipse him. In fact, just the opposite. They support Mann's choice of this multivalent character to bear the rich associations with which he invests his book. As a figure of universal validity, Joseph so lends himself to various identifications that he best serves Mann's purpose of writing an "abbreviated history of mankind," a book of world history.[10] The Joseph theme, through the many facets of its nuclear story, allows for constant reactualization. What Mann was able to do through his own identification with the Joseph character, he would be able to do with other historical figures and moments as well—that is, realize the myth, reveal the enduring patterns of human experience and emotions that make for heightened recognition.

It is only right then that from within the book Joseph, the author's and reader's surrogate, should show us the way to this aesthetic use of myth. Beset by Potiphar's wife, the lovesick Mut-em-enet, he recognizes that they are in effect "realizing" the story of Gilgamesh and Ishtar, and that when he rejected the present of a special feast-day garment from her, he had unconsciously replied in the words that Gilgamesh had used against Ishtar's similar offer. Disturbed on one hand, Joseph is also reassured by this recognition, by the consciousness that their reality is resting upon the solid ground of myth. He came to understand why it was that Gilgamesh had said what he said, just as he came to understand the dimension of his own position in the former story: "for in him I see myself, as through myself I understand him." (III.509/II.845) As we have seen earlier, myth is like history in being a two-way street; in enduring and appealing patterns it shows the present in the past and the past in the present. It historicizes the eternal and brings permanence as well as texture to history and immediate events. And this transaction seems to be the essential one of the literary imagination.

Joseph as a figure, of course, is a link between the Tammuz-Adonai-Osiris story and that of Christ. From the beginning, with the episode of Joseph and Benjamin in the sacred grove of Adonis, to the end, when in *Joseph the Provider* young Sarah unconsciously sings the great songs of resurrection, the form of the Christian story is clearly visible in the precedent ones. But Joseph's story is also one of secular success, and Mann reminds us how truly congenial were Jerusalem, Athens and Rome. When Joseph rejects Potiphar's wife he does so for reasons of future promise, and a kind of individual integrity and male authority that brings to mind other versions where the discipline and purpose of the West are contrasted with the supposed laxness of the East: stories such as those of Aeneas and Dido, or Antony and Cleopatra. But their actual exchange makes even more explicit how much Joseph is speaking as a

Westerner, one with whom Modernists might have a particular affinity.

Since the presence of Potiphar is an obstacle to their love, she suggests that he might be done away with. Joseph is horrified by the suggestion, declaring that to consent to such an action would be like killing his father and sleeping with his mother. This draws out the matriarchal fury of Mut-em-enet, and she calls Joseph a fool: does he not realize that "with his mother each man sleeps—the woman is the mother of the world. . . ." Joseph's response is that of an archetypal Westerner, and, of course, the descendant of Abraham. He cannot be master by way of the mistress. "The Father of the world is no mother's son, nor is he the Lord by a lady's grace." (III.554-555/II.877) Many Modernists, as we have seen, would strive to make the same assertion, to rescue their own purpose and virility from mother dominance. In Joseph's case he is also following Abraham's principle of service only to the Highest, but this conception of the Highest is dependent upon the realization of human dignity. The precondition for Abraham's discovery of God was the claim of the human ego to central importance. In this connection, then, the rejection of the dominance of the mother principle (which is, in effect, what Mut-em-enet's "incestuous" suggestions amount to), manifestly joins in Mann's historical imagination the growth of Joseph with Odysseus and Telemachus, with Orestes and even, finally, in the horrors of the incest theme, with Oedipus. Mann is the Modernist master of such syncretism, where a single episode can come to epitomize so much.

The reverberations of the Joseph theme extend to modern times as well. Joseph is the prototype of an innocent come to an older land, to a country whose ways are more complicated, more sophisticated, and yet, not surprisingly, static, even enervating. Joseph, while a newcomer and simple (although not naïve), is somehow in his thinking more advanced. His devotion to Abraham's God, his concept of the Highest, has not, as the Pharoah's mother recognizes, debilitated him. The forms of the past, so preponderant in the older Egyptian manner, have not strangled his capacity in the present. Culturally, of course, the land of Egypt is the equivalent of the nineteenth century—"the prevailing atmosphere . . . was *fin-de-siècle*." (III.196/II.627)[11] And the confrontation is similar to the one into which the Modernists were cast, and in which they conceived themselves, as Mann did Joseph, as playing a revitalizing role, in religious as well as physical terms. Joseph in Egypt is somewhat like Stephen in the library, bringing living imagination to "timeless essences." And throughout their works Modernists have suggested the power of human sexuality. Nietzsche's assertion that in modern times all values shall be brought before the bar of Dionysus is pitifully realized in the damage done to Potiphar by his parents, who wanted to make him more easily a son of the light, of which action Mut-em-enet is the exonerated victim. Against such impotence and the general paralysis of culture the Modernists, in their earlier works, were compelled to contend. As a type Joseph was well fitted to represent this war on two fronts, which helps explain the special delight Mann derived from Jacob's blessings on his favorite son. The heavens above and "the deep that lieth under" join to enhance this at once spiritual and worldly man.

The associations around Joseph are brought up to date when racial overtones infect Mut-em-enet's raging and disordered accusations. She gives vent to elements of a mass psychosis that the malicious dwarf, Dudu, strutting and puffed up with cockiness, would only too willingly exploit, as did his counterpart in the thirties. The offended Mut becomes the raped Germany, to whose aid all true-born males are called. In this far distant story another version of social resentment and revenge is played out, as the aliens, who for too long played the master in the house, finally receive their punishment. Joseph, the representative now of his race, receives for the first time (to be repeated thereafter) the charges of untold sexual crimes and social élitism that Dudu can now triumphantly unfurl.

But Joseph's thematic possibilities are so multifaceted that he can also serve as his own champion, showing forth in many of his qualities characteristics that Thomas Mann admired in

President Franklin Roosevelt (as well as in his vice-president, the master of hybrid corn production, Henry Wallace). Particularly, what he finds identical in Joseph and President Roosevelt is a kind of enlightened shrewdness in dealing with drastic social crises. Joseph's double-dealing is part of his aristocratic temperament. He combined liberality and exploitation, "crown politics and a concern for the little man." (IV.369/III.1316) "Joseph's economic system, in short, was an astonishing mixture of socialization and freehold occupancy by the individual—a mixture which the children of Egypt thought of as 'magic,' a manifestation of a divinity benign and cunning at once." (IV.374/III.1321)[12] In more modern terms, Joseph's economic policy smacks very much of the planned economy of the welfare-capitalism introduced by the New Deal.

While not denying certain dictatorial features (which, however, he exculpates as probably necessary given the times), in an admiring and sympathetic way Mann felt drawn to the personality of Franklin Delano Roosevelt. In 1941 following a breakfast and later cocktails with the president, Mann wrote that "He once again made a strong impression upon me, or, shall I say, aroused my sympathetic interest: this mixture of craft, good nature, self-indulgence, desire to please and sincere good faith is hard to characterize. But there is something like a blessing upon him. . . ."[13] In a more public piece, written after Roosevelt's death in April, 1945, Mann is even more laudatory in his comparisons: Roosevelt had the aristocratic "life-worthiness" of Caesar and still was a friend of the "small man." Resorting to an association that was dear to him, Mann sees in Roosevelt a "Hermes-nature" one which engaged by virtue of "nimble and cheerfully artful mediation" in effecting the art of the possible, who made concessions to fact in order to realize his ideals. Devoid of interest in intellectual or aesthetic matters, he was, like Caesar, a great man, himself a product of "perfectly aesthetic magic." ("war aber selbst eine Erscheinung von vollkommen ästhetischem Zauber.")[14] Throughout his correspondence with the great mythographer Karl Kerenyi, Mann's interest in Hermes as the type of Joseph is decidedly present. This supple, airy nature, so playful and resourceful, and yet in its magic so difficult to pin down is the mediating figure for the artist as well as the great public leader. And Mann often signed his letters to his children with a Z, meaning *der Zauberer*, or magician.

3. Finnegans Wake

Like *Joseph and His Brothers*, *Finnegans Wake* is a comic epic aspiring to total vision; it is an abbreviated world-history told through the accretion of identities that gather like rings of a tree around character and event. This tendency in Joyce was present in *Ulysses*, where, behind the rappprochement of *Geist* and *Natur*, of Stephen and Bloom, is implied the vision of the All-father, while the final, if indiscriminate, "yes" of Molly seems to provide the sustaining movement to life required of the All-mother. These are intimations of the *Wake*, where the vision of totality is spread over the vast and dim subcontinent of sleep—into which Molly is lapsing—and where the great father lies dreaming, hearing incoherent voicings and aware of the lives that are taking shape around him, while the All-mother, Anna Livia Plurabelle, is the fluid element that holds the entire story together. No Modernist work goes farther into this land of psychic richness nor expresses more fully the strange wonders there to be found. And yet the *Wake* does not stop there—its meaning, like that of dreams, casts light on the land of the living. It was called by Joyce his great myth of the everyday.

Joyce takes his cue from the confused language of sleep, those gestures of sound that are not without significance and strong, if obscure, intent. His method is not actually to imitate these mutterings, but to simulate them and fill them with meanings that can be approximated by the conscious reader. As was the case with *Ulysses*, Joyce's focus is consistently biplanar but here the words themselves carry extra meanings, and are, in the language of the *Wake*, "Doublings"—a characteristic word that suggests the double meanings in expressions as well as the Dublin origin of the experiences. *Finnegans Wake* is in effect a Dublin story that spreads by the language and fiction of dreams out through the cosmos and human history, "the first literary instance of myth utilization on a universal scale."[15]

Finnegans Wake most grandly fulfills the Modernist goal of bringing together the spectre and the passer-by. In the last section of the *Wake*, where the night world is waning and giving place to day and the stage is being set for the recommencement of the entire process we have just followed, Joyce seems to be saying farewell to these possibilities of juxtaposition:

> It was allso agreeable in our sinegear clutchless, touring the no placelike no timelike absolent, mixing up pettyvaughan populose with the magnumoore genstries, lloydhaired mersscenary blookers with boydskinned pigttetails and goochlipped gwendolenes with duffyeyed dolores; like so many unprobables in their poor suit of the improssable. (609)[16]

His pleasing method had been one of mixing up the petty populace with the great gentry, touring the absent-absolute that is like no place nor time in a car that needs neither gear nor clutch—since there are no teeth in time. But of course Joyce's method does not only include such agreeable juxtapositions, it also implies identifications, where in the midst of a boozing feast in a tavern, we participate in the dismemberment of the hero. For Joyce such mythic collocations are daily fare, and with particular justification in this case, as the clandestine opposition between drinkers and tavern owner is a facet of mass *ressentiment* against the hero, and, as in the case of Parnell, mass enjoyment of his fall. Proust's "eternal pantomime," Woolf's "eternal processions"—the whole Modernist preoccupation with avatars and atavisms amid our daily living and city streets finds in the *Wake* its fullest statement. We might begin to forget it, but that is no matter, Joyce tells us in Part IV, the past has its pull: "It will remember itself from every sides, with all gestures, in each our word." (614) Inadvertence is the very point of such recurrence. That it will happen willy-nilly, and is important precisely because we do not consciously make it happen, is the crucial recognition in this third phase of Modernism.

Quotations from Eliot and Mann have repeatedly made this point. So, too, *Finnegans Wake* is teeming with the pressures and presences that unwittingly we express: "The Vico road goes round and round to meet where terms begin." Yet we, in our individual lives, "still onappealed to by the cycles and unappalled by the recoursers we feel all serene, never you fret, as regards our dutyful cask." (452) But even the Modernist quest for such simultaneity and identity does not leave us prepared for the remarkable and multiple superimpositions of the *Wake*, and the accumulations of layer upon layer of presences that fit the essential patterns of life. Tim Finnegan, from the Irish ballad, is joined with Finn MacCool, a legendary warrior, and they with Humpty Dumpty and their modern reincarnation H. C. Earwicker, Here Comes Everybody, Haveth Childers Everywhere, and with all heroes from ancient times to modern history, Swift and Parnell, who have fallen.

The theory to support his imagination Joyce of course found in Giambattista Vico's *New Science*. Vico had great faith in poetic imagination and its ability to present "imaginative universals"—what we would call "types"—whereby human customs may be apprehended in terms of characters made famous by luminous examples. But this poetic faith is dependent upon an intellectual faith in comparisons, particularly between the ancient and the modern times. When he traces the history of the Greeks and the Romans Vico is not so much concerned with "particular history" but "by virtue of the identity of the intelligible *substance* in the diversity of their modes of development [with] the ideal history of the eternal laws which are instanced by the deeds of all nations in their rise, progress, maturity, decadence and dissolution. . . ."[17] This poetic and intellectual belief is at the heart of *Finnegans Wake* (even when it is skeptically mocked):

Our wholemole millwheeling vicociclometer a tetradomational gazebocroticon ... autokinatonetically preprovided with a clappercoupling smeltingworks exprogressive process, (for the farmer, his son, and their homely codes, known as eggburst, eggblend, eggburial and hatch-as-hatch can) receives through a portal vein the dialytically separated elements of precedent decomposition for the verypetpurpose of subsequent recombination so that the heroticisms, catastrophes and eccentricities transmitted by the ancient legacy of the past, type by tope, letter from litter, word at ward, with sendence of sundance ... all, anastomosically assimilated and preteridentified paraidiotically, in fact, the sameold gamebold adomic structure of our Finnius the old One, as highly charged with electrons as hophazards can effective it, may be there for you. . . . (614-615)

Through the four Viconian stages of human history (the vicociclometer, a tetradomational gazebocroticon)—theocratic, aristocratic, democratic, and chaotic, back again for another cycle—the human material, almost seminally, carries on the same atomic (Adamic) structure of Old Finn the hero, and as a consequence we go through the same processes dictated by the heroeroticisms of the past. Joyce's theme of time is the return of habit: "Themes have thimes and habit reburns." (614) "The sehm asnuh" (620)—the same anew, the same as you. "Teems of times and happy returns. The seim anew. Ordovico or viricordo." (215) Such is the order of Vico.

The pattern of communication is complicated, since each generation has something that the preceding did not have, and that is the presence of that former generation itself. This implies not only sameness but sameness in different circumstances, and this is how history becomes a process of change:

> So that when we shall have acquired unification we shall pass on to diversity and when we shall have passed on to diversity we shall have acquired the instinct to combat and when we shall have acquired the instinct of combat we shall pass back to the spirit of appeasement? (610)

For our purposes we shall only concentrate on the break-up of unity, the emergence of the combative instinct, since it is when brothers divide that human history begins, and because onto the ancient theme of Cain-Abel, Esau-Jacob, Romulus-Remus, and through its many other variations in the *Wake*, Joyce adds the modern temporal problem of spatialization; that is, the basis of divisions between the Shems and the Shauns confirms—with good cause, as we shall see—the notion of the paradox of time set out in the second chapter of this study.

The essential Shem-Shaun duality is the kind of universal theme that held great appeal for Joyce. Further point to this brother-strife was occasioned by Joyce's on-going quarrel with Wyndham Lewis, who had attacked him in *The Art of Being Ruled* and in *Time and Western Man* (the running account of which is told by Geoffrey Wagner in his *Wyndham Lewis: A Portrait of the Artist as the Enemy*).[18] This literary dualism is based upon a fundamental duality, that of time as against space. For Lewis, from the birth of Bergson to the middle twenties, "one vast orthodoxy has been in the process of maturing in the world of science and philosophy."[19] This orthodoxy represents the triumph of the "time-mind" whose chief representatives have been Bergson, Einstein, Whitehead and Alexander. For Lewis, all of their combined efforts—and he does seem to treat them in concert—tend to reduce the reality and validity of the external world. Whether we are dealing with duration or general theories of relativity, their common purpose is to subjectivize experience and to damage that kind of common sense that Lewis feels prevailed among the Greeks and the medieval schoolmen (a surprising conjunction). Since Bergson and Whitehead felt that time had become spatialized, Lewis uses space—representing solid, incontrovertible objective reality—to counter this new "time-mind." Lewis is professedly more concerned with the consequences of this time-philosophy. As such he undertakes an "Analysis of the Mind of James Joyce," in which he finds the torrent of matter presented in *Ulysses* to be really part of "einsteinian flux" and correspondent to an internalization of experience, to defining all experience as mental and psychological rather than physical.[20]

Time and Western Man is unquestionably an extremely valuable book. Perverse in its accusation, unsubstantiated in its opinion, it is nevertheless a case of an adversary who accurately describes, with abundant quotation, what in fact has occurred. As a casebook it is a mine of information and even, finally, proof of that which its instinctive purpose was to combat, the predominance in the twentieth century of a new time-philosophy. As a consequence, then, Joyce in responding to Lewis in *Finnegans Wake*, can truly represent what we had called the paradox of time, the fact that what had formerly comprised the attitudes of time had in the course of their development become spatialized.

Throughout the character contrasts in the *Wake*, the antagonist of the Joyce- and Shem-like figure is associated with space. In fact the hostile portrait of Shem in the seventh section of Book One is provided from the perspective of a "spatialist," who, while allowing that some might find respectability in his background, is convinced that "every honest to goodness man in the land of space knows that his back life will not stand being written about in black and white." (169) So, too, the tale of the Mookse and the Gripes is narrated by a Professor Jones, himself a space adherent (and unfortunately kin to the scholars anathematized by Nietzsche, Virginia Woolf and Yeats, those for whom history and time had become static). His professional antagonist is a Professor Loewy-Brueller, or Levi-Brullo (Levy-Bruhl, the student of the primitive mind whose work was favorably cited by Eliot in connection with the close association between the primitive experience and the making of poetry), who is dismissed for placing emphasis on "when" questions—that is, matters of time and history. (151) Professor Jones alludes to the work of a fellow Welshman, Professor Llewellys ap Bryllars (Wyndham Lewis) who argues against such Romantic posh as being mere subjectivism implicit in time. "Since his man's *when* is no otherman's *quandour*": this would mean that time experience is no valid guide to reality, but space is: "the all is *where* in love as war...." (151) Such comical-satirical presentation of course has a Rabelaisian way of mocking the quarreling while at the same time suggesting a truth.

The Professor then tells his version of the Fox and the Grapes, where the aggrandizing Roman expansion is associated with space and the more passive, Celtic, even Eastern Christianity of the Irish Church is associated with time. Such associations can cause confusion, and these confusions come from the changes brought about in the conception of time. The Shem-line is a time-line, but not that of the West since the Renaissance, or even that associated with Roman imperialism. The space-line of Shaun is more typical in its attitudes of the argument of time, with its ingredients of will, ego, and with its sense of hard struggle and the need to make provisions. As a consequence the Ant, in the tale of the Ondt and the Gracehoper, is more representative of the need for careful provision and foresight associated with the older conception of time—a time that now has become spatialized—while the Gracehoper, as his epiphanic name would imply, is representative of the newer attitude toward time found in the Modernist writers. The Gracehoper does not husband time, rather he is prodigal, as Shem had been: "Where is that little alimony nestegg against our predictable rainy day?" (192) the narrator of the Shem section (as "Justice") asks. His attitude toward time is not then one of daily care and accumulation, the expression of will and ego, but rather he "was always jigging ajog, hoppy on akkant of his joyicity," where Joyce acknowledges the Kantian background to this "subjectivism." (414) Following his own impulses of delight, his own subjectivity, has landed him in "chronic despair," he has prodigiously wasted time:

> He had eaten all the whilepaper, swallowed up the lustres, devoured forty flights of styearcases, chewed up all the mensas and seccles, ronged the records, made mundballs of the

ephemerids and vorasioused most glutinously with the very timeplace in the ternitary.... (416)

Joyce is about his creative habit of converting painful accusations into the matter of art. At this time foe and even former friends and admirers were convinced that *Finnegans Wake*, then appearing as *work in progress*, was a disastrous miscalculation, a waste of time. Joyce had, as he expressed it, "tossed himself in the vico." The hostile reporter of Shem's activities (summarizing Joyce's life) is mockingly incredulous of the stunts of this "Esuan Menschavik,"—dispossessed and disinherited parts of an antinomy who had no sense of real power—this "alshemist" who

> wrote over every square inch of the only foolscap available, his own body, till by its corrosive sublimation one continuous present tense integument slowly unfolded all marryvoising moodmoulded cyclewheeling history (thereby, he said, reflecting from his own individual person life unlivable, trans-accidentated through the slow fires of consciousness into a dividual chaos, perilous, potent, common to allflesh, human only, mortal).... (185-186)

Fallen into the vico, and given his sense of time and history, the work Joyce is writing is not *Finnegans Wake*, in Shaun's spatialized telling, but rather *Ho, Time Timeagen, Wake!* (415)

In contrast, the Shaun-half as represented in the Ondt, "was a weltall fellow, raumybult and abelboobied.... He was sair sair sullemn and chairmanlooking when he was not making spaces in his psyche, but, laus! when he wore making spaces on his ikey, he ware mouche mothst secred and muravyingly wisechairmanlooking." (416) Physically able and even charming ("chairmanlooking"), when he was not intent on space, he becomes administrative and chairman-looking when space takes over his ego. In short, there is something very conformist in Shaun, as in the Ant. Hence it is that he is an ablebooby. Since Romanticism, and particularly Byron's *Cain*, the Cain-Abel theme underwent tremendous transformations, one of which made Abel, formerly the representative of Christ—the figure of the sacrificial hero—now merely an upholder of the normal rounds of experience and domesticity, and Cain the metaphysical quester sacrificed in his search of truth. This aspect of the duality then fits into the Modernist scheme, where the Shem-Cain figure finds only boredom and stultification in the standardization of experience represented by the "able" chairman. This is why Joyce, relying on the god of drunkards, Saint Martin, can ask the Ondt, from the vantage point of joy, why he cannot beat time. His devotion to space leads only to repetition and so banal has his experience become that Shaun's successor is notoriously Yawn.

But our purpose, even with this clear evidence of Joyce's understanding of how the argument of time had become spatialized, does not end here. As we have suggested, the Modernist vision was concerned with turning opposites, dualisms, into complementarities.[21] The meaning for time of this new concern with dualism is clear. Joyce explains it in this same Ondt and Gracehoper episode of *Finnegans Wake*. His theme is "time and time again."

> For if sciencium (what's what) can mute uns nought, 'a thought, abought the Great Sommboddy within the Omniboss, perhops an artsaccord (hoot's hoot) might sing ums tumtim abutt the Little Newbuddies that ring his panch . . . for O'Cronione lags acrumbling in his sands but his sunsunsuns still tumble on. (415)

The very basis of dualism resides in the Modernist skepticism of ever finding the "master negative" of experience, or of reaching an absolute perspective suitable to an observer-elect. If Chronos (O'Cronione, or Father Time) is dead then there is no absolute perspective other than that made up compositely of his many fragmentary sons. If we cannot know the great Somebody, the Omni-Boss, then Chronos is tumbled, Humpty-Dumpty is fallen, and the scattered pieces are in fact the egg. Thus it is in Gracehoper's contribution to the quarrel that the dualism becomes a mutually defining relationship.

Relying on the encounters of the prodigals and the avaricious in Dante's *Inferno* VII, the wasteful Gracehoper reminds the thrifty Ondt that "the prize of your save is the price of my spend." He can only gain what the other loses. Such complementarism is the continuing theme of the tale: "We are Wastenot with Want, precondamned, two and true...." Even space and time cannot be separated: "An extense must impull, an elapse must elopes...." (418-419) The opposites are really twins, the Dioscuri, Castor and Pollux, and together they establish the horizons, the full dimensions of an area.

CHAPTER VII

The Bite of Time

1. *The Coming of Day*

Wyndham Lewis's *Time and Western Man*, while a useful compendium of quotation and descriptively accurate as to the prevalence of a new conception of time in early twentieth-century thought and literature, hardly does justice to that theme's full development and importance in Modernism. Joyce's own reaction to his inclusion in that gallery of malefactors is instructive: grant Lewis all his points, does it cover more than ten per cent of Joyce's material? Like many hardheaded, nononsense critics, Lewis had the habit of substituting simple statement for a reasoned explanation of his evaluations. For instance, it is not enough to condemn the time-mind for producing a "phalanstery of selves" if one does not go on to show how this is in reality pernicious.[1] In the Modernist works with which we dealt it was shown how the complex central consciousness actually was quite open to the multiple richness of the external world, more so than its foil, the character of determined will and ego, who seemed to reduce all things to a uniform status. Moreover, we saw how this "protean" personality contained a strong fibre of selfhood, by virtue of which he was able to assert his independence from that same oneness, restrain his will, and keep his own counsel. And in their development, Modernists rendered moot Lewis's criticism by themselves showing a need to transcend simple pluralism. They too feared that susceptibility to the many facets of experience might result in a barren cosmopolitanism, that one might become a "mélange adultère de tout."[2] As a consequence they

THE BITE OF TIME

cherished and found sustenance in those moments of revelation when identity seemed to be assured, or those recognitions which seemed to legitimize the self in relation to mythic and historical patterns. And in this, their fourth stage, where they seem to gain renewed cognizance of the full brunt of external time and history—beyond mere subjectivity—they show how much fuller their conception of things was than Lewis's criticism allowed.

In commencing this chapter that deals with the return of the sense of historical reality, one should consider whether the Modernists—despite their initial repulsion from the values of historical continuity, their concern with the complexity of the mind's conscious (and unconscious) reflections, and their attempts to establish supra-historical connections and identifications—ever did deny, or ever could have denied, the unavoidable reality of immediate experience that has been the stamp of consciousness in the West. Even Dante, in his *Paradiso*, was obliged to reflect that Henry of Luxembourg, Italy's last hope and great deliverer, had indeed failed in his objective, had come before Italy was ready for his mission. And in *King Lear*, Edmund does not send in time the lifesaving reprieve for Cordelia. In its passive reflectiveness the Modernist consciousness was indeed myriad-minded, and its impressions are, as Virginia Woolf declared, "trivial, fantastic and evanescent"; but she also provides a clue to this fourth phase when she adds that some impressions are "engraved with the sharpness of steel."[3] In the complex shadings of Kafka's world, where the most terrible of imaginings are realized, one is at a loss to understand whether what is supposed to have happened really happens. Against Fraulein Bürstner's complaint to Joseph K. that he is never serious, he must concur, only to add, "But I was arrested in earnest."[4]

This renewed recognition of historical reality had much to do with the new economic and political situations of the thirties (even Joyce felt the effect of the Depression, and the market's plunge figures in the *Wake*). Yet such recognition had been long before part of the basic Modernist make-up. In the second phase, we have seen how Modernists rejected subjective idealism and affirmed the coordinate realities of the external world and the separate self. And if, for reasons related to the paradox of time, Modernists needed to break through the chain of historical value, that very rupture may have forced them all the more intently into the present. Even in their most mythical works, covered in the previous chapter, the center of reference is still the self in the present: "History is now and England." (*LG*, V) This hold of the historically given may even have saved Eliot from ill-fated misadventures into reliving or redoing the past. Most particularly in *Four Quartets*, given its astringent spiritual humility and historical sense, one could not "summon the spectre of a Rose. . . . Or follow an antique drum." (*LG*, III) By a similar acquiescence to the realities of history and of his own time (although with somewhat different emotional effect), T. E. Hulme denied that his preachments involved a return to a past classicism (and certainly not Byzantium); such an indulgence could only have resulted in sterility.[5]

Just as throughout this study we have been aware of interpenetrations and continuities (and they turn out to be quite significant since they indicate a constant concern, an essential nucleus to Modernist development), so, too, we have called special attention to the new levels of interest. A renewed awareness of time and history is a discernible stratum of Modernist development. This renewed awareness seems to have distinct placement, coming after the most intense experiences, after those moments of supra-historical simultaneity and personal coherence. Just as the discovery of the mythic was a relatively late event in Modernist development, so, too, does this rediscovery of time and history come as a late event. This is a fact of some importance. Such reassertions of what could be called a more common-sensical approach to time and history occur either late in a major text or late in a career; never are they present in early works nor do they occur early in a major work (that is, one occurring at the height of an author's powers, or one extending over a large part of his career). This

THE BITE OF TIME

shows that a primary and early task of Modernism was to upset orthodox assessments of time; but it also shows that these reevaluations were temporary and to be understood as part of a larger picture of events and human attitudes. For such reasons as this we suggest that Modernism must be understood in the full patterns of its development.

To do so means that we are not obliged to separate the Modernists from the new literature of social seriousness and political and economic consciousness that emerged in the thirties. As a matter of fact, the Modernists suffered no loss of reputation or following in that politically active decade. Whatever the political climate, they were still revered not only as writers with an honorable past but also for their present achievements. In an entirely different political atmosphere, "they were still our heroes," wrote Stephen Spender.[6] This makes for an essential continuity between the thirties and the fifties, both generations, with all their political differences, willing to pardon the Moderns for writing well, and, even more than that, acknowledging them as masters. By the extraordinary genius of their own development the Modernists annexed to themselves more generations than one. They outlived the fifteen- or twenty- or thirty-year hegemony permitted to one generation. And they continued to overshadow other later talents right into the sixties. They enjoyed their literary afterlife—with no sense of being superseded—in their own lifetime.

This literary longevity (matched in some authors by their physical longevity) is due to their on-going responsiveness to the changing conditions of the twentieth century. Their technical innovations have not been surpassed, and they so captured in their latest development the changed attitudes of the pre-World War II epoch that they continued to dominate even after that war. In works that are the most mythical, or the most technically advanced, the Modernists reassert their normal, day-to-day identities. At the greatest moment in Mann's tetralogy, Joseph must turn to his brothers and affirm his human reality: "Your brother is no god-hero, no harbinger of spiritual salvation. He is just a farmer and a manager." (IV.312 / III.1261) Tragic dualistic antagonisms yield, as they do in Joyce, to the complementarities of shared identity. In *Finnegans Wake*, after the long nighttime world of giants and fears and obsessive guilt, day must return, "Here is your shirt, the day one, come back." (619) Finally both Mann and Joyce must close the Book of the Dead: "The book of the depth is. Closed." (621) Thus in the *Wake* Joyce records the coming to a close of those great cycles of death and rebirth that since Frazer's *Golden Bough* have caught the imagination of Modernists. His syntax suggests that these *are*, that is, they exist, and will always do so, but that now they have come to the end of their relevancy as a new daytime cycle of historical experience recommences.

Neither Proust nor Lawrence, because of their earlier deaths, can fit into the same historical chronology, yet the pattern of their works is the same. At length, in the culminating last book of the *Recherche*, the rational intellect is acknowledged for the service it performs in the construction of a work. As we shall see, much more is at stake than this, but clearly a changed direction is indicated from that Proust who wrote in *Contre Sainte-Beuve*, "Chaque jour j'attache moins de prix à l'intelligence."[7] And as for his characters, he comes to see them as living under the dimension of historical change. Lawrence, too, had a post-mythic stage, renouncing his "leadership" novels as being a "back number," and in *The Man Who Died* regaining much of the calm and separate intelligence admired in the earlier second phase.[8]

2. *The Swing of the Pendulum*

Poets have always, I am sure, valued the spontaneous, that which comes along unprompted and seems to write itself. Joyce was not mistaken when he called them "Gracehopers." For Milton the wonder of the muse's nightly visitations was largely that they came "unimplored," that they seemed to yield so easily the "unpremeditated verse." In Modernism, almost cer-

THE BITE OF TIME

tainly because the outer world was becoming controlled to an insufferable degree, the unconscious and the involuntary were made even more visible and extensive parts of their writings. Modernists set themselves in opposition to will, whether they called it the bourgeois will to action and efficiency, or the Romantic will to emotion, sentimentality. So volatile were the contents of consciousness and so suspect the products of willed emotion, that only what was involuntary seemed unquestionably true and authentic. This was the aspect of Modernism stressed in the last chapter. But, of course, this is only part of the picture. Even in the moments of transcendent awareness that the coming of *Death in Venice* had been, Mann carefully adds that the writing "as always" had been a "long-drawn-out job."[9] Eliot himself had his doubts about automatic writing. And "Kubla Khan" he feels has an exaggerated poetic reputation based on faith in mystical inspiration; Eliot acknowledges that the poem's imagery has indeed been "saturated" in Coleridge's psyche, but that it had not been "used: the poem has not been written." Along with Proust he adds that "even the finest line draws its life from its context. Organization is necessary as well as 'inspiration.' " And while emphasizing the primitive echoes of great poetry, he holds that poetry only *begins* "with the savage beating a drum in a jungle."[10]

Enough of something like the Protestant ethic inhered in all of these writers so that they were practically work-compulsive. In Proust, work is a vocation and a sign of redemption—it seems to provide a special kind of concentration, a firmer knowledge, a way of bringing into consciousness what would ordinarily be lost. It saves from insignificance in a moral way as well: those lost in the parties and the changes of time along the Guermantes' way have reduced all experience—even death—to a common level. For them, death was a means of simplifying duties; it also afforded survivors the opportunity for self-congratulation. These maxims, of which the *Recherche* is an inspired source book, are, however, followed by the terribly sober contrast with the serious artist: "And yet this was not the manner in which Elstir had received the news of the death

227

of M. Verdurin." Proust's work is based on these sharp divisions between the dilettantes lost in distraction, and hence vulnerable, like a Swann, and those having an artistic sense of seriousness, even of virility and paternity in relation to his work. In real life there were models for this wastage—Robert de Montesquiou for Proust's group providing the "counterpart" that Desmond McCarthy did for Bloomsbury.[11]

The bourgeois element in Joyce was very strong, extending not only to his household furnishings but to the final values of work and family that held, as his biographer tells us, his primary interests.[12] And all of these writers were extremely regular in their work habits. Mann was a self-professed *Leistungs-ethiker*, and in his correspondence he frequently remarked upon the slowness of his work tempo. The chronicler of the decline of the bourgeois ethic, he was himself, as *Tonio Kröger* reveals, very much caught in its creative grasps. His portrait of Gustav von Aschenbach is largely an ironic partial self-portrait (as will be that much later depiction of Serenus Zeitblom, although from a quite different point of view). Mann, the creator of those large and slowly unfolding complex works, tells his secrets in the work habits of Aschenbach; perseverance is the word. Aschenbach's works were not the product of a breathless inspiration,

> for the truth was that they were heaped up to greatness in layer upon layer, in long days of work, out of hundreds and hundreds of single inspirations; they owed their excellence, both of mass and detail, to one thing and one alone; that their creator could hold out for years under the strain of the same piece of work, with an endurance and a tenacity of purpose like that which had conquered his native province of Silesia, devoting to actual composition none but his freshest and finest hours.[13]

Schopenhauer, always an object of self-identification for Mann, illustrates the same kind of complex nature. This genius of the irrational was bourgeois to the core:

THE BITE OF TIME

One need only look at his life, his Hanseatic merchant origin. The settled life of the elderly man, in Frankfurt-am-Main, dressed always with old-fashioned elegance, his angular, pedantic, immutable, and punctilious daily course; his care for his health . . . his exactness as a capitalist (he wrote down every penny, and in the course of his life doubled his patrimony by shrewd husbandry); the calm tenacity, sparingness and evenness of his methods of work (he produced for print exclusively during the first two hours of his morning . . .).[14]

It was perhaps in Goethe that Mann recognized his own need for slowly developing, long time. In "Goethe's Career as a Man of Letters," he writes, "Goethe needed time for everything. His native slowness, his inherently hesitating nature, has, curiously enough, been recognized only in our own epoch. His life was based on time—on duration. It was ruled by an instinct to leave himself plenty of time, it even shows traces of indolence and irresolute time-wasting." And he goes on to speak of Goethe's prodigious achievement, "growing like a tree." And in the major essay, "Goethe as Representative of the Bourgeois Age," Mann records Goethe's sentiment expressed in *Dichtung und Wahrheit* that all the pleasure we have in life derives from the "regular occurrence" of outward things, of days, seasons, organic growth.[15]

In Mann's self-in-other portraits we see that his early definition of Modernism, as combining both the humanistic and the pessimistic, extends to the most practical areas of work habits, where the temporal husbandry of the Renaissance is used to explore, develop and produce for print thoughts that qualify or even radically attack that heritage. With Virginia Woolf the same was true. Any reader of her published *Diary* will be astonished at the amount of sheer scheduling her overburdened workday required; her serious fictional writing was done in the morning; she attended to the Hogarth press after lunch. Later afternoon was devoted to casual reading and essay writing, and then later hours were spent on proofreading.

THE BITE OF TIME

In Renaissance fashion, the variety of her interests called for close attention to time.

What we observe in Modernists is an attempt to reintegrate faculties they feared had become dissevered. (The use of T. S. Eliot's phrase, "dissociation of sensibility," can be extended to this subject as well.) Their development attests to this principle. Through all of these various phases what we can detect is the felt need to right the balance, to correct the damage, to revive the innovative along with the predictive aspect of time and then, when the innovative seems excessive or even menacing, to reassert the roles of reasonable intelligence and orderly occurrence. (In this sense, the second and fourth stages are clearly related, relying as they do upon the role of consciousness in each, and some sensible concern with the everyday.) Writing to Kerenyi, in a context where he wishes to disassociate himself from the "fad" of irrationalism and its expropriation of myth, Mann writes, "I am a man of balance. I instinctively lean to the left when the canoe threatens to capsize on the right, and vice versa...."[16] This shifting complexity of Modernism must be responsible for its rich development, and for the fact that Modernists tended not to repeat themselves but in the course of their full careers actually completed an *oeuvre*. The several demands they had working upon them created tensions which then sought further solutions.

This dual capacity—and its fruitful results—is made plain by Leonard Woolf when he refers to "two markedly different—even antithetical—phases in Virginia's creative process." The one, indicating a calm rationality of mind and power of casting and calculation, was used in preparation for the writing and in the revision that followed. The other involved periods of excitement and passion, a mood where the impressions of life were brought to cohere around a strong central feeling: "there were long periods of, first, quiet and intense dreamlike rumination when she drifted through London streets or walked across the Sussex water-meadows or merely sat silent by the first, and secondly of intense, analytical critical revision of what she had written." Both phases, however antithetical they may have been in abstraction, he regarded as necessary to his wife's creativity and to that of others as well:

> This swing of the pendulum in the mind between the conscious, rational, analytical, controlled thought and an undirected intuitive or emotional process almost always takes place when the mind produces something original or creative. It happens with creative thinkers, scientists or philosophers.[17]

The pendulum of Mrs. Woolf's career seemed to parallel these swings in the creative process. Speaking only of her larger works, she followed the poetic, experimental *To the Lighthouse* with the historical *Orlando*, and her most innovative work, *The Waves*, with the chronological narrative, *The Years*.

3. *Time and History in the Works of the Thirties*

Like the other full works of the thirties, *Four Quartets*, *Joseph and His Brothers* and *Finnegans Wake*, *The Waves* contains the vacillations that Leonard Woolf described and, especially in its final pages, comes to a renewed appreciation of time and history. In fact, as in other Modernists, a kind of double dialectic operates in Virginia Woolf whereby sets of terms receive twofold evaluations. On the one hand, as part of the routines that have become worn by habit, the values of continuity and settled assurances of narrative story become false-seeming and tiresome. Bernard, the writer, who becomes spokesman for the assemblage in the final chapter of *The Waves*, expresses his fatigue with stories. What delights him, as in a storm, is the "confusion, the height, the indifference and the fury." At this moment, heights and depths—the qualitative alternation of emotional intensities—seem far preferable to the orderly continuity of time and history. (341-342)

At other times, however, and these significantly occur late in the novel, when the experiences of the abysses of space and time are most acute, Bernard values differently the comforts of predictable existence, the known and the familiar. The mechanism of the clock now becomes like the systole and diastole of the pulse; the succession of days, Tuesdays following Mondays, seems like the growth of rings around a sturdy identity. (355-357) Even trains now give off an atmosphere of orderliness: "How satisfactory the atmosphere of common sense and tobacco." (364) All of the elements of mechanical routinization, that appeared to lead to nothingness, have now become parts of a reliable human society. There are even greater coherences in this return of an earlier pattern. Within the same few pages his thoughts turn to children. The normal fierce "tick-tack "of his mind is now filled with the "majestic rhythm" that turns his thoughts to historical continuity and children. "I roamed down Oxford Street. We are the continuers, we are the inheritors, I said, thinking of my sons and daughters." And being a Modernist he cannnot entertain this instinctive feeling without some awkwardness—"and if the feeling is so grandiose as to be absurd one conceals it by jumping on a bus or buying the evening paper, it is still a curious element in the ardor with which one laces up one's boots . . ." And in the next paragraph biographical narrative and conventional epistolary styles are defended: "One cannot despise these phrases laid like Roman roads across the tumult of our lives." (356) If life is tumultuous then that which is orderly and stable receives new recognition and value. But what is mostly remarkable in all of this is the consistency of the recurring elements, the days and months, the clock and the train, even the Roman roads, the children, and narrative style—all of which were specifically part of the time-world that Modernists first attacked but which return *together*—now not associated with mechanization, but rather humanized and regarded as necessary to the comforts and continuities of civilized life.

Almost immediately in the third and largest section of *The Past Recaptured*, Proust follows his succession of timeless revelations—those that would form the inspiration of his work—with another discovery: "I made the discovery of the destructive action of time at the very moment when I had conceived the ambition to make visible, to intellectualize in a work of art, realities that were outside Time." (VII.179/III.930) In this sense, then, the French title, *Le Temps retrouvé* communicates a double meaning not present in the English translation. This last volume is not only about recapturing the past, it is also about rediscovering the realities of time. In relation to the first kind of inspiration, Proust clearly establishes his own tradition, that of Chateaubriand, Gérard de Nerval and Baudelaire—the poetry of magical reminiscence. He is convinced that he can figure in that poetic line of descent (even while participating in society, there being no real reason why solitude should be more conducive to creation), when his appearance at the Duchesse de Guermantes' party presents him with a veritable *coup de théâtre*, the "spectacular and dramatic effect" of time on individuals. And these impressions of individual change lead to the larger sense of change in the networks of human society, that is, they are proofs of the reality of history. (VII.205/III.964) As we have already indicated was the case with Virginia Woolf, this discovery has implications for the method and materials of his book: "For I had decided that [the book] could not consist uniquely of the full and plenary impressions that were outside time, and amongst those other truths in which I intended to set, like jewels, those of the first order, the ones relating to Time, to Time in which, as in some transforming fluid, men and societies and nations are immersed, would play an important part." (VII.181/III.932) The surprise, but definitely not the pleasure, of these discoveries is diluted for the reader by the fact that we have already benefited by their results—that is, they have produced the novel we have just been reading. But this does not diminish the importance of the last pages of the *Recherche* since, in the first case, what Proust is really doing is presenting us with his *art poétique*, and, in the second, with his *art historique*. We get some impression of the importance of the latter when we recall that his poetics was already presented in *Contre Sainte-Beuve*, the small work that serves as a prelude to the *Recherche*, whereas the great fullness (Proust would have called it pleni-

THE BITE OF TIME

tude) of his major effort can only be accounted for by Proust's sense of himself as an historian.

The two inspirations have decidedly different effects. The epiphanic moments seem to remove all temporal urgency and anxiety about the future; life seems to come together, and Proust declares himself at these times as being indifferent to death. The post-mythic discovery of time and of history, however, fills him with anxiety—in fact, we see Proust recapitulating elements of the argument of time standard since the Renaissance. As his own book takes shape—and this is a fairly common experience among authors—he is more and more possessed by the fear of death, a death that would prevent him from finishing his nearly completed task. He becomes increasingly conscious then of time, as a factor of life as well as a theme. It is noteworthy that in the Renaissance both the fear of the individual death, as distinguished from the more medieval communal sense of dying, and the recognition of time as a "loan" for which the individual was solely responsible emerged coincidentally. Care for time was required if the individual were to make a satisfactory accounting of his life.

In each of these two approaches to experience, Proust's enemy is habit, the quotidian assumption that things have always been as they now seem to be. But the nature of time reinforces this assumption: its perspective is distorting, it is invisible, "colorless and inapprehensible" (VII.259/III.1031) until, in a sudden flash we are presented undeniably with realities that reveal its hard design and purpose. This new dimension of time shows life as it is, "not as it appears to us, that is to say, permanent." (VII.174/III.924) Furthermore, there seems to be some complicity between the deceptively silent nature of time and the nature of the complex central consciousness. By a strange twist this latter is so involved in ordinary day-to-day existence that these aspects of a life are not regarded as changeful but rather assume the characteristics of permanence. "The manner by which . . . we take cognizance of this moving universe whirled by Time, has the contrary effect of immobilizing it" (V.205/III.963-969)—and Proust's example is that of a photograph which we constantly carry with us, and with which we always identify ourselves. In our minds we are always twenty-three, until we see ourselves suddenly in a mirror, or in a newspaper story, and we seem to see another person or are surprised to be reminded that instead of 23, the number behind this other person's name is 50. Proust himself is like the man

> who, from idleness and perhaps also because of poor health, has perpetually put off [the one idea that has been the goal of his life] every evening striking out as though it had never existed the day that has slipped away and is lost, so that the illness which hastens the aging of his body retards that of his mind, such a man is more surprised and more appalled to see that all the while he has been living in time than one who lives little inside of himself and, regulating his activities by the calendar, does not in a single horrifying moment discover the total of the years whose mounting sum he has followed day by day. (VII.178/III.930)

Indeed, the consciousness of Modernism is bound to register the lives we live, "de jour en jour, de minute en minute," but, reversing Montaigne in this last stage, Proust is brought to reflect and notice the larger lines of life, "de sept en sept ans," that in the blur of habit and daily existence we fail to recognize. Time, ordinarily without qualities in our normal lives, suddenly emerges as a destructive demon in these last pages of the *Recherche*.

As it was in the Renaissance, so in this Modernist reactivation, time is part of an objective reality that brings home truths independent of consciousness. Lending more coherence to this pattern of time is the fact that in three of our writers, Joyce, Mann and Proust, the experience of the objectivity of time is associated with an awakening. In fact, in Proust and in Joyce's *Ulysses* a minor analogue becomes Rip van Winkle (while in *Finnegans Wake*, the implied doubling of the title means "awake," as Joyce, in a pregnant association made it: *Ho, Time Timeagen, Wake!*). In *The Magic Mountain*, Hans, with his time-obliviousness, endures the sleep of the Seven Sleepers before he is awakened by the thunderbolt of World War I.

Eliot does not use these folkloric figures but he, too, particularly in *Four Quartets*, is engrossed in the problem of our consciousness of time and its objective reality. Moments of agony are permanent, "with such permanence as time has." But usually we are not so aware of our own experience; rather it is more apparent in the experience of others:

> We appreciate this better
> In the agony of others, nearly experienced,
> Involving ourselves, than in our own.
> For our own past is covered by the currents of action,
> But the torment of others remains an experience
> Unqualified, unworn by subsequent attrition.
> People change, and smile; but the agony abides.

And the final lines of this verse-paragraph express some of the complexities of time—time may be "as you like it," but this amorphousness only serves to conceal its terrible destructive reality. It is like the "ragged rock in the restless waters,"

> Waves wash over it, fogs conceal it;
> On a halcyon day it is merely a monument,
> In navigable weather it is always a seamark
> To lay a course by: but in the sombre season
> Or the sudden fury, is what it always was.
>   (*DS*, II)

Lastly, to return to Proust, as with the involuntary revelations of the *moments bienheureux*, this dramatic discovery of time and of history shows a significance and coherence—life is, after all, something worth writing about. "How much more worth living did it appear to me now, now that I seemed to see that this life that we live in half-darkness can be illumined, this life that at every moment we distort can be restored to its true pristine shape, that a life, in short, can be realized within the confines of a book." (VII.259/III.1032) Time, even in its destructiveness—and it is not only that—at least carries with it meaning, matters of moment. It also lays a responsibility upon the writer. Not only in spite of but because of the effects of habit and error and illusions of permanence, Marcel finds his vocation in being the faithful son of memory, one who writes true histories, who remembers Swann and Charlus and Oriane de Guermantes and all the others as they were indeed. Memory for Proust is not only a force of individual liberation, but one of social redemption as well, redemption even of a society whose very values he had transcended. An artist, for Proust, is a person who must first save himself and in so doing he will save others—he will realize their own wasted potentials and remember their true beings, from which they were distracted. But in order to do so, like Dante, Marcel must separate himself (voluntarily in his case) from his society in order to become its faithful registrar and chronicler:

> Was it not surely, in order to concern myself with them that I was going to live apart from these people who would complain that they did not see me, to concern myself with them in a more fundamental fashion than would have been possible in their presence, to seek to reveal them to themselves, to realize their potentialities . . . ? Was it not more worthwhile that I should attempt to describe the curves, to educe the laws which governed these gestures that they made, these remarks that they uttered, their very lives and natures? (VII.223/III.986)

From events dominated by forgetfulness, error and failed potentialities the artist rescues true memory; this is his bequest to the race, and Proust's final justification of his vocation. The sheer passage of time itself lends such importance to the historical role of the artist. His cargo of history is rendered precious by virtue of the fact that the most singular attribute of time is that it is irreplaceable. That which has been lived through, thought and seen will never be done so again—it is this finality that makes the artist's historical function so necessary.

Place after all is replaceable, in turn held by many people and successive generations. It is turned up and over, whereas time is once and only—hence it is the most distinctively human and individual commodity. It is all we have. The melancholy that pervades the last section of the *Recherche* as well as the famous final book of the *Wake* is based upon the cruel equation that we can only achieve identity in relation to time and that this very act carries with it a clear sentence of termination, finality and replacement. Such is the tragedy of man's historical existence and the one that we encounter most acutely in this final phase. Mythic time is, after all, no time at all, but space. Ritualistic patterns repeat one time recurrently, as Joseph instructs Benjamin in Mann's novel. (II.73/I.338) Hence myth is associated with place or with that which endures. The flow of the river in *Finnegans Wake* returns us by a "commodius vicus of recirculation back to Howth Castle and Environs." H. C. E., the hero of the work, is really an abiding place (as it had already become in Bloom's intimations of the mythic in *Ulysses*), in relation to which all generations become as one. Individuals are lost in timelessness; only in relation to time does the self define itself, but this self-definition amounts to eventual annihilation. Not accidentally, the Renaissance, that epoch which reintroduced history *and* tragedy to the West, also saw the individual define himself in a new way toward the forces of time and death.[18]

Following the episodes of timelessness, of All-people as omnipresent, the last section of the *Wake* makes these connections, showing along with the reemergence of time, other Renaissance time-patterns (not to mention one very distinct Renaissance voice). It is time to wake up. "Time!" He is called again, that figure from song and legend, "Time-o'-Thay!" The "time of day" is coming; but what is it by the clock—"But wherth, O clerk?" and "Whithr a clonk?" (599) Such wakeful inquiry clearly denotes passingness.

> Passing. One. We are passing. Two. From sleep we are passing. Three. Into the wikeawades warld from sleep we are passing. Four. Come, hours, be ours!
> But still. Ah diar, ah diar! And stay. (608)

The wide-awake world is a wicked one since the very time that brings the self into being will also take it away. The Renaissance allusion confirms this. In order for the hours to be ours they must have motion, but after they are "ours" we then wish for them to be still, like the dramatic prayer of Marlowe's *Doctor Faustus*: "Stand still, you ever-moving spheres of heaven. . . ." But time (pathetically, "Oh dear, Oh dear") passes day by day ("Ah diar, Ah diar!") and is as a consequence so precious (dear).

These last moments are bitter ones ("O bitter ending") as the sustaining fluid and resolving flux of existence, ALP, the very river and waters of life, now becomes a dying old woman, who feels that she has never been understood (". . . is there one who understands me?") and who now scorns her hero-husband ("I thought you the great in all things, in guilt and in glory. You're but a puny"). (627) And yet, martyr to the end, she tries to slip off without trouble before her family is awake. The waters of life now represent, as the tide has always done, the forces of replacement in existence. At her back she feels another rising current, "a daughterwife from the hills again. . . . And she is coming. Swimming in my hindmoist. Diveltaking on me tail." It is to this younger beauty that her husband will now turn.

The definition of self in relation to time is the real *felix culpa* of Joyce's work. "It's something fails us," ALP reflects, "First we feel. Then we fall." (627) The fall into time is a fall into self—by which the self becomes sensitive to his separation from his environment. Bloom's fall is a similar tale. To define himself personally Bloom must encounter his destiny—to be cuckolded is his history and his fall, his doom and his redemption. In this definition there is moral and emotional substance, especially when contrasted with Blazes Boylan, who is obscene by virtue of his lack of personal definition. He is known only by a congeries of flashing glitter and jangling sounds. His freedom is secured by an absence of feeling and identity that saves him from a fall but not from frivolousness.

4. *Humanism and Development*

Not quite as political as they would seem, neither Proust nor Joyce nor Woolf ever had any serious flirtations with the reactionary resurgence in twentieth-century philosophy and politics. With Mann and Eliot the issues are a bit more complex, particularly in the need they obviously felt to maintain the metaphysical and religious dimensions of experience as against the social and ethical. In the thirties, however, the strong humanistic bias of their work reasserted itself; along with their renewed interest in time can be associated their conviction, which circumstances only strengthened, of the need for reason and culture and ethics.

Hans Castorp himself explains to Naphta what it means to be hermetically sealed: "The magic part of it lies in the fact that the stuff that is conserved is withdrawn from the effects of time, it is hermetically sealed from time, times passes it by, it stands there on its shelf shut away from time." (511/538-539) But, of course, well before the war intervenes to shatter this alchemical enhancement, Mann begins to cast doubts on any immunity from the effects of time. As it is his wont to upstage pedagogy by experience, even Hans's great "dream-poem of humanity," the real fruit of his hermetical experience, is followed by the chapter dealing with the death of Joachim, where Hans's vision must be tested in fact. The return of the dignity of the soldier, that alter-ego that Hans had earlier to transcend, is coincidental with the counter-current in the book, one that holds within it not the needed experience of the timeless, but rather that of time and its consequences for actions.

The very next chapter, "By the Ocean of Time," makes this clear. Formerly the subjective aspects of time, the deceptiveness of what in the West was normally taken to be temporal reality, were stressed; now, however, Hans's own illusions are revealed. Mann's narrative voice intercedes to provide another basis of judgment for his young hero's immersion in the heady experiences of the mountain: "Time, however weakened the subjective perception of it has become, has objective reality (sachliche Wirklichkeit), in that it brings things to pass"—how potently suggestive is that word "zeitigen" (sofern sie tätig ist, sofern sie "zeitigt"). (544/573) Even upon Seven Sleepers, the narrator assures us, time does it work. He cites evidence of a young girl who slept thirteen years, "but who still bloomed into ripe womanhood as she slept."

Time engenders change and change is history, and this occurs not only in the biology of the individual but also, as Proust saw, in the more extraordinary developments of external events. World War I was the thunderbolt that shattered the sleep and the illusions of the mountain. (It is noteworthy that in one of the first works of the Renaissance to discuss the role of time in relation to poetry, Petrarch's "Coronation Oration," time is compared to a thunderbolt.)[19] They must abandon their metaphysical freedom, as their lives and that of Hans in particular are now taken up and determined by the course of Europe's destiny.

Even that translucent, Ariel-like, "Hermesnatur" of Joseph cannot endure forever in the fluidity of his playful consciousness. He, too, must endure the casualty of his choice, the limitation of his virtue. After their long separation, the confrontation between the ancient Jacob and the son who managed so well in an alien land reveals all the more starkly the differences that separate them. Joseph is a secular link in a religious chain: his worldly genius has in effect disinherited him. As a provider he is not a saint. In another moving exchange, both father and son recognize this fact. God has raised Joseph above his brothers—as the dreams foretold—but, Jacob now sees, "He has raised you in a worldly way, not in the sense of salvation and inheritance of the blessing. You know that. . . . You are blessed, my dear one . . . blessed from the heavens above downward and from the depths that lie beneath, blessed with blitheness and with destiny, with wit and with dreams. Still, it is a worldly blessing, not a spiritual one. Have you heard the voice of self-denying love?" (IV.357/III.1305) The very playfulness of Joseph's intelligence closes to him the total belief and even calling, exemplified in the determination of

Tamar. In this most mythic of books, history intervenes bitterly and sadly, to exact the kind of exclusion that typifies its domain.

Yet here, too, Joseph continues to serve for the portrait of the Modernist author. Mann's statement is similar to that of Eliot at the conclusion of *Dry Salvages*: Joseph's reversion is genuinely toward the temporal, and his calling not that of the saint. As Joseph assumes his larger social function, so Mann and Eliot as well acknowledge their own vocations to be allied with mankind in its earthly and historical natures. Worldliness, and mediation, incorporating that which comes from below as well as aspiration toward that which is above (if such spatial metaphors are at all useful)—it is in regard to these virtues and talents that the civilizing role of the artist reveals itself.

Humanism itself, a word that had been trampled upon for so long, regarded as at best a superficial way of regarding existence, comes in for reappreciation. For Mann, of course, this is not so much a radical departure as a continuation of basic directions. Still, the essay on Goethe "as representative of the bourgeois age," emphasizes his Erasmian side and not, as had the earlier "Goethe and Tolstoy" (with its very clear affinities with *The Magic Mountain*), the Lutheran dimension.[20] This portrait of Goethe's "Wohlwollen für das Menschliche," however, recalls similar sentiments expressed by Tonio Kröger. And in his mythic phase, it is significant that Mann should have chosen that bright spirit, Joseph—a signal guide in Mann's attempts to take myth away from the "intellectual fascists" and transpose it into the humane.[21] The renewed sense of time and historical consequences thus serves to reinforce the ethical—terms which in the Renaissance were associated with humanism.

In his prose works of the late twenties Eliot felt compelled to attack the humanism of Irving Babbit and of others. He did so in order to establish his sense of the need for religious ordering of experience. After having established that position, however, and in an atmosphere of growing fanaticism, Eliot,

THE BITE OF TIME

much given to second thoughts (witness his revised thinking on Milton and Goethe), had second thoughts on humanism as well. In fact, he redefined humanism so that it became less of a program and more of an attitude that Eliot felt was short on supply in those passion-filled times. Like Mann, Eliot came to regard the humanist legacy as one of reasonableness and good will. True humanism, he now argues, in "Second Thoughts About Humanism," "makes for breadth, tolerance, equilibrium and sanity. It operates against fanaticism." On the one hand Eliot can declare, "Culture, after all, is not enough," only to add, "even though nothing is enough without culture."[22] In *Four Quartets*, part of whose temporal reversion involves a scrupulous ethical consciousness, "right action" as well as just vision is a means of liberation from past and future. The more modulated voice of the *Quartets*, relatively free from the rich allusiveness of *The Waste Land*, itself indicates some of the larger public concern of Eliot, who had already tried his hand at drama, the most social of literary art forms. And the "tone" of the *Quartets* indicates Eliot's growing responsiveness to the times and his sense of "humiliation" brought about by the rise of the Nazis and a feeling of helplessness toward the coming World War II.

A new sense of tolerance on the parts of almost all of our writers for virtues that had formerly been despised—the orderly, the practical, the common-sensical—should in this last phase come as no surprise. Given the conviction of discontinuous levels of existence, the assignment of appropriate virtues to their suitable sector of experience would seem to be a natural consequence. So, in Joyce, the Shem-personality is able to see the Shaun-type as his complement rather than his antagonist. Eliot, given his own "temporal reversion" and his mediating role between the experience of the saint and normal error-prone existence, can distinguish between two kinds of wisdom and now give greater scope to the worldly:

There is worldly wisdom, and there is spiritual wisdom. Wisdom which is merely the former may in the end turn out to be folly, if it ignores, or aspires to judge those things which are beyond its understanding; wisdom which is purely spiritual wisdom may be of no help in affairs of this world.[23]

Such tolerance even enters into Eliot's own historical judgments, based as they are on phases of growth, each with varying needs. Milton, or even Goethe, harmful when certain functions were required for poetry, can at later stages be readmitted. Eliot denies that this amounts to a recantation—rather it is a question of different needs at different times. Whereas at the time of his own developing style he felt a personal affinity with the works of Laforgue, Donne and minor Elizabethan and Jacobean dramatists, now when his own aims seem to have been accomplished and his valuations require permanence and universality, he reads more readily Mallarmé, or Herbert or Shakespeare.[24] He has passed from the language and attitudes of break-through to those of consolidation and assimilation.

This appreciation of discontinuous levels of experience is further responsible for two formidable qualities of Modernist achievement—its range and its development. And these connections, as we have seen in the usefulness of T. E. Hulme's thought as a general paradigm, are not accidental or random. The Modernist vision was not directed toward unity and fusion, but rather toward diversity—toward that which is multiple and heterogeneous (in the words of Lawrence and Proust). But my further suggestion is that this Modernist range of experience, this sensitivity to the discontinuous levels of existence, somewhat like a ladder laid on its side, is responsible for the stages of Modernist growth and development. In this sense, vertical multiplicity is the basis for horizontal succession; and proteanism is the principle of metamorphosis.

The Modernists' remarkable metamorphic attributes derive from the range of experiences that they were able to envision as well as from the heat that these conflicting pressures were able to generate. The liberal-conservative, narrative-poetic, event-consciousness, time-timeless, history-myth polarities fostered an atmosphere of reassessment. So aware were they of alternative ways, so empathic with other modes of thought or belief, that it was difficult for them to rest content with that which had been accomplished, with standpoints or staying-points. Once outside the determinations of time and the dimensions of history, they were all explorers. Exploration is the natural factor of the intense Modernist sense of change. Having written *Ulysses*, Joyce had before him in 1922, "the almost totally unexplored expanse" of dream and sleep.[25] Clearly the genius of Modernism, from its own internal pressures, was developmental. In this they resemble their Renaissance forebears whose own reactions to the contradictory pressures brought about by a wide range of experience were themselves conducive to remarkable self-transformations. It is no accident that time, so related to change and to history, should be a primary figure of literary address in both epochs.

CONCLUSION

Purviews and Purposes

One can best summarize the nature and contributions of Modernism by recalling the charges made against that movement (and which were alluded to frequently in the course of this study). Not unexpectedly, given the complex nature of Modernism, the accusations are contradictory. The first kind of charge would deny any substantial character or value-change to Modernism (here we think of Frye—"post-Romanticism," or Hough—Modernism only wrought stylistic changes), or, if a character is allowed Modernism, that character is marked by negativity and ephemerality. The second, and to my mind quite interesting kind of criticism, partly because the response it elicits involves questions of aesthetic and moral value, belongs to the perspective of post-Modernism. Its argument, nominalistic in the extreme, holds that Modernism is an institutionalization, a congealment, if you will, of an impulse of *modernité* that must always be shifting, always changing. In this sense, Modernism became a betrayal of *modernité*: it abandoned its avant-gardistic roots and became "established." These separate kinds of criticisms need to be considered individually: their value may be in the rejoinders they provoke, rejoinders that help us determine the enduring character of Modernism.

By now there can be little doubt that the Modernist shift in style was inseparable from the Modernist shift in values. This is brought out in the ways that the complex central consciousness grew out of the shattering of the powerful will and unified ego presented in the first two chapters. Modernism did not take particular delight in the accelerating mobility of modern times; rather, it found such mobility to be based upon unitary sameness and not the genuine shifts and jumps in values and qualitative experiences that the new order of consciousness required. Similarly, the argument is clear that the very fragmentation of the ego was a step on the way to the apprehension of the mythic and a more integrated self. There are other connections. For instance, just as in the first two chapters we saw the ultimate antagonist to be the industrial will, so in the chapters dealing with style and sensibility we saw the corollary of that industrial drive to be willed emotion, sentimentality, terminating in a repugnant need for fusion. In a similar way, the spatialization of experience that was a product of the repetitive will is comparable (although put to different effects) to the "dread of space" that upset natural humanistic at-oneness. All along the way, then, the "stylistic" and the "ideological" are interrelated.

This argument is supported by two other facts: (1) the corroboration the Modernist shift in values received from other disciplines and (2) their own historical consciousness that they were challenging previous epochs and, in so doing, marking off their own terrain. In chapter 2, section 4 and chapter 3, section 2 ("The Paradox of Time" and "Perspectivism and Relativity" respectively) I have shown the way several of the Modernist positions (the "spatialization" of the paradox of time, the kinship of Whitehead's "manifold of prehensions" with the networks of relationships established in Proust, Joyce and Lawrence) were echoed or prompted by innovative thinking in allied disciplines. This mutuality of interest contributed greatly to the overall strength and confidence of Modernism as a movement, a sense shared by its adherents that they were not only making stylistic innovations but valid contributions to the fuller understanding of their society.

Historically, Modernists did much to establish their own positions, setting themselves off quite consciously from Renaissance developments that resulted in the industrial mind of the nineteenth century (of which Gerald Crich might be regarded as a prime representative) as well as from Romantic style and sensibility. They were not only defining themselves in relation to superficial habits and inherited social customs, but to the very underpinnings of a society, its notions of time, causality and historical values. By confronting these tendencies that had their origins in the Renaissance, the Modernists were quite consciously asserting their own identities, and attaching these identities to cultural shifts of massive proportions.

This is one of the reasons why Modernism, at least in its earlier and middle phases, emphasized to such an extent the depiction of troubled young people. Of course, this should generically represent nothing too different from Romanticism. Nevertheless the Modernist young (Stephen, Paul Morel, Ursula and others) were troubled because the ideas they found uncongenial and were struggling to alter were precisely holdovers from Romanticism, whether in aesthetics or ideology. By another kind of measurement, unlike those of so many characters in nineteenth-century fiction, their problems did not emerge from a set of circumstances or characters that blocked them from their inheritance or their fortunes—they are surprisingly indifferent to such matters. Furthermore, young Modernists felt themselves severed not only from their antecedents but also from their cohorts: they were not part of any youth movement. Their purpose was not to assert the values of youth but rather a new set of cultural values. The problems they encountered arose because they wished to alter normative thought and value. Theirs was not a temporary stage in the process of growing up, but rather a temporary stage in making known and accepted new conditions in art and belief. Probably no area is greater than this—the struggles of young people—in showing that the concern of Modernism was to bring about a fundamental shift in cultural values.

That this shift proved to be enduring is equally clear. Modernism succeeded in evolving a typology wherein we continue to mirror and recognize ourselves (even though we may no longer quite as consciously form ourselves there). There are several typologies to Modernist evolution. The first was that of the "negative" heroes, the suffering ones like Prufrock or Kafka's characters, Thomas Buddenbrook, Gustav von Aschenbach or Gerald Crich, from which the Modernists separated themselves. More important characters, quite responsive to the complex conditions of late industrial life, were those evolved in the works of the twenties: Leopold Bloom, Hans Castorp, Marcel (really spanning more than a decade) and even Tiresias. These figures may be characterized as tolerant, selfless, passive witnesses, and if we consider the hazards of the aggressive will (of which World War I provided some illustration) we see how responsive these character types were to the needs of their times. But in another sense, rather than regarding their passivity, perhaps we ought to regard as their primary trait their *disponibilité*, a new kind of complex register marked by an openness to multiple and various experiences. Perhaps in all of these characters we can see the format of the Hermes-like, mediating and secular nature of Joseph, the provider not the saint, a mediating figure bringing together what is "above" with what is "below," that is, a fuller picture of man's human nature. This "temporal reversion" in its vision of man might be Modernism's most important bequest.

Fredric Jameson described Modernism by means of its "strategies of inwardness," and to a certain extent the phrase is apt.[1] However, it is much too limited, as we have seen. Rather do we not find that their openness, described above, is an openness that includes inwardness but much more importantly a transparency that is thus a reflecting device for all the changeful conditions of human existence? The two go together: the apparent inwardness is actually a window out onto the world. In support of this contention, I find it hard to conceive that the enduring longevity of Modernism—and certainly this longevity is one of the critical facts we need to consider in assessing Modernism—could be accounted for merely by "strategies of inwardness." Arguably, it is this "openness" to ranges of experience, including of course, the changing times, that helps account for their extraordinary development.

Here we can use the phenomenon of the sixties as an example. To a great extent, the sixties, as a period of new singular moral commitment, marked the end of Modernism. Yet, even here, we find some evidence of the rich "social" inclusiveness of Modernist thought. I frequently ask myself why it is that to those of us who had read and studied the Modernists, the theories of writers like Marcuse or Adorno came as no surprise.[2] One particular reason for this is that the Vietnam War recalled many of the issues of our technological culture that had been glossed over in World War II and the fifties. But these very issues had already been exposed in the works of the major Modernists—think only of D. H. Lawrence. So, once again, in the sixties we heard of the dominator dominated, the master of spectacular technical power apparently willing its own destruction, of a tragic lack of suppleness in thought, and of deadly obsessive narrowness and fixation. These analyses were not new to any reader of the Modernists; what was new, and tragically so for the generation of the fifties, was the manifestations of justifiable protest they engendered.

Modernism has been characterized by its "negativity"; its stance being essentially adversarial vis-à-vis human institutions, or, more radically, in regard to meaning itself and the assumption of any position. Modernism breathes a kind of discontent, according to this view, and consequently, and almost by definition, is committed to negating any prevalent style or position, including its own. It is charged with adopting a "continuing adversary stance."[3] Daniel Bell, the particular critic whom I am quoting, goes on to identify Modernism with manifestations of the sixties, manifestations from which his own liberalism seems to recoil. "In the theoretical writings of Norman O. Brown and Michel Foucault, in the novels of William Burroughs, Jean Genet, and to some extent Norman Mailer, and in the porno-pop culture (more vulgar and more brassy) that is played out in the world of drugs, rock music, and oral sexuality, one sees a culmination of modernist inten-

PURVIEWS AND PURPOSES

tions."[4] Quite a list of sins with which to afflict the departed Modernists, even extending, mind you, to oral sexuality, the appeal of which would seem to have very little to do with the goings-on of culture and most certainly antedated Modernism, let alone the sixties.

In the first stage of Modernist negative critiques, we can see formed a position of hostility to the dominant codes of their culture, but we can also see that this position was remarkably reasoned, that it was responsive to conditions of their society, and that by itself it was incomplete, necessary wrecking work on the way to a fuller more positive expression of their needs. But also in the second stage we can see why Modernism could be identified with the need to participate in never-ending self-interrogation, interrogations not only of one's own tenets (which is always laudable) but also of the very need to be ever interrogating itself. (One quickly discerns what a shabby intellectual game this can become.) To the great credit of the Modernists, while certainly exploiting the technical and intellectual possibilities of this stage, they went beyond it into the zones of the mythic and personal identity. They felt a need for personal coherence. But here, too, the means by which they attained this personal coherence (in their works, of course) reflected the prior stages of their growth. It could not come through an act of the conscious will, but rather had to be involuntary, and the more authentic for having come without their bidding. What this need for authenticity reveals is a bias toward reality. That which comes unbidden is not an invention, or a concoction, but rather bears the patent of reality. This abiding commitment to external reality and even historical consciousness reveals itself at length in the last phase of Modernist development, where, almost without exception, the major Modernists reassert the realities of time and of history. In short, to answer criticism of the sort offered by Daniel Bell, we should look to the full development of Modernists, to the complexities of their various responses, as well as to the internal dynamic and coherence of their changes.

The error of those who recoiled in horror from the happen-

251

ings of the sixties (somewhat like Satan being shown his offspring by Sin), is to confuse the high Modernists with some of their followers. Later post-Modernists themselves do not make this error. Their view—the counterpart to that of Bell—is that *modernité* (a long-abiding "impulse," or aesthetic need, that goes back to Baudelaire if not Romanticism) is committed to ever renewing itself and that Modernism, far from being the progenitor of the sixties, is actually an historical congealment of that protean impulse. To this view, the high Modernists do not sit well with the anarchic sixties. Modernism is a *modernité* that has become crystallized.

In response I can only argue that it was better, certainly from the viewpoint of their artistic accomplishment, that the Modernists did, as it were, come into their estate, did take the risks of historical identity. In the stages of their growth do we not find a fuller, more accurate and more satisfying depiction of the human life cycle? Can we, for instance, only know dispersal and not unification? And is there not something eternally young, unrisking, even virginal in that refusal to accept identity? Does this not amount to fearing too much the Greater Dispersal, as if we must always be jogging, afraid of the cancer at our back, as if not to have an identity would shield us any better from age or death?[5]

These considerations return us to a very elementary point, one I raised in preliminary fashion in the preface to this study: the particular combination of features that we discern in Modernism and that helps account for the greatness of individual Modernists and the strength of the movement. They were committed to depicting the changing truths of their time and their experience, but they also had a remarkable sense of history, understood in a critical and comprehensive way. They rendered the momentary and the fleeting, the here and the now, but they also interpreted these events in the light of more permanent forms. The fullness and complexity of their responses yielded a total picture of reality that was deeply satisfying and that helped account for the longevity of their continuing appeal as a significant movement and period of our culture.

AS WE TURN from critical purviews to historical purposes, we have an impression of leaving an embattled zone and of entering a freer air of accomplishments and legacies. More important than the prior contentions are the new possibilities of freedom in subject matter and style that Modernism brought to art in the twentieth century. So wide is the range of their register, so heterogeneous their style, so multiple and complex their reference that their ultimate bequest to the generations that followed is precisely this tremendous range of reflexive and reflecting freedoms. Can we really imagine Saul Bellow, the late John Cheever, John Updike (to mention only a few of the talented heirs of today), the easy, almost unself-conscious reflective mobility of their styles, the fluid juxtaposition of radically different subject matters, the great sense of the contingent and then suddenly, unexpectedly a jostling movement of significance that brings tears, can we imagine this taken-for-granted possibility without the achievement of the Modernists? The legacy is there for all to delight in and use.

Related to this individual range of styles is a kind of cultural pluralism that may be the product of Modernism. Leonard B. Meyer has made this the thesis of his brilliant study, *Music, the Arts, and Ideas*. His idea is that "the coming epoch . . . will be a period of stylistic stasis, a period characterized not by the linear cumulative development of a single fundamental style, but the coexistence of a multiplicity of quite different styles in a fluctuating and dynamic steady-state."[6] While our ideas may appear to be contradictory (I follow the internal dynamic of Modernism's growth and he declares that the quintessence of the artistic movement at present is the absence of any single development) in fact they are quite complementary. I think he accurately describes the artistic situation since the end of Modernism, and that in fact the sign of the end of a movement is precisely this break-up of the coherent development and inclusive forms into a variety of singular aspects and forms. What was a composite whole in Modernism, or at least part of their development, has been singled out by their followers into a series of individual styles. This helps us explain why we are still under the Modernist sway, and that the absence of stylistic hegemony also means the lack of any new styles or break-throughs.

In this regard my position on post-Modernism may be thought to be contradictory. On the one hand, I deny that Modernism is post-Romantic in any derivative sense, but I do not think that post-Modernism has achieved the same breakthrough. I say this despite the work of Ihab Hassan, whose "The Culture of Post-Modernism" is the most compelling synthesis of the post-Modernist position I know.[7] Certainly there are differences and the differences are crucial. But in a specific sense post-Modernists do not define themselves by a counter-Modernity in the way the Modernists defined themselves by a counter-Romanticism. To be a counter-Romantic was part of the Modernist point of departure, a *prise de position* by which they identified themselves. I see no similar counter-Modernism in the work of post-Modernism. Instead, what I see and what Leonard B. Meyer has described is precisely this breaking-away into a plurality of fluctuating styles, each with its point of origin in some aspect of Modernist development.

While the great Modernists are dead, their works and the issues they addressed have not disappeared. In 1981 I attended a debate in Florence (the debate was subtitled, History and Philosophy) between Eugenio Garin and a young university professor, who had previously been a Marxist but subsequently became something of an Italian *nouveau philosophe*. Garin, our premier student of Renaissance humanism, spoke of the importance of history, and of cultural continuity, while the younger man, more radical in his theological philosophy, spoke of empty spaces in Nature, of schisms in historical events. Later I had occasion to mention to Garin that I had been present at the debate before, since Thomas Mann had given us the form of the twentieth-century debate between liberal humanist and reactionary radical in the stirring clashes Settembrini and Naphta generate in the *The Magic Mountain*.

Clearly one of the larger historical purposes of Modernism was political, a purpose whose ambivalance and dialectic—as the above anecdote illustrates—we continue to share. In effect, for the Modernist writers, the triumph of liberal humanism in the nineteenth century was a secular triumph, where all the dimensions of experience were absorbed into the middle level. And yet the Modernists felt the need to make room for other aspects of experience as well, for the supra-historical as well as the infra-historical, the religious and mythical as well as the subhuman and unregenerate. All of this amounted to a challenge to liberal humanism and the extremely dangerous starting point for Modernism (hence the pressing scholarly need to separate the style and character of Modernism from those of Fascism). Yet, on the larger screen of history I think we can discern three stages of Modernist development (and here I am referring to political, or ideological development, not aesthetic), if the first is to be considered that of the inherited liberal humanism. The second is that necessary yet perilous one of repudiating that faith, of turning to religion and philosophy, which finally itself must then be qualified and directed by what Mann called "love of truth and human sympathy" and what Eliot called simple tolerance and sanity. The need to balance these conflicting tendencies is the ideological factor responsible for the phases of Modernism's development.

The notion of development helps us to unravel these ambiguities that were inherent in the very beginnings of Modernism and, at the same time, address a prominent crux of contemporary criticism, a crux that is central to the nature of Modernism. Two of the outstanding critics in post-World War II America, Harry Levin and the late Lionel Trilling, may be taken as spokesmen for these divergent views as to the origins and basic purposes of Modernism. Trilling, from *The Liberal Imagination* onward, has emphasized the Modernist insight into the more irrational sides of human experience, thus associating Modernism, in what we call its first phase, with the theories of Nietzsche and German philosophy. Levin, on the other hand, has underscored the consciousness of Modernism, with its roots in the Enlightenment. His version of Modernism suits well with the great classics of the twenties. The theory of development advanced in this study seems to accommodate each of these views, explaining why each was necessary at different stages of Modernist growth and how each contributed to the fuller range of the Modernist vision. The unsettling early critiques, with their negative heroes, were as necessary as they were temporary in their creators' evolutions. They looked forward to further development, the fuller purpose of Modernism that would be expressed in the complex central consciousness (which is still very different, as Virginia Woolf reminds us, from the ease, even blitheness, of the Enlightenment personality). In terms of personal dynamics the development of the complex central consciousness seems to be the crucial Modernist phase. Those who would proceed to the "mythic" without knowing the supple flexibility and the range of reference of the complex consciousness, its abstention from willfulness, would doom themselves to barren repetition, or worse. Perhaps, then, we should give greater heed to Levin's insights into the ethical consciousness of the Moderns.[8]

One can also see that what we referred to as "ideology" is the expression of needs that were making themselves known in broader areas of human experience. The primary Modernist encounter is with history, and not only with history as a discipline of knowledge but with historical values, the very flow and continuities of life itself, or, at least, the particular Western construction that was placed on that flow since the time of the Renaissance. At their points of departure, following Nietzsche, Modernists rejected historical values and historical knowledge as linear development. This is the substance of the Modernist quarrel with the nineteenth century. History was not a sufficient bulwark of support against the growing sense of cosmic void and personal futility. It was not enough to know; one needed to bring a density and texture of personal apprehension to knowledge. We can gauge how threatening had become the standardization of experience (and this is the cause of Nietzsche's great complaint), and how paper-thin historical knowledge by the intensity of this Modernist need to redeem history through the self. Historical themes needed to be given a psychic root in order for them to take hold; a personal affinity had to be established before the past could gain significance. This is the act of legitimation that all Modernists needed to experience: only through such nonhistorical means could history be salvaged. The gates of horn require the close proximity of the gates of ivory, as historical themes need myth.

If the first of the several historical purposes of Modernism was to "temper" liberal humanism with other kinds of experience, and another was to restore the primacy of the individual self in the present as against the claims of history and historical values, a third purpose, not quite so apparent, yet far-reaching in its effect, was to slow down the Western dynamic that had been unleashed in the Renaissance. In that period of energetic reawakening, of exhortations to exploit all available time, as well as resources, the intellectual background was laid for an age of industrial expansion. Even Burckhardt, taking another look at the relations of the Middle Ages and the Renaissance in his later reflections, could say that the earlier time was a period of "salutary delay" in the history of the West, suggesting thereby that he himself had doubts as to where that energetic code of values was taking us.[9] (As my text has made clear repeatedly we are not talking about the full Renaissance achievement, which was quite balanced, but about "tendencies" in their thought and the later development of these tendencies.) Was not Modernism, in line with Burckhardt's revised thinking, an attempt to put a brake on the linear movement of the will toward simple expansion? By their exploration of the virtues of passivity, tolerance and selflessness, by their pathetic pictures of the self-destructive powers of the will, did they not provide for us the basis in personality of the type best calculated to effect such a slowdown?

PURVIEWS AND PURPOSES

More so than the social theories of communism or capitalism, was not Modernism operating at what Ortega called the "height of the times," and focusing on problems that were common to each of these competing industrial systems? In "The Human Prospect," a book-length article that received wide attention, Robert Heilbroner declared that "the values of an industrial civilization, which have for two centuries given us not only industrial advance but a sense of *élan* and purpose, now seem to be losing their self-evident justification." He finds the problems of industrial civilizations common to both capitalism and communism (or socialism). They range from the deification of efficiency and production to the "unthinking pillage of nature." "All these values," Heilbroner sums up, "manifest themselves throughout bourgeois and socialist styles of life, both lived by the clock, organized by the factory or office, obsessed with material achievements, attuned to highly quantitative modes of thought—in a word, by a style of life that, in contrast with the non-industrial civilizations seem dazzlingly rich in every dimension except that of the cultivation of the human person."[10]

If Heilbroner's analysis is appealing without being surprising (in ways similar to those of Adorno or Marcuse), it is because we have already had in the works of Modernism a clear dramatic presentation of reasons why this *élan* had lost its justification as well as a preview of the mental attitudes needed to revise the industrial outlook "lived by the clock." What must be impressive in the works of Modernism is the range of their realizations, the radical shifts in their emotional register. It is as if they were suggesting to us by the fabric of their works a model to cope with a world where single-mindedness is increasingly easy and increasingly dangerous. By the mental attitudes of their new personality-types and their own range of sensibility they suggest the human need for a multiplicity of times, and for activities that would feed all of the dimensions of the human personality. This foresightedness is the kind of prophecy Joyce may have had in mind when he declared that the real supermen are the historians of the future.[11]

Notes

Introduction

1. For the history of the term "modern" or its variants, see Franco Lombardi, *Nascità del Mondo Moderno* (Asti: Casa Editrice Arethusa, 1953), pp. 316-320; Herbert Anton, "Modernität als Aporie und Ereignis," in *Aspekte der Modernität*, ed. Hans Steffen (Göttingen: Vandenhoeck and Ruprecht, 1965), pp. 7-13. See also Matei Calinescu, *Faces of Modernity: Avant-garde, Decadence, Kitsch* (Bloomington, Ind.: Indiana University Press, 1977), pp. 14-58 for a literary survey.

2. Randomly one can point to such works as Lyndall Gordon's *Eliot's Early Years* (London: Oxford University Press, 1977), Ronald Bush's *The Genesis of Pound's "Cantos"* (Princeton, N.J.: Princeton University Press, 1976), and Paul Delany's *D. H. Lawrence's Nightmare: The Writer and His Circle in the Years of the Great War* (New York: Basic Books, 1979). These works, far from closing their subjects off in isolated uniqueness, reveal how elaborate were the patterns of connection. See, for instance, the section in Bush's book, "Stages of Revision," where he shows how the periodical publication of chapters of *Ulysses* prior to 1922 strongly influenced Pound's *Cantos* and Eliot's *Gerontion* and *The Waste Land* (pp. 205-246).

3. First published in *The Massachusetts Review* (August, 1960), reprinted in *Refractions: Essays in Comparative Literature* (New York: Oxford University Press, 1966), pp. 271-295, where it has the company of a related essay, "Reflections on the Final Volume of *The Oxford History of English Literature*," pp. 151-170. See also the "Epistle Dedicatory" to *Memories of the Moderns* (New York: New Directions, 1980).

4. Cambridge, Mass.: Harvard University Press, 1972.

5. Edited by Malcolm Bradbury and James McFarlane (London and New York: Penquin, 1976), p. 50.

6. See the very useful study by Wilson Martins, *The Modernist Idea: A Critical Survey of Brazilian Writing in the Twentieth Century*, trans. Jack E. Tomlin (New York: New York University Press, 1970). The Futurist fascination with the "modernist age" may be represented by Rubens Borba de Moraes, who shows genuine delight in twentieth-

NOTES TO INTRODUCTION

century time and speed: "The intensity of modern life has sharpened our notion of material time. . . . The speed of modern life forces the artist to depict quickly what he felt quickly, before the intelligence intervenes. From that condition was born the synthesization of modern art. Time!" (pp. 31-33) The Modernist movements in countries like Italy and Spain—and to them could be added Russia—had some purposes that obviously differed from those of the northern, more industrialized countries. And these differences derived from basic historical conditions, namely, that the former countries were much more belated in their transition from a feudal to an industrialized society. See my *Renaissance Discovery of Time* (pp. 499-500) for a brief discussion of Italy and Spain. For a vibrant and, one must say, inspired study of the nature of the Spanish discontent (called Quixotism) with the "rationalism" of the Renaissance, see Miquel de Unamuno's *Tragic Sense of Life*, trans. J. E. Crawford Flitch, 1921 (New York: Dover Publications, 1954), pp. 322, 326. For ancillary evidence from a closely related but much more quantifiable area, witness this paragraph from David S. Landes's splendid study, *Revolution in Time: Clocks and the Making of the Modern World* (Cambridge, Mass.: Harvard University Press, 1983):

> In all these countries [Germany, Great Britain, the United States and even Austria-Hungary] the large and growing demand for timepieces was an accompaniment of urbanization and industrialization—indeed, for the adoption of all the values that we commonly associate with modern living. In this sense, the consumption of timepieces may well be the best proxy measure of modernization, better even than energy consumption per capita. . . . The need to know the time is independent of all of these, and data on consumption of timepieces have the additional advantage of quantifying the imponderable. They sum up, in effect, a whole bundle of new work and life requirements and the inculcation of values and attitudes that make the system go. (p. 325)

Speaking of time as a "centering device" intellectually! While its subtitle is something of a misnomer, nevertheless, this book provides valuable information for the development of time-telling, and the clock and watch industries in the early modern and modern periods. A similar study, devoted to the early modern period, from the middle of the seventeenth to the end of the nineteenth centuries, and cov-

NOTES TO INTRODUCTION

ering the concept of time as a cultural factor, is now one of our greatest needs.

7. See Georges Poulet, *Studies in Human Time*, trans. Elliott Coleman (Baltimore and London: The Johns Hopkins University Press, 1956); Hans Meyerhoff, *Time in Literature* (Berkeley, Calif.: University of California Press, 1955); A. A. Mendilow, *Time and the Novel* (London and New York: P. Nevill, 1952); for fuller coverage and bibliography, see *Aspects of Time*, ed. C. A. Patrides (Manchester and Toronto: Manchester University Press and University of Toronto Press, 1976); and, for a somewhat different approach, Sharon Spencer, *Space, Time and Structure in the Modern Novel* (New York: New York University Press, 1971). Another book of interest that has recently appeared is that of Stephen Kern, *The Culture of Time and Space: 1880-1918* (Cambridge, Mass.: Harvard University Press, 1983), which is, as its title suggests, more of a sociological study, in which most of the movements of this epoch are uniformly entwined.

8. See Calinescu, p. 41.

9. From *The Birth of Tragedy*, see below chapter 1, section 2 and n. 11.

10. See below n. 26. Incidentally, this sense of the "struggle of the modern" may be distinguished from Poggioli's sense of the "agonistic" avant-garde, which is masochistic in its willingness to throw itself in the abyss for the sake of posterity. This sense of being necessary, even willing, victims at the barricades, present in Nietzsche, is somewhat antipathetic to what I would consider the Modernist consciousness. See *The Theory of the Avant-garde*, trans. Gerald Fitzgerald (Cambridge, Mass.: Harvard University Press, 1968), pp. 66-68.

11. *Speculations*, ed. Herbert Read (New York: Harcourt, Brace and Co., 1924), pp. 97-98.

12. The point of departure represents certain psychic conditions and moral patterns rather than an absolute chronological beginning. In our great sense of the continuities of historical flux, there are always beginnings before beginnings, falls before the Fall. This is of course the crux of the problem in any diachronic study—antecedents and precursors and continuities are always coming into sight, hard to dismiss. The point of departure represents more of a decisive turn in the consciousness of an author or of a period—that by which their mark becomes distinctive. Rather than a chronological beginning, the point of departure represents the core conditions of break-through, those conditions by means of which the author asserts the character-

NOTES TO INTRODUCTION

istics that are identifiably his and by which he will be known. This explains why, in contrast to a simple beginning, the point of departure will be recapitulated in later works, as if the writer felt compelled to reiterate the vital commencement of his development. (For an example, see chapter 6, section 1.)

13. Lyndall Gordon, *Eliot's Early Years*, p. 66.

14. Specifically, see "Farinata and Cavalcante," in *Mimesis: The Representation of Reality in Western Literature*, trans. Willard Trask (Princeton, N.J.: Princeton University Press, 1953), and "Figura," in *Scenes from the Drama of European Literature* (New York: Meridian, 1959).

15. One gathers that it is in exactly such a nexus between historical geneticism and structuralism that René Girard would place his work. See the chapters on Freud and Lévi-Strauss in *La Violence et le sacré* (Paris: Bernard Grasset, 1972). His interest in establishing causal connections between theory and reality may be summarized as a return to Freud without renouncing structuralism. See *La Violence*, p. 329. On the most recent impetus to "rehistoricize" literary studies, see the sophisticated essay by Jerome J. McGann, *The Romantic Ideology: A Critical Investigation* (Chicago and London: The University of Chicago Press, 1983).

16. *In Search of Cultural History*, The Phillip Maurice Deneke Lecture of 1967 (Oxford: The Clarendon Press, 1969), p. 46.

17. See *The Renaissance Discovery of Time*, pp. 181-186, where I explain these phrases taken from Cassirer's work and attempt to show their adaptability to Renaissance developments. In brief, "graduated mediation" implies a state of religious, ontological at-oneness with the world and with God, or even a practical sense of belonging; it evidences no metaphysical disquiet. Chorismos, on the other hand, shows epistemological as well as practical disturbances, radical skepticism. Man is totally separated from a God, who is totally other. This is the basis for tragedy, *Hamlet* and *King Lear*, with their roots in Montaigne's *Apology for Raimond Sebonde*. In both Shakespeare and Montaigne, the experience of this tragic separation (or chorismos), leads to a post-tragic world of renewed participation (methexis), shown by Shakespeare's last plays, and Montaigne's great *Third Book of Essays*.

18. See Monroe K. Spears, *Dionysus and the City: Modernism in Twentieth Century Poetry* (New York: Oxford University Press, 1970); Maurice Beebe, "Ulysses and the Age of Modernism," *James Joyce*

NOTES TO INTRODUCTION

Quarterly, 10 (1972), p. 172; and " 'A Mirror Carried Along the Road of Life?' Reflective and Reflexive Trends in Modern Fiction," a paper read to the American Society for Aesthetics, 1973.

19. See conveniently *The Mirror of Art: Critical Studies by Charles Baudelaire*, trans. and ed. Jonathon Mayne (Garden City, N.Y.: Doubleday Anchor, 1956), pp. 130, 223. For the *Painter of Modern Life*, see *Baudelaire as a Literary Critic*, trans. Lois Boe Hylsop and Francis E. Hylsop (University Park, Pa.: Pennsylvania State University Press, 1964), p. 296.

20. *The Use and Abuse of History*, trans. Adrian Collins, The Library of Liberal Arts (Indianapolis, Ind.: Bobbs-Merrill, 1957), pp. 29, 39, 49; *Friedrich Nietzsche: Werke*, ed. Karl Schlechta, 3 vol. (Munich: Hanser, 1954), I. 238-239, 249, 260. For a much fuller analysis of Nietzsche's complex legacy to Modernism, see John Burt Foster, Jr., *Heirs to Dionysus: A Nietzschean Current in Literary Modernism* (Princeton, N.J.: Princeton University Press, 1981).

21. See "Why *Four Quartets* Matter in a Technologico-Benthamite Age," *English Literature in Our Time and the University* (Cambridge University Press, 1979), p. 111.

22. Quoted by Michael Roberts in his *T. E. Hulme* (London: Faber and Faber, 1938), p. 18. Anna Balakian makes these very pertinent remarks about Baudelaire:

> ... one must recognize that Baudelaire's most salient characteristic is his diversity, his very lack of a salient trait, his virtual reversibility and multiplicity of character. The student of literary criticism could go through his verse and prose writings and find enough substantiation, compile enough quotes, to make him a Swedenborgian poet, after which, he could go back again and find enough proof to arrrive at a diametrically opposite conclusion.

The Symbolist Movement, A Critical Appraisal (New York: New York University Press, 1977), p. 31.

23. "Schopenhauer," in *Essays of Three Decades*, trans. H. T. Lowe-Porter (New York: Knopf, 1947), pp. 407-410; *Thomas Mann: Schriften und Reden zur Literatur, Kunst und Philosophie*, vol. 2 (Frankfurt-am-Main: Fischer, 1968), pp. 285 ff., esp. 287, 289, 290.

24. This is the suggestion by Bradbury and McFarlane, *Modernism*, pp. 37-44; what follows is indebted to their essay. See in particular Georg Brandes, *Friedrich Nietzsche* (Heinemann, 1914). A specific case of the impact of Nietzsche is detailed in Carl E. Schorske's *Fin-*

NOTES TO CHAPTER I

de-siècle Vienna (New York: Knopf, 1980). See the chapter, "Gustav Klimt: Painting and the Crisis of the Liberal Ego," pp. 208-278.

25. Oxford: The Clarendon Press, 1969, pp. 35-38.

26. Paul Valéry, "The Crisis of the Mind," trans. Denise Folliot and Jackson Mathews, *History and Politics*, vol. X, *The Collected Works of Paul Valéry*, ed. Jackson Mathews, Bollingen Series XLV (New York: Pantheon, 1962), p. 27; Stephen Spender, *The Struggle of the Modern* (Berkeley and Los Angeles: University of California Press, 1963), pp. 71-78.

27. While the critical order of the day is the necessity to reassess and reassert the achievements and the accomplishments of the "high" Modernists, I emphasize that these concerns do not exhaust my interest or awareness of Modernism in all of its broader senses—witness my roles as co-organizer of The Claremont Colleges' Comparative Literature Conference on Modernism (April, 1982) and as co-editor of the forthcoming proceedings of that conference.

28. See above n. 10.

29. *Opus Posthumous*, ed. Samuel French Morse (New York: Knopf, 1957), p. 177.

30. *A History of Modern Poetry: From the 1890s to Pound, Eliot and Yeats* (Cambridge, Mass.: Harvard University Press, 1976), pp. 599, 601. Doubtlessly, Yeats represents a major problem for my text, almost requiring a small monograph or a sizeable essay. I do mention the importance of Yeats in the development of the Modernist epiphany, as well as the mythic method. "Sailing to Byzantium" is a remarkable Modernist poem, as is the entire *Tower* volume.

31. One of the pleasures that derives from a study such as this, one dealing in patterns and paradigms, where the illustrative examples are of necessity limited in scope and number, occurs when readers with expert knowledge in other areas of literature or related subjects—those not covered in the study at hand—find application and use for the patterns developed.

I. *The Collapse of Historical Values*

1. Geoffrey Barraclough, *An Introduction to Contemporary History* (Baltimore, Md.: Penguin Books, 1967), p. 61.

2. Alan Bullock, "The Double Image," in *Modernism*, ed. Bradbury and McFarlane, p. 60.

3. "Reflections on a Literary Revolution," *Image and Experience*

NOTES TO CHAPTER I

(Lincoln, Neb.: University of Nebraska Press, 1960), pp. 74-78. As will be clear throughout this study, my purpose is to form a bridge between the "political" and the social, on one side, and the aesthetic and artistic on the other. Frankly, in practical terms, I have always found such divisions to be artificial. In this attempt, I am heartened by the bold, imaginative speculations of Marshall Berman in his *All That Is Solid Melts into Air: The Experience of Modernity* (New York: Simon and Shuster, 1982), particularly where he writes: "Our vision of modern life tends to split into material and spiritual planes: some people devote themselves to 'modernism,' which they see as a species of pure spirit, evolving in accord with its autonomous artistic and intellectual imperatives; other people work within the orbit of 'modernization.' . . . This dualism, pervasive in contemporary culture, cuts us off from one of the . . . facts of modern life: the interfusion of material and spiritual forces, the intimate unity of the modern self and the modern environment." (pp. 131-132)

4. "Humanism and the Religious Attitude," *Speculations*, p. 36.

5. "Goethe and Tolstoy," trans. H. T. Lowe-Porter, *Essays of Three Decades* (New York: Knopf, 1947), p. 170; *Thomas Mann: Werke, Schriften und Reden zur Literatur, Kunst und Philosophie* (Frankfurt-am-Main: Fischer, 1967), I. 212.

6. "Goethe as Representative of the Bourgeois Age," *Essays of Three Decades*, p. 68; *Schriften und Reden*, II. 64. Some of Eliot's comments on the nineteenth century are relevant here: "Tennyson lived in a time which was already acutely time-conscious: a great many things seemed to be happening, railways were being built, discoveries were being made, the face of the world was changing. That was a time busy in keeping up to date." "In Memoriam," *Selected Essays* (New York: Harcourt, Brace and Co., 1950), p, 294. "In the middle nineteenth century, the age which (at its best) Goethe had prefigured, an age of bustle, programmes, platforms, scientific progress, humanitarianism and revolutions which improved nothing, an age of progressive degradation, Baudelaire perceived that what really matters is Sin and Redemption." "Baudelaire," *ibid.*, p. 378.

7. *Essays of Three Decades*, pp. 74-75; *Schriften und Reden*, II. 71-72.

8. *The Birth of Tragedy*, trans. Francis Golffing (Garden City, N.Y.: Doubleday Anchor, 1956), p. 140; *Friedrich Nietzsche: Werke*, 3 vols. (Munich: Hanser, 1954), I. 128.

NOTES TO CHAPTER I

9. *The Birth of Tragedy*, pp. 95, 104, 120-121, 123, 139, 140; *Werke*, I. 87, 95, 110, 112, 128.

10. *The Birth of Tragedy*, pp. 109, 139-140, 110; *Werke*. I. 99-100, 128, 100.

11. *The Birth of Tragedy*, p. 111; *Werke*, I. 101.

12. *The Birth of Tragedy*, pp. 138-139; *Werke*, I. 127. For a more direct personal connection, see Nietzsche's hostility to the less enterprising academic endeavors: "Those university teachers who have not exhausted their energies in the emendation of classical texts or the microscopic inspection of linguistic phenomena will assimilate Greek antiquity by "historical" methods, along with other antiquities, with the conscious superiority of up-to-date scholarship." (p. 122, *Werke*, I. 111)

13. "Myth Becomes History," in *Myth and Meaning* (New York: Schocken Books, 1979), pp. 42-43.

14. *The Renaissance Discovery of Time*, summary, pp. 494-496; see also pp. 13-16, 72-84, 135-146, and 300-311. These points are summarized in my "Time and Historical Values in the Literature of the Renaissance," *Aspects of Time*, ed. C. A. Patrides (Manchester and Toronto: Manchester University and University of Toronto Presses, 1976), p. 38.

15. "A Song for Simeon," and "Ash Wednesday," in *T. S. Eliot: The Complete Poems and Plays, 1909-1950* (New York: Harcourt, Brace and Co., 1952), pp. 70, 64.

16. Baltimore, Md.: Johns Hopkins University Press, p. 42; also Jerome Buckley, *The Triumph of Time* (Cambridge, Mass.: Harvard University Press, 1966), p. 6. Friedrich Meinecke's *Historism: The Rise of a New Historical Outlook*, trans. J. E. Anderson (New York: Herder and Herder, 1972), is valuable since it traces the development in the late eighteenth century from the "paradigmatic" generalized view of human nature that dominated in the Enlightenment to the more "individualized" historical view. There is much of use in Peter Allan Dale's *The Victorian Critic and the Idea of History* (Cambridge, Mass.: Harvard University Press, 1977). On the decline of historical drama, see Herbert Lindenberger's *Historical Drama: The Relation of Literature and Reality* (Chicago and London: University of Chicago Press, 1975).

17. *The Use and Abuse of History*, p. 10; *Werke*, I. 217. As the next paragraph makes clear, by "process" Nietzsche means the loss of the individual to some higher historical group development. Thus, there

NOTES TO CHAPTER I

is no real contradiction between opposition to this kind of process and the widespread favor of Whitehead's "process philosophy" in twentieth-century thought. The same thing might be said of the antihistoricist bias of Modernism (with some qualifications) and my own "developmental" method of approach. Obviously, one can adhere to a developmental approach (as most Modernists did in relation to their own works) and still be opposed to the scheme of historical values that Nietzsche, among others, opposed. For one, development, particularly from the perception of Modernists, is something realized after the fact (see below, the chapter "The Songs That I Sing"); it is not an *a priori* commitment, nor does it require the subjection of the self. Rather, it follows the self in its integral phases of development.

18. *Speculations*, p. 3.
19. By M. S. Watanabe at the Second World Conference for the Study of Time, July, 1973, Mt. Fuji, Japan.
20. Page 330, *Jacob's Room and The Waves* (New York: Harcourt, Brace and World Harvest rpt., 1959).
21. *The Renaissance Discovery of Time*, pp. 74-75, 133-135, 326, 513.
22. *Man's Fate*, trans. Haakon M. Chevalier (New York: Random House Vintage, 1961), p. 313; *La Condition humaine* (Paris: Gallimard, 1946), p. 265.
23. All page citations that follow in the text refer, first, to the English language edition of *The Magic Mountain*, trans. H. T. Lowe-Porter (New York: Random House Vintage, 1967), and, secondly, after the slash, to the German language edition, *Der Zauberberg*, 1924 (Frankfurt-am-Main: Fischer, 1967). This procedure will be followed with all continuous quotations from Mann.
24. The watch that Leopold gave to Molly Bloom, "never seems to go properly," *Ulysses*, and Quentin Compson in Faulkner's *The Sound and the Fury* breaks the crystal and wrenches off the hands of his watch.
25. *The Renaissance Discovery of Time*, pp. 6, 11, 148-149, 162, 347, 354, 412, 496, and 512.
26. Quoted from the abstract of Masanao Toda's paper at the Second World Conference for the Study of Time, July, 1973, at Mt. Fuji, Japan. The hypothesis that "the habit of predicting and planning is something of a newcomer in western culture," is presented, along with evidence of the growth of "prediction," by Edward M.

NOTES TO CHAPTER II

Jennings in "The Consequences of Prediction," *Studies on Voltaire and the Eighteenth Century*, CLI-CLV (1976), pp. 1131-1150.

27. "Time and Entropy," in *Time in Science and Philosophy*, ed. Jiri Zeman (Prague: Academia, 1971), p. 29.

28. *The Use and Abuse of History*, p. 46; *Werke*, I. 251.

II. The Family, the Machine and the Paradox of Time

1. *The Complete Poems and Plays: 1909-1950*, p. 97.

2. *Phoenix II*, ed. Warren Roberts and Harry T. Moore (New York: Viking, 1970), p. 400.

3. *T. S. Eliot: Selected Essays* (New York: Harcourt, Brace and Co., 1950), p. 295.

4. *The Critical Writings of James Joyce*, ed. Ellsworth Mason and Richard Ellmann (New York: Viking, 1964), p. 185.

5. *Jacob's Room* (New York: Harcourt, Brace and World, 1959), see pp. 45, 99.

6. In *The Heart of Darkness and The Secret Sharer* (New York: Signet, 1950), pp. 119, 117.

7. *"Death in Venice" and Seven Other Stories* (New York: Random House Vintage, 1954), pp. 9-10. There is perhaps no greater link between the nineteenth century and the energetic qualities of the Renaissance than this faith in the redeeming qualities of labor. The Renaissance usage of the parable of the talents tells the story. (See my *Renaissance Discovery of Time, passim.*) In an excellent chapter on the "The Problem of Work," Karl Löwith quotes from Zola's address to young people, "I had only one faith, one source of strength: work. I was held up only by the immense task I laid upon myself. . . . The work of which I speak is regular work, a lesson, a duty I have assigned myself to make some progress in every day, even if only a step forward. . . . Work! Consider, gentlemen: work forms the only law of the world." (See below section 3, n. 31.) And in another chapter also entitled "Work," Alexander Welsh (*The City of Dickens*, Oxford: Clarendon Press, 1971) quotes similarly from Dickens: "My own invention and imagination, such as it is, I can most truthfully assure you, would never have served me as it has, but for the habit of commonplace, humble, patient, daily, toiling, drudging attention." (p. 75) When Thomas Mann designed the character of Aschenbach, he was able to find examples for this stalwart worker not only in himself but in his immediate cultural past. (See below chapter 7,

NOTES TO CHAPTER II

section 2.) Only Nietzsche, that radical reactionary, set himself against this doctrine of work, seeing it as opposed to religion and philosophy, and he does so in the same section of *Beyond Good and Evil* (58) where he attacks the scholar's commitment to history and his reliance on mere industry.

8. Part of the revenges exacted against unremitting toil must occur in the erotic life. Gregor Samsa has one pleasure in his otherwise drab existence and that is offered by the picture of the woman dressed in fur. Joseph K. seems desperate in his assaults on the women in *The Trial*. In Modernism Dionysus will force his way. Perhaps the most prescient of all Nietzsche's remarks comes from *The Birth of Tragedy*: "All that is now called culture, education, civilization, will one day have to appear before the incorruptible judge, Dionysus." (p. 120)

9. *Op. cit.*, p. 18.

10. *Ibid.*, p. 68.

11. See below section 3 of this chapter.

12. See the chapter, "Thy Death," in *Western Attitudes Toward Death: From the Middle Ages to the Present*, trans. Patricia M. Ranum (Baltimore and London: Johns Hopkins University Press, 1974), pp. 53 ff.

13. "The American Family in the Past Time," *American Scholar*, 43 (1974), p. 432.

14. *Buddenbrooks*, trans. H. T. Lowe-Porter (New York: Random House Vintage, rpt., 1961); *Buddenbrooks: Verfall einer Familie*, 1901 (Frankfurt-am-Main: Fischer, 1967). All citations in the text refer in order to these two volumes.

15. See subsection, "The Age of History," in *The Order of Things: An Archaeology of the Human Sciences*, trans. (none given) (New York: Random House Vintage rpt., 1973), pp. 220-221. See chapter 1, n. 16 above.

16. By Henry Hatfield in *Thomas Mann* (New York: New Directions, 1951), p. 33. For a study of the "genealogical patterns" in *Buddenbrooks* (as well as Lawrence's *The Rainbow*), see Patricia Drechsel Tobin's *Time and the Novel: The Genealogical Imperative* (Princeton, N.J.: Princeton University Press, 1978). While stressing the involvement of linearity with lineality, we can also note that other forces figure prominently in the Modernist rejection of "historical values." In this regard, Professor Tobin's slip in paraphrasing Stephen's famous declaration is intriguing: "*A Portrait* . . . pictures at its end

NOTES TO CHAPTER II

Stephen saying his *non serviam* to the paternal authority of father, church, and nation. . . ." (p. 27) Actually, Stephen declares his unwillingness to serve "that in which I no longer believe whether it calls itself my home, my fatherland, my church." The home presumably would include the mother's domain.

17. Cambridge, Mass.: Harvard University Press, 1971, p. 139.
18. New York: The Free Press, rpt., 1967, pp. 96, 97, 101.
19. From an ambience similar to that of Freud, that of a Central European German Jew, Kafka shows the problem of family life in the cruel dynamic of his works. Rather than nurturing continuity the family seems to have the effect of a see-saw: Georg Bendemann rises as his father falls; during Gregor Samsa's reversion the father, a bankrupt, resumes wearing his smart uniform, the mother and father are reunited, and the sister at last, no longer under the care of the brother's solicitous patronage, is like a butterfly emerging into a new life.

Following René Girard's insights in his *La Violence et le sacré* there may be even greater significance in Kafka's stories. In pages that strike fire, Girard places his theories of sacrifice, ritual and myth in an historical and contemporary setting, and makes of Kafka the true spokesman for the modern age, itself beset by the "dissolution des différences" that is so similar to the primitive "crise sacrificielle." This crisis is marked primarily by the "effacement complet du rôle paternel." From my own studies I have been struck by the disappearance of the father; others have written with good evidence of his overwhelming presence. It is perhaps Girard's theory that accommodates both conceptions and does so by placing them in a fuller theory. The father serves as model and obstacle and he becomes more of an obstacle the more the differences between father and son disappear: "Et le père ne peut devenir obstacle qu'avec la diminution de sa puissance paternelle qui le rapproche du fils sous tous les rapports et le fait vivre dans le même univers que celui-ci. L'âge d'or du 'complexe d'Oedipe' se situe dans un monde où la position du père est affaiblie mais pas complètement perdue, c'est-à-dire dans la famille occidentale au cours des derniers siècles." (259) Kafka's theme is precisely the loss of structure that Girard describes. Not a strong father, not an absent father, but a sadly weakened one, who in turn creates the malaise of his son, not the malaise deriving from oppression but rather from guilt. The model presents an inverse obstacle, the guilt of supercession. This same "destructuration" affects the law: "Ce n'est pas la loi . . . qu'on peut rendre responsable des tensions et aliena-

NOTES TO CHAPTER II

tions auxquelles l'homme moderne est exposé, c'est l'absence toujours plus complète de toute loi." (260) Not Freud, not Nietzsche, it is Kafka who recognizes that it is this absence of law (which is the same thing as the law gone mad) which is "le vrai fardeau qui pèse sur les hômmes." (260-261) Kafka is the true spokesman for the "whatever" culture, that non-culture which Girard associates with the modern (here I gather he is not speaking of Modernism but of the modern world).

20. New York: Viking, 1960, p. 327, to which all future citations in the text refer.

21. *Phoenix I*, ed. Edward McDonald (New York: Viking, 1936), p. 621. The following sentence is also indicative: "Romulus and Remus had all the luck. We see now why they bred a great, great race: because they had no mother: a race of men." (p. 637)

22. New York: Knopf Vintage, 1955, p. 247.

23. I refer to Modernism here as an aesthetic. But see the marvelous statement from Ortega's *Dehumanization*: "The aspect European existence is taking on in all orders of life points to a time of masculinity and youthfulness. For a while women and old people will have to cede the rule over life to boys ... the world grows increasingly informal." (52) And we all wear jeans.

24. Included in the volume, *"The Sea and Sardinia" and Selections from "Twilight in Italy"* (Garden City, N. Y.: Doubleday Anchor, 1954), pp. 241-242.

25. *Ulysses* (New York: Random House Vintage, corrected, 1961), p. 10.

26. *A Portrait of the Artist as a Young Man*, in *Viking Portable James Joyce*, pp. 520, 474. While the birth of a child, in itself, is a potent thing in Joyce (see *Ulysses*), what Stephen objects to is the whole schema of social values and extended obligations built around it.

27. All citations in the text refer to *The Rainbow* (New York: Viking, 1961).

28. In *Phoenix II*, 410. Harry T. Moore, *The Priest of Love* (New York: Farrar, Straus and Giroux, rev. ed., 1974), p. 235.

29. For valuable material in regard to this point, see David J. Kleinbard, "D. H. Lawrence and Ontological Insecurity," *PMLA*, 89 (1974), pp. 154-163, esp. 158.

30. "The Crown," *Phoenix II*, p. 412.

31. Trans. David E. Green (Garden City: N.Y.: Doubleday Anchor, 1967), p. 260.

NOTES TO CHAPTER II

32. Quoted from Löwith, p. 302.
33. In *Phoenix I*, to which all citations in the text refer.
34. Trans. anon. (New York: North, 1957), p. 32.
35. New York: Harcourt, Brace and Co., 1928, pp. 288-289.
36. *Phoenix II*, p. 373: "Anything that triumphs, perishes."
37. *The Grand Design of God: The Literary Form of the Christian View of History* (London: Routledge and Kegan Paul, 1972), p. 132.
38. *Apocalypse*, 1931 (New York: Viking rpt., 1966), p. 87.
39. *The Revolt of the Masses*, p. 33.
40. *Science and the Modern World*, pp. 50-51, 124. Whitehead expresses his difference with Bergson as to the nature of the error on pp. 50-51.
41. Trans. F. L. Pogson (New York: Harper rpt., 1960), p. 90, to which all citations in the text refer.
42. Trans. Cloudesley Brereton and Fred Rothwell (New York: Macmillan, 1928), to which citations in the text refer.
43. "Bergson's Theory of Art," in *Speculations*, pp. 149, 147.
44. "Romanticism and Classicism," *Speculations*, p. 137.
45. In *History and Class Consciousness*, trans. Rodney Livingstone (Cambridge, Mass.: MIT Press, 1971), pp. 88-91. The passage from Marx can be found in *The Poverty of Philosophy* (Moscow: Foreign Languages Publishing House, n.d.), pp. 58-59.
46. *Ibid.*, p. 88.
47. See Colin Clarke's *River of Dissolution: D. H. Lawrence and English Romanticism* (London: Routledge and Kegan Paul, 1969).
48. *The Principles of Scientific Management*, 1911 (New York: Norton rpt., 1967), see pp. 38 and 118, 7 and 62, and 140. See also Emma Rothschild, *Paradise Lost: The Decline of the Auto-Industrial Age* (New York: Random House, 1973), p. 34, reviewed by Richard Barnet in *The New York Review of Books*, May 2, 1974, p. 33; and Martin Braverman, *Labour and Monopoly Capitalism: The Degradation of Work in the Twentieth Century* (New York: Monthly Review Press, 1974), reviewed by Robert L. Heilbroner, in *The New York Review of Books*, Jan. 23, 1975, p. 6. For the reference to Henry Ford, see *Phoenix II*, p. 583. Important corroboration of this argument is provided by Hubert Zapf in "Taylorism in D. H. Lawrence's *Women in Love*," *The D. H. Lawrence Review*, 15 (1982), pp. 129-139, more particularly the specific conclusion that "the concrete measures Gerald takes to implement his new scheme agree almost point by point with the measures proposed in Taylor's book."

NOTES TO CHAPTER III

49. For similar instances in Henry James, see R. W. Stallman's Afterword to *The Ambassadors* (New York: Signet, 1960), pp. 377-381.
50. *The Renaissance Discovery of Time*, p. 37.
51. "The celestial machine," wrote Kepler, "is not to be likened to a divine organism . . . but rather to a clockwork." Quoted in J. T. Fraser, *Of Time, Passion and Knowledge: Reflections on the Strategy of Existence* (New York: Braziller, 1975), p. 65.

III. Transformations

1. This trope offers more than the normal tensions of nineteenth-century dualisms; it offers a remarkable range of differing and contradictory emotions. The usual phrase, something like, "*les grandeurs et misères*," does not fill the Modernist range, either, since such terminology is used to describe grand things, of a common level, that are imbued with a great and perhaps fatal destiny. This is not at all like the Modernist concern with objects from different levels of experience. The quotation from Ortega comes from *The Revolt of the Masses*, p. 33.
2. *Joseph Conrad: The Three Lives* (New York: Farrar, Straus and Giroux, 1979), p. 460. Ian Watt's *Conrad in the Nineteenth Century* (Berkeley and Los Angeles: University of California Press, 1979) traces the emergence of Conrad's qualified "modernity."
3. *The Viking Portable James Joyce*, pp. 432-433.
4. *The Use of Poetry and the Use of Criticism*, p. 106.
5. In *Jacob's Room and The Waves* (New York: Harcourt, Brace and World Harvest rpt. 1959), p. 342. Bernard is directed by whispers to that "which is outside our predicament, to that which is symbolic and thus perhaps permanent, if there is any permanence in our sleeping, eating, breathing, so animal, so spiritual and tumultuous lives." p. 349.
6. *George Herbert*, British Council and National Book League (London: Longmans, Green and Co., 1968), pp. 16-17.
7. In *Complementarities*, ed. John Paul Russo (Cambridge, Mass.: Harvard University Press, 1976). See D. H. Lawrence's description of the "rather bony, bloodless drama" written by the "rule and measure mathematical folk" (Shaw, Galsworthy and Barker), in a letter to Edward Garnett (1 Feb. 1913), *The Letters of D. H. Lawrence*, vol.

NOTES TO CHAPTER III

I, 1901-1913, ed. James T. Boulton (Cambridge: Cambridge University Press, 1979).

8. "Ulysses, Order, and Myth," *The Dial* 75 (1923), p. 480.
9. "The Name and Nature of Modernism," *Modernism*, p. 27.
10. See n. 2 above.
11. See Harry Levin's essay, "What was Modernism." *Refractions, op. cit.*, pp. 287-288 for this useful idea.
12. "The Ideology of Modernism," in *Realism in our Time*, trans. John and Necke Mander (New York: Harper and Row rpt., 1971), pp. 31 and 43.
13. *Loss of the Self in Modern Literature and Art* (New York: Random House Vintage, 1962), p. 36.
14. See "Notes from the Underground," trans. David Magarshack, *Great Short Works of Dostoevsky* (New York: Harper and Row Perennial Classic, 1968), pp. 265, 272.
15. *Phoenix II*, p. 384.
16. *The Letters of James Joyce*, ed. Richard Ellmann, vol. 2 (New York: Viking Press, 1966), pp. lv-lxii. Almost at random one can leaf through articles or books treating twentieth-century authors and come across such geographical mobility as part of their own personal and aesthetic *disponibilité*. See the Introduction by Monique Chefdor to a recent issue of *Studies in Twentieth Century Literature*, 3 (1979), devoted to Blaise Cendrars.
17. *The Collected Essays, Journalism and Letters of George Orwell*, ed. Sonia Orwell and Ian Angus (New York: Harcourt, Brace and World, 1968), IV. 489-490. That this influence from abroad has not been universally accepted as an entire package in England has helped to promote a far-reaching and very fruitful *querelle* between the adherents to a native English tradition in poetry (Wordsworth, Hardy and Larkin) and apologists for Modernism. England ought well to be a kind of battleground of serious resistance to the code and canon of Modernism since it is largely the great things of nineteenth-century England—from the Crystal Palace to Victorian literature (that peaceful leisurely reading of the great long novels) to, moving back, the essential genius of English Romantic poetry—that primarily figured as objects of Modernist attack. The legacy of native traditions as well as critical "common sense" spared England from uncritical acceptance of Modernism. Frank Kermode has written that one of the main issues of the modern poetic is "the unformulated quarrel between the orthodoxy of symbolism and the surviving elements of an

NOTES TO CHAPTER III

empirical-utilitarian tradition which, we are assured, is characteristically English." *The Romantic Image* (London: Routledge and Kegan Paul, 1966), p. 152. We may further note the absence of any interesting literary theory emanating from England. Fortunately, another generation of English critics, now somewhere in their forties, is producing excellent insight into the theory and practice of Modernism. I cite the volume edited by Bradbury and McFarlane, and the recent volumes of David Lodge and Peter Faulkner. What makes Lionel Trilling's *Sincerity and Authenticity* so intriguing a work is precisely its attempt to bestride this quarrel. See also Samuel Hynes, "The Hardy Tradition in Modern English Poetry," *Sewanee Review*, 78 (1980), pp. 34-51.

18. Frank Budgen, *James Joyce and the Making of "Ulysses"* (Bloomington, Ind.: Indiana University Press rpt., 1960), pp. 15-17.

19. John Bayley recognized the common type among Modernist characters when, writing in the *New York Review of Books*, March 6, 1975, he showed that Leopold Bloom and Marcel "are brothers under the skin." (p. 24) See also Meno Spann, *Franz Kafka*, pp. 106-107.

20. E. R. Curtius, "T. S. Eliot: I" in *Kritische Essays zur europäischen Literatur*, 2nd ed. (Bern: Francke, 1950), p. 326.

21. *The New Science*, trans. Thomas G. Bergin and Max Harold Fisch, revised and abridged (Ithaca and London: Cornell University Press, 1970), p. 192.

22. Page numbers following quotations refer first to *Remembrance of Things Past*, 2 vols., trans. C. K. Scott Moncrieff (New York: Random House, 1934) and, secondly, to *A la Recherche du temps perdu*, 3 vols. (Paris: Pléiade, 1954), with the exception of volume seven, *The Past Recaptured*, where I refer to the recent translation of Andreas Mayor (New York: Random House, 1970). Since I cite the standard French *Pléiade* edition, I see no reason to incorporate Terence Kilmartin's valuable revised version of Scott Moncrieff's older translation. But every reader of Proust in English must now use *Remembrance of Things Past*, 3 vols., trans. Terence Kilmartin (New York: Random House, 1981).

23. See n. 8 above.

24. *The Social History of Art* (New York: Vintage, n.d.), IV. 238.

25. See the pamphlet by Harry Levin, "*The Waste Land:* From *Ur* to *Echt*" (privately printed, New Directions, 1972), pp. 8-9.

26. Dostoevsky's heroes have a different function. Despite their

NOTES TO CHAPTER III

urban location, they do not open onto the world of the city. Rather, the city only presses us deeper into their consciousness. Kafka's Joseph K. also seems to be different. Normally his trials would constitute a tour of the professions, in the manner of Everyman (which he is not). As he tries to unravel the mysterious summons of his existence he moves among lawyers, tradesmen, painters and priests. Yet, his misery is left unsolved and his "counsellors" remain at the level of inscrutable accusations. His interviews do not open out onto, rather they seem to close off. See the remarkable essay by Renato Poggioli, "Mythology of Franz Kafka," *The Spirit of the Letter* (Cambridge, Mass.: Harvard University Press, 1965), p. 254.

27. All page citations in the text refer to *Mrs. Dalloway* (New York: Harcourt, Brace and World, 1925).

28. See the excellent essay by Morris Philipson, "*Mrs. Dalloway*: 'What's the Sense of Your Parties?'" *Critical Inquiry* I (1974), p. 123.

29. How many of Woolf's characters—those whose consciousness we follow—must forge the courage of existence in the face of discontinuity. Supremely important, as the basic matter of realization, is childlessness, or singleness.

30. Valéry Larbaud, "James Joyce," *Nouvelle Revue française*, 103 n.s. (1922), 385; Richard Ellmann, *James Joyce*; J. F. Revel, *Sur Proust* (Paris: Julliard, 1960); Roger Shattuck, *Marcel Proust* (New York: Viking Press, 1974); Mark Van Doren, "*Joseph and His Brothers*: A Comedy in Four Parts," rpt. in *Thomas Mann: A Collection of Critical Essays*, ed. Henry Hatfield (Englewood Cliffs, N.J.: Prentice-Hall, 1964), p. 96; and Erich Heller, *The Ironic German* (Boston: Little, Brown, 1958).

31. See *Souvenirs and Prophecy: The Young Wallace Stevens*, ed. Holly Stevens (New York: Knopf, 1977), pp. 165, 166, 167.

32. See the section "The Modern as Vision of the Whole" in *The Struggle of the Modern* (Los Angeles and Berkeley: University of California Press, 1963), p. 80.

33. See Bertrand Evans' *Shakespeare's Comedies* (Oxford: Clarendon Press, 1960).

34. *Sur Proust*, pp. 161 ff.

35. Here we can see why Dostoevsky, if not a Modern, as I believe is clear, is nevertheless something of a precursor. In *Crime and Punishment* there are two scenes, the death of Marmeladov and the funeral meal, that reveal the Modernist disunity, separate planes and

NOTES TO CHAPTER III

fractured interests, a sense of variety that prevents emotional unity. The death scene shifts from Mrs. Marmeladov's refusal to indulge in sympathy ("Got what he asked for"), to Mrs. Lippewechsel's lodgers gathered to gawk and gossip, the long-standing war between Mrs. Marmeladov and her landlady, to Mrs. Marmeladov's own pathetic flights of fantasy, and yet her refusal to allow her husband's gestures toward reconciliation ("Shut up! I don't want it! I know what you are going to say!"). The scene at the funeral meal is similar. Yet curiously enough (and showing Dostoevsky's intermediate position), each does end with a "gesture" (Raskolnikov's extraordinary gift of twenty rubles to Mrs. Marmeladov and Lebezyatnikov's courageous denunciation of Luzhin's ugly trick to embarrass Sonya and hence Raskolnikov). *Crime and Punishment*, trans. David Magarshack (London: Penguin, 1951), pp. 204, 411. The country fair scene in *Madame Bovary*, for all its technical innovations, is still on the level of old-fashioned satire. Its purpose is not to register multiple levels, but rather to debase one level, to bring it down by its context and interspersed ironies.

36. See the chapters, "Doctrine of the Point of View" and "The Historical Significance of the Theory of Einstein," *The Modern Theme*, trans. James Cleugh, pp. 92, 139; also Julian Marias, *José Ortega y Gasset: Circumstance and Vocation*, trans. Francis M. Lopez-Morillas (Norman, Okla.: University of Oklahoma Press, 1970), pp. 373 ff.

37. *The Modern Theme*, p. 92. See the more complex development of this idea in Marias, pp. 373-379, for valuable distinctions, and also Kern, *The Culture of Time and Space*, pp. 150-152.

38. *The Modern Theme*, p. 143.

39. *Oeuvres complètes* (Paris: Presses universitaires de France, 1959), pp. 1280-1283. See John D. Erickson, "The Proust-Einstein Relations: A Study in Relative Point of View," *Marcel Proust: A Critical Panorama*, ed. Larkin B. Paul (Urbana, Ill.: University of Illinois Press, 1973), p. 247.

40. *Criterion*, 10 (1930), p. 28. For the background of relativity in Eliot's thought, see Steven Foster, "Relativity and *The Waste Land*: a Postulate," *Texas Studies in Language and Literature*, 7 (1965), p. 77.

41. *Science and the Modern World*, p. 118.

42. "Time, Distance and Form in Proust," trans. Irving Singer, *The Hudson Review*, 11 (1958), p. 504; "Ulysses, Order and Myth,"

NOTES TO CHAPTER III

The Dial, 75 (1923), p. 480; *The Literary Essays of Ezra Pound* (London: Faber and Faber, 1954), pp. 5, 6, 17.

43. "Marcel Proust," especially in the subsection entitled "Relativismus" in *Französischer Geist in zwanzigsten Jahrhundert* (Bern: Francke, 1952), p. 343; "Ortega y Gasset: I" in *Kritische Essays*, pp. 258-259 and 263-265, where Curtius gives credit to Ortega for first showing the significance of "perspectivism" for modern times. See also Robert Wohl, *The Generation of 1914*, pp. 156-157, and Suzi Gablik, *Progress in Art*, pp. 80-86.

44. *The Modern Theme*, p. 90.

45. *Science and the Modern World*, p. 71.

46. *Axel's Castle* (New York: Scribner's, 1931), pp. 157, 189. "(Proust) has recreated the world of the novel from the point of view of relativity: he has supplied for the first time in literature an equivalent on the full scale for the new theory of modern physics." (p. 189)

47. See Foucault, *The Order of Things*, "Our culture crossed the threshold beyond which we recognize our modernity when finitude was conceived in an interminable cross-reference with itself." (p. 318)

48. See the essays by Maurice Beebe, "Ulysses and the Age of Modernism," and " 'A Mirror Carried Along the Road of Life?' Reflective and Reflexive Trends in Modern Fiction," Preface, and n. 18; John Fletcher and Malcolm Bradbury, "The Introverted Novel," *Modernism*.

49. *Sincerity and Authenticity* (Cambridge, Mass.: Harvard University Press, 1972).

50. *The Modern Theme*, p. 94.

51. *Mimesis*, trans. Willard Trask (Princeton, N.J.: Princeton University Press, 1953), p. 550.

52. One might of course ask, and indeed it has been asked at learned conferences I have attended and helped organize, why this urgent need to distinguish between the styles of Modernism and fascism. The contention is that to ignore the style of communism, to have no similarly urgent requirement to mark the differences from that "style," is itself a political act of omission, one that fails to note that both fascism and communism are regressive when it comes to the style of Modernism. I have heard Martin Esslin make this point with remarkable cogency. Nevertheless, judging from its own inner dynamic, it does seem that the important distinction to be made is that between Modernism and fascism. The more serious charges

NOTES TO CHAPTER IV

brought against eminent Modernists (Yeats, Lawrence, Eliot, Pound, to mention only the English-language "reactionaries")—their abrogation of the ethical, their disagreement with the melding of the religious, the human and the organic, their disgust with liberal humanism—all seem to make them more vulnerable to accusations of fascistic tendencies. However, when we witness the key role played by the negation of the will, by the dispersal of the ego into the complex central consciousness, the insistence on development, we can see how these signals of the Modernist position can have little in common with fascism.

See the useful comments by Russell Berman in his "Fascist Literature and the Modernist Paradigm," in the forthcoming publication of the proceedings of the Claremont Colleges' Comparative Literature Conference on Modernism (University of Illinois Press): "If the fascist political movements intended to overcome the chaos of liberal capitalism by returning to the ideological vision of a primitive stability and homogeneity, the fascist work of art appropriated this regenerative goal for itself. . . . It is the world of change and exchange that the fascist work denounces; neither the diversity of difference nor the transformation of history is tolerated. . . . This explains the anti-modernist gesture of fascist literature." Mr. Berman, however, apparently includes Lawrence and Eliot with Pound, Céline and Hamsun. He hardly reassures us on the first two in taking *Lady Chatterley's Lover* to be typical of Lawrence, or when he refers to Eliot's need to return to the seventeenth century. We see how important it is to have the full picture of Modernist development, their originating positions, as well as their exposition of the complex central consciousness. Of course, we can see instances of a need in Eliot to restore the great religious epoch of the seventeenth century ("Little Gidding"), but that is only part of the picture. In his valuable review of *Ulysses*, Eliot emphasized not only the mythic but also the anarchic in modern life, but for whose representation the mythic, or classical, would be mummified. In short, I agree with Mr. Berman's terms of analysis but not with all of his examples.

IV. *The Modernist Sensibility*

1. "The Drunken Boat," in *Romanticism Reconsidered*, Selected Papers from the English Institute, ed. Northrop Frye (New York and London: Columbia University Press, 1963), p. 24.

NOTES TO CHAPTER IV

2. *After Strange Gods* (New York: Harcourt, Brace and Co., 1934), pp. 50-51.

3. "Climbing Down Pisgah," *Phoenix I*, p. 744.

4. See "Wordsworth's Preface of 1800, with a Collation of the Enlarged Preface of 1802," in *Wordsworth and Coleridge: Lyrical Ballads, 1798*, ed. H. Littledale (London: Oxford University Press, 1953), pp. 240-241.

5. "The Dehumanization of Art," in *The Dehumanization of Art and Other Essays on Art, Culture, and Literature* (Princeton, N.J.: Princeton University Press, 1968), p. 5.

6. *The Priest of Love*, pp. 48-53.

7. For Mann, see *The Story of a Novel*, trans. Richard and Clara Winston (New York: Knopf, 1961), pp. 25, 39.

8. Philip Kolb, "The Birth of Elstir and Vinteuil," in *Marcel Proust: A Critical Panorama*, p. 153.

9. "The Limits of Joyce's Naturalism," *The Sewanee Review*, 53 (1955).

10. For Eliot, See *Selected Essays*, "John Dryden," pp. 267-268; "Baudelaire," pp. 377-379; and "Swinburne as Poet," p. 258. For Joyce, see Richard Ellmann, "The First *Waste Land*," in *Eliot in His Time*, ed. A. Walton Litz (Princeton, N.J.: Princeton University Press, 1973), p. 51.

11. In *Opus Posthumous*, ed. Samuel French Morse (New York: Knopf, 1957), p. 176.

12. This sentiment might be contrasted with that of the English Romantic painter John Constable, "Every tree seems full of blossom of some kind and the surface of the ground seems quite living—every step I take and on whatever object I turn my Eye that sublime expression of the Scripture, "I am the resurrection and the life," etc., seems verified about me." Quoted by Hugh Honour, *Romanticism* (New York: Harper and Row Icon, 1979), p. 87.

13. *James Joyce and the Making of "Ulysses,"* p. 13.

14. For Stevens, see *Adagia*, in *Opus Posthumous*, p. 164. The anecdote from Joyce is quoted by Ellmann in *James Joyce*, pp. 576-577. For Hulme, see *Speculations*, pp. 229, 231.

15. *The Modern Theme*, p 151.

16. "The Metaphysical Poets," *Selected Essays*, p. 250.

17. *Romanticism*, p. 319.

18. See Calinescu, *Faces of Modernity: Avant-garde, Decadence, Kitsch*, pp. 37-41, for this "modernist" impetus of Romanticism.

NOTES TO CHAPTER IV

19. *Wordsworth and Coleridge: Lyrical Ballads*, ed. H. Littledale, p. 226.

20. See Samuel Hynes, "The Hardy Tradition in Modern English Poetry," pp. 39, 55.

21. It is reassuring to find this passage in the major work of one of our authorities about Romanticism:

> In this, as in earlier chapters, I have stressed analogues in post-Romantic literature to the ideas and forms that were developed during that period of astonishing creativity, the several decades after the French revolution. Such an emphasis may appear to align my point of view with the recent tendency to break down the traditional opposition between what is Romantic and what seems to be distinctively "modern" in literature. . . . The fact is, however, that many of the chief figures of the modernist movement—including, in England and America, Hulme, Pound, and Eliot—identified themselves as, explicitly, counter-Romantic; and from any comprehensive view of their basic premises and literary practice, it seems to me that in this judgment they were manifestly right.

M. H. Abrams, *Natural Supernaturalism: Tradition and Revolution in Romantic Literature* (New York: Norton, 1971), p. 427.

22. See David Perkins's section on Frost, "Unsaying the Romantics," in *A History of Modern Poetry*, pp. 243-247.

23. See Herbert Weisinger, "The Self-Awareness of the Renaissance as a Criterion of the Renaissance," *Papers of the Michigan Academy of Science, Arts, and Literature*, 29 (1944), p. 561; and "Who Began the Revival of Learning? The Renaissance Point of View," *ibid.*, 30 (1944), p. 625. See also Margaret Davies, "La Notion de la modernité," *Cahiers du 20e siècle*, 5 (1976): "Il ne s'agit pas ici de savoir si la nature humaine avait vraiment changé. L'important pour cette étude est qu'au début de ce siècle il y eut dans tous les domaines le sentiment qu'on assistait à un de ces moments qui changent le cours de l'évolution humaine . . ." p. 9.

24. Quoted in "Humanism and the Religious Attitude," *Speculations*, p. 54 (where Hulme, incidentally, is himself quoting Worringer, see below n. 53).

25. See Wordsworth and Coleridge: *Lyrical Ballads*, ed. H. Littledale, p. 239.

26. How appropriate is Ortega's comment, in *The Dehumanization*

NOTES TO CHAPTER IV

of Art, about metaphor: "The weapon of poetry turns against natural things and wounds or murders them." (p. 35)

27. Michel Décaudin, in a conference held at Scripps College, Spring, 1980.

28. Tennyson's "Flower in the Crannied Wall" continues this thought: ". . . if I could understand / What you are, root and all, and all in all, / I should know what God and man is." This "reflective" Tennyson has been the object of Modernist attack, most significantly in Eliot's "The Metaphysical Poets," *Selected Essays*, p. 247. For a vindication of Tennyson's other qualities, see the review-article by John Bayley, "The All-Star Victorian" (*The New York Review of Books*, Dec. 18, 1980, p. 42). This article marks yet another instance in a recent trend to restore Victorian and later poets, unjustly covered by Modernist obloquy.

29. See "The Metaphysical Poets," *Selected Essays*, pp. 246-247.

30. See M. H. Abrams's "Structure and Style in the Greater Romantic Lyric," in *From Sensibility to Romanticism: Essays Presented to Frederick A. Pottle*, ed. Frederick W. Hilles and Harold Bloom (New York: Oxford University Press, 1965), pp. 527-560. A recent and welcomed work, placing greater emphasis on the fragmentariness of the Romantic psyche, is Thomas McFarland's *Romanticism and the Forms of Ruin: Wordsworth, Coleridge, and Modalities of Fragmentation* (Princeton, N.J.: Princeton University Press, 1981). McFarland does not deny unity, he simply emphasizes the "diasparactive triad" of fragmentation, incompleteness and ruin—primary human experiences—out of which the Romantic need for wholeness, unity and completion grew. See pp. 7, 17, 19, for the sense of longing in Romanticism ("which is an inner form of the perception of reality as diasparactive"); pp. 23, 28, for the straining after the infinite ("The logic of incompleteness is ultimately the logic of infinity," and "the prospects of infinity so cherished by Romanticism," p. 234); p. 47, for the need for unity: "Here, as elsewhere in the structure favored by the Romantic consciousness, a diasparactive form is evident: an actual incompleteness striving toward a hypothetical unity. . . ." Romanticism and Modernisn do not diverge over the general data of experience (the stylistic presentation of that data is another matter), but largely over the Romantic need to strive against the disunities of existence. While Professor McFarland rightly discerns much evidence of fragmentariness (where is it not?), the point is that there is no criticism in Romanticism itself of this need to sublimate. With Mod-

NOTES TO CHAPTER IV

ernists, on the other hand, one primary area of conflict, and a point of self-definition, was precisely this abhorrence of Romantic striving and longing for the infinite.

31. *Sincerity and Authenticity*, pp. 59-60.
32. Konstantin Mochulsky, *Dostoevsky: His Life and Work*, trans. Michael A. Minihan (Princeton, N.J.: Princeton University Press, 1967), p. 312.
33. William James, in a letter to Henry James, quoted by Whitehead, *Science and the Modern World*, p. 3. See Frederick Karl above, chapter 3, n. 2.
34. *Civilization and Its Discontents*, in *The Complete Psychological Works of Sigmund Freud*, trans. and ed. James Strachey (London: The Hogarth Press, 1961), XXI. 64-72. See the interesting juxtaposition of Freudian analysis with Wordsworth in John A. Lester, Jr., *Journey Through Despair: 1880-1914* (Princeton, N.J.: Princeton University Press, 1968), pp. 169-170.
35. *Science and Poetry* (New York: Norton, 1926), pp. 53 ff. On April 30, 1926, Virginia Woolf made this entry in her diary, "Yesterday I finished the first part of *To the Lighthouse*." On May 25 she writes that she has "finished sketchily" the second part. *A Writer's Diary*, ed. Leonard Woolf (New York: Harcourt, Brace and Co., 1954).
36. *Kangaroo*, 1923 (New York: Viking rpt., 1960), to which all page citations in the text refer.
37. See Introduction n. 18. With quite specific interests throughout the study I show significant areas of agreement "in premise and in practice" between Lawrence and the other Modernists, including even here T. E. Hulme. Harry T. Moore seems more to the point when he quotes Pound ("Lawrence learned the proper treatment of modern subjects before I did") and when he goes on to indicate areas of Modernist solidarity. See *The Priest of Love*, pp. 199-200.
38. See Kleinbard, "D. H. Lawrence and Ontological Insecurity," *op. cit.*, pp. 156-157.
39. In *Phoenix II*, to which the page citations refer.
40. Dorothy van Ghent writes of Lawrence's world that it is multiple rather than dual: ". . . there is a creative relationship between other people and between people and things so long as this 'otherness' is acknowledged. When it is denied—and it is denied when man tries to rationalize nature or society, or when he presumptuously assumes the things of nature to be merely instruments for the expres-

NOTES TO CHAPTER IV

sion of himself, or when he attempts to exercise personal possessorship over people—then he destroys his own selfhood and exerts a destructive influence all about him." From *The English Novel: Form and Function*, rpt. in D. H. *Lawrence: Sons and Lovers*, ed. Julian Moynahan (New York: Viking Critical Library, 1968), p. 536.

41. In this section of running quotation, citations in the text refer to T. E. Hulme, *Speculations*, ed. Herbert Read (New York: Harcourt, Brace and Co., 1924).

42. ". . . Love was Once a Little Boy," *Phoenix II*, p. 452 and *Aaron's Rod*, 1922 (New York: Viking rpt. 1961), p. 162, to which all further citations refer.

43. See Gabriel Josipovici, "Modernism and Romanticism," in *The World and the Book* (London: Macmillan, 1971), p. 193.

44. "The Drunken Boat," *Romanticism Reconsidered, op. cit.*, p. 19. For the Romantic dissolution of self, see Honour, *Romanticism, op. cit.*, pp. 80, 116, 280.

45. See Honour, p. 42. Lawrence, as usual, is blunt; "I've no sympathy with starvers, Gissings or Chattertons." Letter of 12 Jan. 1913, *The Letters of D. H. Lawrence*, ed. James T. Boulton (Cambridge: Cambridge University Press, 1979), I. 501. Curiously enough, many of the major Modernists enjoyed remarkable physical longevity, a sad contrast with the subsequent generation, particularly the American poets. Graham Hough ignores much evidence when he singles out Yeats as the "outstanding exception" to his notion that "there are no Goethes in modern literature, and few poets whose lives show a long-sustained development, a perpetual re-creation of the self continued into late maturity or old age." "The Modernist Lyric," in *Modernism*, ed. Bradbury and McFarlane, p. 321. See Eliot's 1940 lecture on Yeats, rpt. in *On Poetry and Poets* (New York: Farrar, Straus, 1957), pp. 297-298, for his own sense of development.

46. "Nietzsche, Freud et Marx," *Nietzsche* (Paris: Minuit, 1967), p. 186.

47. Ortega, *The Dehumanization of Art*, p. 47.

48. "Romanticism and Classicism," in *Speculations*, p. 127.

49. *Orlando*, pp. 226 ff.

50. "Nietzsche, Freud et Marx," *Nietzsche*, pp. 186-187.

51. *Speculations*, pp. 222, 223, 228, 230.

52. See the piece "Insouciance," *Phoenix II*, p. 532.

53. *Abstraction and Empathy*, trans. Michael Bullock (London: Routledge and Kegan Paul, 1953), p. 29.

NOTES TO CHAPTER IV

54. In "Traditon and the Individual Talent," Eliot wrote, "The point of view I am struggling to attack is perhaps related to the metaphysical theory of the substantial unity of the soul." *Selected Essays*, p. 9.

55. The incident is recounted in *Contre Sainte-Beuve* (Paris: Gallimard, 1954), pp. 173 ff.

56. *Contre Sainte-Beuve*, pp. 165, 178.

57. "The *Pensées* of Pascal," *Selected Essays*, p. 363.

58. "Spatial Form in Modern Literature," *The Widening Gyre: Crisis and Mastery in Modern Literature* (New Brunswick, N.J.: Rutgers University Press, 1963), p. 50.

59. Albert William Levi, "The Concept of Nature," *The Origins of Modern Consciousness*, ed. John Weiss (Detroit: Wayne State University Press, 1965), p. 56. See the opening sentence of the Nausicaa episode in *Ulysses*, "The summer evening had begun to fold the world in its mysterious embrace." (p. 346) See McFarland, *Romanticism and the Forms of Ruin*, pp. 145-150.

60. Donald J. Schuchard, "Eliot and Hulme in 1916: Toward a Revaluation of Eliot's Critical and Spiritual Development," *PMLA*, 88 (1973), p. 1083.

61. "T. E. Hulme, Mercenary of Modernism, or, Fragments of Avant-garde Sensibility in pre-World War I Britain," *ELH* 47 (1980), pp. 355-385. See also A. R. Jones, *The Life and Opinions of T. E. Hulme* (Boston: Beacon Press, 1960); Frank Kermode, *The Romantic Image* (London: Routledge and Kegan Paul, 1961), pp. 119-137.

62. *Phoenix II*, p. 413.

63. *Beyond Good and Evil*, trans. Walter Kaufman (New York: Vintage, 1966), #41; *Werke*, II.

64. *The Dehumanization of Art*, p. 11.

65. *Orlando*, p. 229.

66. Pittsburgh: University of Pittsburgh Press, 1971, p. 13.

67. *Dr. Faustus*, trans. H. T. Lowe-Porter (New York: Random House, 1948), p. 116; *Doktor Faustus*, 1947 (Frankfurt-am-Main: Fischer, 1967), p. 118.

68. Quoted by Carl E. Schorske, "Generational Tension and Cultural Change: Reflections on the Case of Vienna, " *Daedalus*, Fall (1978), p. 120. In his guilty actions, Emil Sinclair suddenly feels superior to his father. Hermann Hesse, *Demian*, trans. Michael Roloff and Michael Lebeck (New York: Bantam, 1970), p. 15.

NOTES TO CHAPTER IV

69. See Robert Wohl, *The Generation of 1914* (Cambridge, Mass.: Harvard University Press, 1979), pp. 205 and *passim*.
70. See *The Priest of Love*, p. 478.
71. *Phoenix I*, p. 615.
72. *The Complete Poems and Plays*, p. 125.
73. See my *Renaissance Discovery of Time*, pp. 16-18.
74. *Ibid.*, p. 206. See also Harold R. Isaacs, "Bringing up the Father Question," *Daedalus*, Fall (1978), where besides noting the sheer predominance of journal articles devoted to the mother, Professor Isaacs reflects on the paucity of criticism showing the viewpoint of the father (p. 194).
75. See chapter 2, nn. 2, 3.
76. See Philippe Ariès, "The Family and the City," *Daedalus*, Spring (1977), pp. 227-235.
77. *Centuries of Childhood: A Social History of Family Life*, trans. Robert Baldick (New York: Random House Vintage, 1965), pp. 398-403.
78. Honour, *Romanticism*, pp. 311-314.
79. *The Image of Childhood: The Individual and Society, A Study of the Theme in English Literature* (Baltimore, Md.: Penguin, 1967).
80. *The Trial*, trans. Willa and Edwin Muir (New York: Random House Vintage, 1964), p. 45.
81. *Childhood and Society*, 2nd ed. (New York: Norton, 1963), p. 396; and *Insight and Responsibility* (New York: Norton, 1964), pp. 179-185.
82. Oxford: Clarendon Press, 1971, p. 197.
83. "Romanticism," *Death, Heaven and the Victorians, ibid.*, p. 14. John Stevens Curl, *The Victorian Celebration of Death* (Detroit: Patridge Press, 1972), also refers to Romanticism, "Melancholy, Decay and Romanticism," pp. 19-26.
84. See chapter 2, n. 2, but also the fuller French version, *Essais sur l'histoire de la mort en Occident du moyen âge à nos jours* (Paris: Editions de Seuil, 1975).
85. London: Cresset Press, 1965.
86. *Virginia Woolf: A Biography* (New York: Harcourt, Brace, Jovanovich, 1972), II. 209.
87. Gertrude regrets in *Sons and Lovers* that in her grief over William she almost lost her younger son: "I should have watched the living, not the dead." (140) Stephen in *A Portrait of the Artist as a Young Man* records this night entry: "Free. Soul free and fancy free.

NOTES TO CHAPTER V

Let the dead bury the dead. Ay. And let the dead marry the dead." (520)

V. "*The Songs That I Sing*"

1. See the excellent pages of William Barrett devoted to Heidegger and Beckett in *Time of Need* (New York: Harper Torchbook, 1973), pp. 370-376—pages that are very useful for the discussion of history and the will throughout this study.
2. "The Philosophy of Intensive Manifolds," *Speculations*, p. 173.
3. *The Use and Abuse*, pp. 11, 69; *Werke*, I. 217, 281.
4. *In Essays of Three Decades*, p. 422; *Schriften und Reden*, II. 225.
5. *Mythology and Humanism: The Correspondence of Thomas Mann and Karl Kerenyi*, trans. Alexander Gelley (Ithaca and London: Cornell University Press, 1975), p. 33.
6. "Freud and the Future," *Essays of Three Decades*, p. 422; *Schriften und Reden*, II. 225.
7. See *Phoenix I*, p. 292, and *The Priest of Love*, pp. 489-493, for the complex history of this very intriguing encounter.
8. *The Priest of Love*, p. 295.
9. "A Letter from Germany," *Phoenix I*, p. 109.
10. 2 June 1914, to A. E. McLeod, *The Collected Letters of D. H. Lawrence*, ed. Harry T. Moore (New York: Viking, 1962), I. 280; this and a subsequent letter to Edward Garnett of 5 June 1914, *Collected Letters*, pp. 281-282, show Lawrence's Modernist directions.
11. "Hymns in a Man's Life," *Phoenix II*, p. 597.
12. *A Writer's Diary*, pp. 96-97. Were it not so obvious and well rehearsed, discussion at this point would require the introduction of the Modernist notion of "epiphany." Indeed, it does fit squarely into the larger concerns that we have been tracing. Two consistent elements in the Modernist sense of epiphany are the ordinary, even trivial, context from which it emerges, and its sudden, involuntary nature. This is obvious from Joyce's uses of the notion and from Yeats's as well, particularly in that quintessentially epiphanic poem, "The Magi." The mystery takes place in the stable—"the bestial floor." And it, too, occurs beyond our will, is involuntary, uncontrollable. The quest of the Magi themselves is paradigmatic, representing a perennial human quest. "Now as at all times," Yeats can picture their figures in his mind, and the quest is made contemporary, entered

287

NOTES TO CHAPTER V

into the present, when, unsatisfied in the midst of the waning Christian era, they hope to find "once more" the revelation that had been shown at its inception. See Morris Beja, *Epiphany in the Modern Novel* (Seattle, Washington: University of Washington Press, 1971), p. 18. See also the Romantic background in M. H. Abrams, *Natural Supernaturalism*, pp. 77-78, 385-390. Joyce's experience of epiphany occurs in *Stephen Hero*, ed. Theodore Spencer (New York: New Directions, 1955), pp. 211-213. For a sense of development in Joyce's attitudes toward epiphany, see Robert Scholes, "In Search of James Joyce," *James Joyce Quarterly*, II (1973), p. 5. "The Magi," in *The Collected Poems of W. B. Yeats* (New York: Macmillan, 1956), p. 124.

13. *Mythology and Humanism*, p. 37.
14. *The Use of Poetry and the Use of Criticism*, p. 148.
15. "New Modes of Characterization in *The Waste Land*," in *T. S. Eliot in Our Time*, p. 95.
16. *Jacob's Room and The Waves*, p. 113.
17. *Mrs. Dalloway*, pp. 122-125.
18. *Orlando*, pp. 310-314.
19. *A Sketch of My Life*, trans. H. T. Lowe-Porter (New York: Knopf, 1960), pp. 44-46.
20. "A Propos of *Lady Chatterley's Lover*," *Phoenix II*, p. 514.
21. *Phoenix II*, p. 457.
22. "Blessed Are the Powerful," *Phoenix II*, pp. 441, 440.
23. *Collected Letters*, pp. 311-312.
24. *Phoenix II*, p. 399.
25. For other accounts of "involuntariness" in Proust see Gilles Deleuze, *Proust and Signs*, trans. Richard Howard (New York: Braziller 1972), pp. 159 ff., and Roger Shattuck, *Marcel Proust*, pp. 120-127.
26. G. K. Hunter, "T. S. Eliot and the Creation of a Symbolist Shakespeare," *Twentieth-Century Literature in Retrospect*, Harvard English Studies: 2, ed. Reuben A. Brower (Cambridge, Mass.: Harvard University Press, 1971). "The revaluation of the last plays as Symbolist masterpieces is one of the great achievements of twentieth-century Shakespeare criticism," pp. 198-199.
27. *The Wheel of Fire*, 1930 (London: Methuen, 4th ed. 1956), p. xviii.
28. *The Use of Poetry and the Use of Criticism*, p. 153; Colin Still, *Shakespeare's Mystery Play: A Study of the "The Tempest"* (London: C. Palmer, 1921).

NOTES TO CHAPTER V

29. Quoted in Elizabeth Drew, *T. S. Eliot: The Design of His Poetry* (New York: Scribner's, 1949), p. 127.
30. *The Use of Poetry and the Use of Criticism*, pp. 146-147.
31. Elizabeth Drew, *T. S. Eliot: The Design of His Poetry*, pp. 126 ff.; Donald Davie, "Eliot in One Poet's Life," *Mosaic*, 6 (1972), p. 238; John F. Lynen, *The Design of the Present: Essays on Time and Form in American Literature* (New Haven: Yale University Press, 1969), pp. 396 ff.
32. "Marina," *The Complete Poems and Plays*, pp. 72-73.
33. *Letters of Wallace Stevens*, ed. Holly Stevens (New York: Knopf, 1966), 12 Jan. 1940, p. 352.
34. "Imagination as Value," *The Necessary Angel* (New York: Random House Vintage, 1965), pp. 140 and 31.
35. *The Collected Poems of Wallace Stevens* (New York: Knopf, 1955), pp. 128-130.
36. For Bloom, see *The Ringers in the Tower: Studies in Romantic Tradition* (Chicago and London: University of Chicago Press, 1971), and *Wallace Stevens: The Poems of Our Climate* (Ithaca and London: Cornell University Press, 1976); for Bornstein, among several works dealing with Romanticism and Modernism, see *Transformations of Romanticism in Yeats, Eliot, and Stevens* (Chicago and London: University of Chicago Press, 1976), of which the introduction, "The Poem of the Act of the Mind," is valuable for its survey of interpretations of Romanticism. Surprisingly, the writer who does seem to carry a special charge from Romanticism to Modernism, Lord Byron, is precisely the writer most ignored by such neo-Romanticists. As usual, though, John Bayley is on the mark: "The fact is that Byron is a modern man, and writer, while Wordsworth and Coleridge increasingly seem men of their time" (*New York Review of Books*, June 2, 1983, p. 27). Deconstructionism represents yet a further stage in the saga of Romanticism and Modernism. It should come as no surprise that, according to Jonathan Culler, "one of the principal efforts of deconstructive criticism has been to disrupt the historical scheme that contrasts romantic with post-romantic literature." He rightly goes on to quote Paul de Man's observation that following the deconstructive mode of Romanticist interpretation would undermine all historiography. *On Deconstruction: Theory and Criticism after Structuralism* (Ithaca, N.Y.: Cornell University Press, 1982), pp. 248-249.

NOTES TO CHAPTER VI

37. For Bornstein, see *Transformations*, pp. 12-14, 25; for Bloom, see *Ringers in the Tower*, pp. 26, 24, 30, 31.
38. *Transformations*, pp. 25, 13.
39. *Ringers in the Tower*, p. 21.
40. *Ringers in the Tower*, p. 17.
41. *Ringers in the Tower*, pp. 17, 22-23, 26-27.
42. See David Perkins, *A History of Modern Poetry*, p. 537.
43. See "The Imagination as Value," *The Necessary Angel*, p. 138. Despite the appropriation of Stevens by the neo-Romantics, it should be remarked that there is a strong critical tradition that places Stevens among the Moderns. R. P. Blackmur: "Stevens' rhetoric is as ferociously comic as the rhetoric in Marlowe's *Jew of Malta*, and as serious." (p. 73) Howard Baker: "Though as a rule his poems are serious underneath, this seriousness is also suffused with the surface gaiety." (p. 82) *The Achievement of Wallace Stevens*, ed. Ashley Brown and Robert Halles (Philadelphia: J. B. Lippincott, 1962). Most recently Helen Vendler shows a Modernist Stevens: "One of Stevens' continuing triumphs is his rapidity of change as he is flicked by various feelings." (p. 71) "The single voice, suggesting a consistency of ultimate reference and attitude, can hardly embrace Stevens' earnest seriousness combined with volatile irony. . . ." (p. 110) "When Stevens moves freely and confidently back and forth among his intuitions, we sense a respect for all versions of experience." (p. 166) *On Extended Wings: Wallace Stevens' Longer Poems* (Cambridge, Mass.: Harvard University Press, 1969).

VI. Three Major Works

1. "From Obsession to Imagination: The Psychology of the Writer," *The Michigan Quarterly Review*, 13 (1974), p. 202.
2. *T. S. Eliot: The Design of His Poetry*, p. 11.
3. In this section—a more detailed look at *Four Quartets*—I change my form of notation, and, instead of citing page number, shall indicate each poem by the initial letters of its title (*Burnt Norton* = BN, *East Coker* = EC, *The Dry Salvages* = DS and *Little Gidding* = LG), followed by a Roman numeral indicating the section within that poem.
4. *The Invisible Poet* (New York: McDowell, Obolensky, 1959), p. 32.
5. See the extremely helpful article by C. A. Patrides, with its

NOTES TO CHAPTER VI

suggestive title, "The Renascence of the Renaissance: T. S. Eliot and the Pattern of Time," *The Michigan Quarterly Review*, 12 (1973), p. 172.

6. See *The Renaissance Discovery of Time*, pp. 152-158, 395-396. While starting from different perspectives, the one involving the "argument of time," and the other, the Modern, "the paradox of time," they both arrive at a more tragic apprehension of experience, although Modernism produced no "tragedy" proper.

7. The citations refer first to the English translations and, after the slash, to the Fischer German language reprints of *Joseph und Seine Brüder*; I = *The Tales of Jacob*, trans. H. T. Lowe-Porter, as in all subsequent volumes (New York: Knopf, 1934); II = *The Young Joseph* (1935); III = *Joseph the Provider* (1944). The Roman numerals after the slash refer to the three-volume reprint of *Joseph und Seine Bruder* (Frankfurt-am-Main: Fischer, 1967).

8. *Letters of Thomas Mann, 1889-1955*, selected and trans. by Richard and Clara Winston (New York: Knopf, 1971), p. 231.

9. *Letters of Thomas Mann*, p. 345.

10. *Letters of Thomas Mann*, p. 231.

11. "Es war spätherbst . . ." is the German original.

12. The German original, while perhaps implying "magic," does not state as much: Joseph's system was "eine Mischung, die durchaus als schelmisch und als Manifestation einer verschlagenen Mittlergottheit empfunden wurde."

13. *Letters of Thomas Mann*, p. 355.

14. *Thomas Mann Werke: Politische Schriften und Reden*, 3 vols. (Frankfurt-am-Main: Fischer, 1968), III. 157-158.

15. Joseph Campbell and Henry Morton Robinson, *A Skeleton Key to "Finnegans Wake"* (Harcourt, Brace and Co., 1944), p. 361.

16. All page citations refer to *Finnegans Wake* (New York: Viking Press, 1955).

17. *The New Science*, pp. 256-257, 372-373. One should beware of the phrase "imaginative universals" since the Italian reads "generi fantastici," which are, however, synonymous with "universali fantastici" (#209), in *Giambattista Vico: Opere*, ed. Fausto Nicolini (Milan-Naples: Ricciardi, 1953), pp. 740/453.

18. New Haven: Yale University Press, 1957, pp. 168-188.

19. *Time and Western Man*, 1927 (Boston: Beacon Press rpt., 1957), p. 87.

20. *Time and Western Man*, p. 103.

NOTES TO CHAPTER VII

21. See above chapter 6, section 2. In my study of *Dante Alighieri*, Twayne World Authors Series (Boston, Mass.: G. K. Hall, 1979), I made brief use of the concept (p. 13). See also James McFarlane, "The Mind of Modernism," *Modernism*, pp. 72, 87, 88.

VII. The Bite of Time

1. *Time and Western Man*, p. 170.
2. T. S. Eliot, *The Complete Poems and Plays*, p. 28.
3. "Modern Fiction," *The Common Reader* (New York: Harcourt, Brace and World Harvest, 1953), p. 154.
4. *The Trial*, Appendix, p. 320.
5. "Romanticism and Classicism," p. 125; "Modern Art and Its Philosophy," p. 93, both in *Speculations*.
6. *The Thirties and After*, pp. 5, 161.
7. *Contre Sainte-Beuve*, p. 53.
8. *The Priest of Love*, p. 397.
9. *A Sketch of My Life*, p. 46.
10. *The Use of Poetry and the Use of Criticism*, pp. 146, 155.
11. Germaine Brée utilized the notion of "counterparts" to bring together Bloomsbury and Gide's circle in a lecture at Scripps College, "Two Vintage Years: France, 1913 and England, 1922," November, 1973.
12. Richard Ellmann, *James Joyce*, p. 756.
13. *"Death in Venice" and Seven Other Stories*, p. 10.
14. *Essays of Three Decades*, p. 400; *Schriften und Reden zur Literatur, Kunst und Philosophie*, II. 280.
15. *Essays of Three Decades*, pp. 60, 70-71; *Schriften und Reden zur Literatur, Kunst und Philosophie*, II. 105-106, 67.
16. *Mythology and Humanism*, p. 38.
17. Leonard Woolf, *Downhill All the Way: An Autobiography of the Years 1919 to 1939* (New York: Harcourt, Brace and World, 1967), pp. 53-54.
18. Philippe Ariès, *Western Attitudes Toward Death*. See the section "One's Own Death," pp. 27 ff.; in *The Renaissance Discovery of Time* see, for instance, pp. 139, 308.
19. *The Renaissance Discovery of Time*, p. 121.
20. "Goethe as Representative of the Bourgeois Age," *Essays of Three Decades*, pp. 68-69; *Schriften und Reden zur Literatur, Kunst und Philosophie*, II. 68.

NOTES TO CONCLUSION

21. *Mythology and Humanism*, p. 100.
22. *Selected Essays*, pp. 436, 435. See also John D. Margolis, *T. S. Eliot's Intellectual Development: 1922-1939* (Chicago: University of Chicago Press, 1972), pp. 124-126 for Eliot's awareness of the dangers of religion without humanism, and p. 210, for the sense of humiliation referred to below.
23. "Goethe as Sage," *On Poetry and Poets* (New York: Farrar, Straus and Cudahy, 1957), pp. 256-257.
24. "To Criticize the Critic" in volume by that title (New York: Farrar, Straus and Giroux, 1965), pp. 22-23.
25. Ellmann, *James Joyce*, p. 729.

Conclusion: Purviews and Purposes

1. "The most influential formal impulses of canonical modernism have been strategies of inwardness." *Fables of Aggression, Wyndham Lewis, the Modernist as Fascist* (Berkeley and Los Angeles: University of California Press, 1979), p. 2.
2. One could of course choose almost any number of the works of Marcuse or Adorno. See particularly, *One Dimensional Man: Studies in the Ideology of Advanced Industrial Society* (Boston: Beacon Press, 1964); some of the phrases in the noted paragraph were taken from *Dialectic of Enlightenment*, Max Horkheimer and Theodor W. Adorno, trans. John Cumming (New York: Herder and Herder, 1972). This work, originally published in German in New York in 1944, might very well, from the viewpoint of science and philosophy, be used to summarize the changes that I have described as taking place from *Henry IV* to *Buddenbrooks* or *Women in Love*.
3. "Beyond Modernism, Beyond Self," in *Arts, Politics, and Will: Essays in Honor of Lionel Trilling*, ed. Quentin Anderson *et al.* (New York: Basic Books, Inc., 1977), p. 214. Professor Bell writes, "This essay continues and enlarges with literary evidence an argument I began on sociological grounds in my book *The Cultural Contradictions of Capitalism*." (p. 213) Even Franklin Baumer in his *Modern European Thought: Continuity and Change in Ideas, 1600-1950* (New York and London: Macmillan, 1977), describes Modernism as not a "normal" revolution comparable to other revolutions like that of science in the seventeenth century or even the Romantic movement. He sees something inherently "problematic "in the twentieth century change of ideas (409-410).

NOTES TO CONCLUSION

4. *Ibid.*, pp. 231-232.

5. See the quite brilliant essay by Claude Leroy, "Modernity and Pseudonymity" in the forthcoming proceedings of The Claremont Colleges' Comparative Literature Conference on Modernism (chapter 3, n. 52 above).

6. *Music, the Arts, and Ideas* (Chicago and London: University of Chicago Press, 1967), p. 98 and *passim*. What Meyer has described in art as a plurality of styles is interestingly enough described by Alvin B. Toffler, in his *The Third Wave* (New York: Bantam Books, 1980), as characteristic of the new wave technological culture. The demassified media, the plethora of limited professional journals, the astonishing spread of small cable TV stations, the regionalization and decentralization implied in such concepts as the "electronic cottage,"—all seem to be a part of the stylistic situation of the arts that Meyer describes. I flatter myself that what I have described in *The Renaissance Discovery of Time* as the proto-industrial mind revealed in the temporal attitudes of the Renaissance, Toffler means by the Second Wave mentality. In that case, the kind of complex consciousness described here in *Mapping Literary Modernism* is very congenial to the condition Toffler perceives us as living under during the Third Wave. Toffler, a seasoned journalist, a diligent and trained observer, has skillfully caught the world's imagination with his *Third Wave*. For further support of this position see the remarkable anthology *Innovation/Renovation: New Perspectives on the Humanities*, ed. by Ihab Hassan and Sally Hassan (Madison, Wis.: The University of Wisconsin Press, 1983), particularly the essays by Matei Calinescu, Malcolm Bradbury and Jean-François Lyotard.

7. Appearing in the forthcoming proceedings referred to in n. 5.

8. See the headnote to "What was Modernism?" in *Refractions* for the delineation of his differences with Trilling, and pp. 294-295 for his defense of the "ethical values" of Modernism. We should not ignore the fact that Levin's headnote, written prior to 1966, could not possibly have taken into account Trilling's strong defence of *Mind in the Modern World*, the 1972 Jefferson Lecture in the Humanities (New York: The Viking Press, 1972). Levin's final question remains a challenging one: "Has it not been the endeavor of his generation [that of Joyce] to have created a conscience for a scientific age?" In another provocative work, that unfortunately appeared too late for me to have fully used, Marshall Berman's *All That Is Solid Melts into Air*, a similar concern is urged: "I have been arguing that those of

us who are most critical of modern life need modernism most, to show us where we are and where we can begin to change our circumstances and ourselves." (p. 128) Levin's thesis receives support from such magisterial works as Jean H. Hagstrum's *Sex and Sensibility: Ideal and Erotic Love from Milton to Mozart* (Chicago: University of Chicago Press, 1980) and Lawrence Stone's *The Family, Sex and Marriage in England, 1500-1800* (New York: Harper & Row, 1977), each work attributing a critical shift in individual values to what was formerly called the Enlightenment.

9. *Judgments on History and Historians*, trans. Harry Zohn (Boston: Beacon Press, 1950). A typical sentence from his reflections: "If [the Middle Ages] had exploited the earth's surface as we are doing, we would perhaps not be around at all." (p. 65) This must be an astonishing revaluation by the greatest Renaissance historian!

10. *New York Review of Books*, 24 Jan. 1974, pp. 22, 27.

11. "Only our supermen know how to write the history of the future," from "Ireland, Island of Saints and Sages," *James Joyce: The Critical Writings*, ed. Ellsworth Mason and Richard Ellmann (New York: The Viking Press, 1964), p. 173.

Index

Abrams, M. H., 281n, 282n, 288n
Adorno, Theodor, 250, 258
Alighieri, Dante, 12, 41, 86, 200, 223, 292n
Anton, Herbert, 259n
Apollinaire, Guillaume, 19
Ariès, Phillipe, 45, 155, 162, 163, 286n
Arnold, Matthew, 88
Auerbach, Erich, 12, 119

Babbit, Irving, 242
Bacon, Francis, 53
Baker, Howard, 290n
Balakian, Anna, 263n
Barraclough, Geoffrey, 264n
Barrett, William, 287n
Baudelaire, Charles, 14, 22, 128, 146, 165, 233, 252, 263n, 265n
Baumer, Franklin, 293n
Bayley, John, 275n, 282n, 289n
Beckett, Samuel, 19
Beebe, Maurice, 262n, 278n
Beja, Morris, 288n
Bell, Daniel, 250-252
Bell, Quentin, 160, 162
Bellow, Saul, 253
Bennett, Arnold, 89
Bergson, Henri, 15, 16, 102, 108, 112, 115, 120, 135, 148, 165, 216
Berman, Marshall, 265n, 295n
Berman, Russell, 279n
Blackmur, R. P., 290n
Blake, William, 155, 164
Bloom, Harold, 187, 189
Bohr, Niels, 120
Bornstein, George, 187-188

Bradbury, Malcolm, 5, 18, 24, 89, 192, 275n, 278n
Bradley, Francis Herbert, 135
Brandes, Georg, 17, 264n
Braverman, Martin, 272n
Brée, Germaine, 292n
Broch, Hermann, 19
Brown, Norman O., 250
Buckley, Jerome, 266n
Budgen, Frank, 124
Bullock, Alan, 91, 264n
Burckhardt, Jacob, 257
Burroughs, William, 250
Bush, Ronald, 259n

Calinescu, Matei, 6, 7, 259n, 280n
Campbell, Joseph, 291n
Camus, Albert, 19, 162
Carter, Frederick, 166
Cassirer, Ernst, 13
Cendrars, Blaise, 274n
Chateaubriand, Françoise de, 233
Cheever, John, 253
Chefdor, Monique, 274n
Clarke, Colin, 272n
Coleridge, Samuel T., 132, 227
complex central consciousness, *see* Modernism
Conrad, Joseph, 21, 40, 41, 42, 87, 90, 94, 95, 123, 189
Constable, John, 131, 280n
Coveney, Peter, 155-156
Culler, Jonathan, 289n
Curl, John Stevens, 286n
Curtius, Ernst Robert, 3, 116

Dale, Peter Allan, 266n
Davie, Donald, 184

INDEX

Davies, Margaret, 281n
death, *see* Modernism
Décaudin, Michel, 282n
deconstructionism, 289n
Delany, Paul, 259n
Deleuze, Gilles, 288n
development, *see* Modernism
Dickens, Charles, 22, 155, 157, 268n
Donne, John, 244
Dostoevsky, Fyodor, 21, 92, 93, 120, 132, 276n
Drew, Elizabeth, 184, 193, 289n

Einstein, Albert, 115-116, 120, 216
Eliot, T. S., 15, 16, 19, 29, 31, 49, 61, 89, 94, 99, 102, 109, 116, 122, 123, 128, 136, 144, 147, 148, 168-169, 176, 184, 199, 214, 217, 227, 230; *Ash Wednesday*, 100, 184; *Choruses from "The Rock,"* 41, 201; *The Four Quartets*, 5, 9, 10, 18, 100, 153, 157, 166, 168, 184, 190, 194, 196-198, 200-201, 204, 224, 231, 243; humanism and, 240, 242, 243; "Journey of the Magi," 170; on James Joyce, 88-89, 116; *The Love Song of J. Alfred Prufrock*, 10, 40, 41, 92, 130, 188, 194, 195; "Marina," 184, 185, 200; on Montaigne, 146; *Murder in the Cathedral*, 100; on Pascal, 146; *Preludes*, 133; and Romanticism, 125, 130, 134, 188; "Second Thoughts About Humanism," 243; on Shakespeare, 183, 184; on Tennyson, 132, 265n; "Tradition and the Individual Talent," 199; *The Use of Poetry and the Use of Criticism*, 170-171; *The Waste Land*, 9, 10, 22, 39, 54, 89, 95, 100, 108, 127, 150, 161, 171, 194, 201, 243; "What Dante Means to Me," 199; on Yeats, 121
Ellmann, Richard, 108, 122, 280n
Enlightenment, the, 127, 256
Erikson, Erik H., 159
Erikson, John D., 277n
Esslin, Martin, 278n
Evans, Bertrand, 276
existentialism, 135

fascism, 151, 278n
Faulkner, Peter, 275n
Faulkner, William, 19, 267n
Fitzgerald, F. Scott, 19
Flaubert, Gustave, 92
Fletcher, John, 278
Foster, John Burt, Jr., 263n
Foster, Steven, 277n
Foucault, Michel, 12, 46, 140, 142, 250
Frank, Joseph, 147
Frazer, James, 226, 273n
Frost, Robert, 9
Freud, Sigmund, 16, 67, 134, 142, 156, 189, 270n
Frye, Northrop, 120, 139, 246
futurism, 19, 66, 167, 260n

Gablik, Suzi, 6, 278n
Garin, Eugenio, 254
Genet, Jean, 250
Girard, René, 262n, 270n
Goethe, Wolfgang, 129, 243, 244, 265n
Gombrich, E. H., 18
Gordon, Lyndall, 259n, 262n
Gorer, Geoffrey, 162
Gorki, Maxim, 159

Hagstrum, Jean, 295n
Hansen, Miriam, 148

INDEX

Hardy, Thomas, 127, 132, 133
Hassan, Ihab, 254, 294n
Hassan, Sally, 294n
Hatfield, Henry, 269n
Heilbroner, Robert, 258
Heller, Erich, 108
Hemingway, Ernest, 19, 142
Herbert, George, 244
Hesse, Hermann, 285n
Honour, Hugh, 125, 280n, 284n
Hough, Graham, 23, 91, 246, 284n
Hugo, Victor, 130
Hulme, T. E., 8, 15-16, 23, 25, 31, 114, 124, 136, 137, 139, 141-142, 144, 147, 148, 165, 176, 224, 244
humanism, 22-24, 118, 146, 148, 163, 240-243, 247, 256
Hunter, G. K., 288n
Hynes, Samuel, 275n, 281n

Ibsen, Henrik, 17
imagism, 19, 123
involuntarism, *see* Modernism
Isaacs, Harold R., 286n

James, Henry, 123
James, William, 135
Jameson, Frederick, 249
Jennings, Edward M., 268n
Job, 203
Johnson, Samuel, 126
Jones, A. R., 285n
Josipovici, Gabriel, 284n
Joyce, James, 5, 29, 41, 55-56, 94-96, 105, 123-124, 159, 169, 188-189, 240, 243, 245, 247, 258; "The Dead," 40-41, 56; *Finnegans Wake*, 9, 10, 18, 118, 212-221, 226, 231, 238; *A Portrait of the Artist as a Young Man*, 128; *Ulysses*, 5, 9-10, 54-56, 61, 109, 121, 123-124, 127, 152, 161, 212, 216, 238
Jung, C. G., 173, 193

Kafka, Franz, 9, 16, 18, 29, 40, 44, 54, 156, 223, 270n
Kant, Immanuel, 51
Karl, Frederick, 87
Keats, John, 126, 127, 139
Kenner, Hugh, 199
Kerenyi, Karl, 166, 169, 211, 230
Kermode, Frank, 274n, 285n
Kern, Stephen, 261n, 277n
Kleinbard, David J., 271n
Knight, G. Wilson, 183
Kolb, Philip, 280n

Laforgue, Jules, 244
Landes, David S., 260n
Langbaum, Robert, 171
Larbaud, Valéry, 3, 108
LaRochefoucauld, Duc de, 146
Lawrence, D. H., 9, 14-15, 18, 29, 44, 49, 53, 55, 66, 89, 105, 117, 121, 122, 136, 137, 149, 167, 178, 179, 244, 247, 250; *Aaron's Rod*, 135-136, 139-141, 152; "The Crown," 41, 60, 148, 179; "The Education of the People," 55, 137, 153; *Kangaroo*, 135, 143-145; "The Lemon Gardens," 55; ". . . Love Was Once a Little Boy," 138, 178; "The Man Who Died," 140; *The Plumed Serpent*, 55; *The Rainbow*, 45, 57-63, 65, 139-140, 157, 179, 188; *Sons and Lovers*, 22, 54, 96, 122, 128, 135, 140; "Study of Thomas Hardy," 66; *Women in Love*, 5, 45, 48, 54, 59, 83, 135, 137, 152, 179, 163; on Wordsworth, 131, 134

299

INDEX

Lasserre, Pierre, 16
Leavis, F. R., 15, 136
Leroy, Claude, 294n
Lester, John A., Jr., 283n
Levi, Albert William, 285n
Levin, Harry, 3, 4, 193, 255, 256, 274n
Lévi-Strauss, Claude, 12, 29, 37
Levy-Bruhl, Lucien, 217
Lewis, Wyndham, 216, 217, 222
Litz, A. Walton, 280n
Lodge, David, 275n
Lombardi, Franco, 259n
Löwith, Karl, 63, 66, 268n
Lukács, Georg, 15, 75, 91
Lynen, John F., 184, 289n

Madame Bovary, 277n
Mailer, Norman, 252
Mallarmé, Stephan, 244
Malraux, André, 19, 33
Man, Paul de, 289n
Mandelbaum, Maurice, 31
Mann, Thomas, 22, 29, 46, 48, 50-51, 57, 100, 108, 111, 122, 144, 176, 188, 211, 212, 214, 226, 228, 230, 240, 242, 254; *Buddenbrooks*, 9, 21, 43-50, 58-59, 63, 65, 68, 87, 93, 94, 178; *Death in Venice*, 27, 40, 42, 44, 45, 178, 228; *Doktor Faustus*, 150; "Freud and the Future," 166; on Goethe, 24, 229, 242; and humanism, 240-242; *Joseph and His Brothers*, 9, 10, 18, 109, 174, 178, 204-211, 225, 231, 242; Kerenyi correspondence, 166, 169, 211, 230; *The Magic Mountain*, 4, 9, 10, 11, 24, 33-37, 44-45, 49, 95, 109, 125, 143, 145, 148, 160-163, 178, 195, 235, 242, 254; mistranslation of, 9, 49, 51; Schopenhauer and, 16, 50, 51, 87, 165, 228; *A Sketch of My Life*, 178
Marcuse, Herbert, 250, 258
Margolis, John D., 293n
Marias, Julian, 277n
Marlowe, Christopher, 239
Martins, Wilson, 259n
Mauron, Charles, 116
Marx, Karl, 15, 74, 75, 142
McFarland, Thomas, 282n, 285n
McFarlane, James, 275n, 292n
McGann, Jerome J., 262n
Meinecke, Friedrich, 266n
Mendilow, A. A., 7
Meyer, Leonard B., 253-254
Meyerhoff, Hans, 6
Milton, John, 126, 161, 226, 243, 244
Mochulsky, Konstantin, 283n
Modernism, 3, 13, 17-21, 27, 42, 44, 61, 63-64, 87-96, 108, 111, 114, 117-118, 120, 123, 137-141, 165, 202, 225, 227, 253; charges against, 14, 91, 246, 250, 251, 279n; complex central consciousness in, 90, 105, 108, 116, 118, 135-137, 144, 164, 168, 171, 222, 234, 246, 249; complex range of, 14, 17, 87, 89, 244, 253; death in, 49-50, 159-163, 195, 228, 234; developmental phases of, 4, 7-11, 13, 17, 40, 90-91, 119, 121, 135, 138, 142, 164, 167-171, 177-179, 189-193, 197, 214, 223-226, 230, 235, 243-245, 250-251, 254-256; family and children in, 33, 49, 51, 54, 57, 59, 65, 156-157; fathers in, 54, 56, 94, 154, 270n; industrialization and, 6, 23, 25, 53, 55, 66; involuntarism in, 169, 177-184, 227; mothers in, 55, 56, 60, 154, 158-160, 209; point of departure, 9, 37,

INDEX

40, 44, 54, 128, 142, 161, 186, 190, 193, 254, 256, 261n; role of artist in, 121-122, 125, 242; science and, 115-117, 120, 125, 128; typology of, 10, 40, 48, 90-92, 95-106, 248-249; values of time and history in, 23, 28-30, 33, 45-46, 48-51, 53, 55-58, 60, 62, 136, 144, 146, 151, 153, 165, 192, 193, 195, 256-257; work habits in, 44, 63, 227-228; World War I and, 9, 59, 77, 160-161, 167, 225, 236, 241, 249; youth and, 8, 36, 128, 150-152, 193, 248
Montaigne, Michel de, 13, 112, 262n
Moore, Harry T., 283n
Moraes, Rubens, 260n
Morley, John, 150
Moynahan, Julian, 284n
myth, 11, 29, 118, 166-176, 183, 185, 192-194, 203, 207-208, 213, 223-224, 230, 238, 242, 247
Musil, Robert, 151

Nerval, Gerard de, 233
Nietzsche, Friedrich, 8, 9, 11, 14-17, 22, 25-29, 31, 38, 40, 49-51, 53, 57, 58, 75, 94, 99, 111, 120, 121, 139, 140, 142, 145, 149, 151, 165, 192, 194, 210, 217, 256, 257, 266n, 269n
nineteenth century, values of and attitudes toward, 22, 28-29, 31, 37, 41, 44, 45, 46, 50, 51, 53, 57, 62, 93, 94, 132, 141, 149, 152, 154, 155, 159, 190, 210, 256

Ortega y Gasset, José, 24, 27, 69, 87, 108, 115-118, 120, 122, 125, 135, 139, 144, 147, 149, 152, 258, 271n
Orwell, George, 94

paradox of time, see time
Patrides, C. A., 261n, 266n, 291n
Paz, Octavio, 6
Perkins, David, 19, 281n
Philipson, Morris, 276n
Piaget, Jean, 12
Poggioli, Renato, 19, 261n, 276n
point of departure, see Modernism
post-Modernism, 7, 187, 246, 252, 254
Poulet, Georges, 6
Pound, Ezra, 9, 18, 40, 94, 95, 116, 122
Proust, Marcel, 5, 9, 18, 55, 61, 90, 92, 97-99, 106, 108, 110-117, 122-123, 146, 148, 152, 168, 180-183, 188, 203, 213, 226, 227, 232, 240, 244, 247; *Contre Sainte-Beuve*, 226

Quinones, Ricardo, *The Renaissance Discovery of Time*, 4, 260n, 262n, 268n, 286n, 291n, 294n

Rabelais, François, 46, 53
Renaissance, the, 4, 7, 15, 23, 25, 28-31, 37, 42, 45, 47, 53, 56, 57, 96, 128, 145, 147, 153, 164, 229, 235, 239, 242, 247, 248, 254, 257; time and, 25, 30, 33-34, 37, 38, 45, 66, 77, 91, 218, 234, 241, 256
Revel, J.-F., 108, 112
Richards, I. A., 89, 123, 128, 130, 135, 147
Rimbaud, Arthur, 22
Roberts, Michael, 263n

INDEX

Robinson, Henry Morton, 291n
Romanticism, 7, 11, 23, 27, 53, 66, 120-122, 126-134, 137-139, 141, 144, 145, 147, 149, 154, 157, 185, 188-190, 219, 227, 248, 252, 254, 282n
Roosevelt, Franklin Delano, 211
Rothschild, Emma, 272n
Rousseau, J-J., 36, 132
Russo, John Paul, 273n

Sartre, J.-P., 18, 143
Schiller, Friedrich, 155
Schlegel, R., 38
Scholes, Robert, 288n
Schorske, Carl E., 264n, 285n
Schuchard, Donald J., 285n
Shakespeare, William, 13, 37, 53, 91, 104, 107, 183, 203, 244, 262n; *1 Henry IV*, 45, 76; *2 Henry IV*, 30; history plays of, 30, 51, 56; *King Lear*, 223; *A Midsummer Night's Dream*, 114; *Pericles*, 183; *Richard II*, 32; *The Tempest*, 54, 161; *Twelfth Night*, 163
Shattuck, Roger, 108, 288n
Shaw, G. B., 17, 89, 188
Slochower, Harry, 206
Sorel, Georges, 148
Spann, Meno, 275n
Spears, Monroe K., 263n
Spencer, Sharon, 261n
Spender, Stephen, 3, 8, 18, 110, 225
Stallman, R. W., 273n
Steffen, Hans, 259n
Stevens, Wallace, 9, 11, 18, 19, 109, 123-124, 185-191
Still, Colin, 183
Stone, Lawrence, 295n
surrealism, 19

Swinburne, Algernon, 123
Sypher, Wylie, 92

Taylor, Frederick Winslow, 76, 81
Tennyson, Alfred, 41, 127, 132, 265n, 282n
Tillich, Paul, 122
time, 4-7, 25, 28, 31, 33, 43, 51, 52, 59, 86, 90, 91, 148, 161, 195, 196, 201-202, 216-219, 222, 237-238, 240-241, 245, 252; as innovative and predictive, 7, 38, 42, 67, 230; paradox of, 7, 27-39, 63, 65, 67, 71, 75, 81, 86, 92, 96, 114, 142, 147, 224, 247; Bergson and, 71-73, 75; Eliot and, 75, 197; Ortega y Gasset and, 70-71; Hemingway and, 74; Hulme and, 73; Joyce and, 216-217, 220, 235; Lawrence and, 63, 65, 67, 70-72, 75-86; Lukács and, 74-75; Mann and, 9, 67-70, 82; Whitehead and, 71; Woolf and, 69, 72; Renaissance and, 5, 7, 9, 41, 67, 71, 92, 111, 230; return of, 114, 231, 233-242, 249; Romanticism and, 7
Tobin, Patricia, 269n
Toda, Masanao, 267n
Toffler, Alvin, 294n
Trilling, Lionel, 52, 118, 128, 132, 255
Turner, J.M.W., 131
typology, Gustav von Aschenbach, 77, 92; Leopold Bloom, 92, 95, 103-105, 127, 188; Will Brangwen, 92, 196; Hans Castorp, 22, 49, 56, 92, 94, 95, 101, 102, 161, 163, 240; Gerald Crich, 40, 41, 92-93, 96-97, 144, 158; Stephen Dedalus, 8, 31, 54, 57, 88, 146, 150-152, 163, 193; Marcel, 95, 100, 102, 105; Paul Morel,

302

8, 22, 57, 96, 137, 150, 162; Tiresias, 92, 95, 106. *See also* Modernism

Unamuno, Miguel de, 260n
Updike, John, 253

Valéry, Paul, 18
values of time and history, *see* Modernism
van Doren, Mark, 108
van Ghent, Dorothy, 283n
Vendler, Helen, 290n
Verlaine, Paul, 128
Vico, Giambattista, 96, 176, 214, 215
Victorianism, 149, 154
Voltaire, François, 176

Wagner, Geoffrey, 216
Wagner, Richard, 180
Watanabe, M. S., 267n
Watt, Ian, 273n
Weisinger, Herbert, 128, 281n
Wells, H. G., 17, 89
Welsh, Alexander, 159, 268n
West, Nathaniel, 134
Whitehead, Alfred N., 53, 116-117, 120, 135, 216, 247, 267n
Wilde, Oscar, 111
Wilson, Edmund, 3, 108-109, 117
Wohl, Robert, 154, 278n, 286n
Woolf, Virginia, 35, 110, 141, 162, 168-169, 173, 190, 213, 217, 223, 229-231, 240, 256; *Jacob's Room*, 9, 41, 95, 160, 172; *Mrs. Dalloway*, 9, 32, 95, 106-110; *Orlando*, 141, 149, 177; *To the Lighthouse*, 5, 95, 106, 110, 134-135, 153, 171, 231; *The Waves*, 9, 18, 32, 53, 95, 152, 180, 231-232; *The Years*, 231
Wordsworth, William, 121-123, 126, 128-134, 138, 155, 157, 186, 188
Worringer, Wilhelm, 24, 145, 147

Yeats, W. B., 18, 19, 108, 128, 146, 186, 188, 200, 217, 264n, 287n

Zapf, Hubert, 272n

Library of Congress Cataloging in Publication Data
Quinones, Ricardo J.
  Mapping literary modernism.

  Bibliography: p.
  Includes index.
  1. Modernism (Literature)   2. Literature, Modern—
20th century—History and criticism.   I. Title.
PN56.M54Q56 1985   809'.91   84-42899
ISBN 0-691-06636-1